The

Man of the

Forest

Zane Grey

1st WORLD
LIBRARY
Literary Society

The Man of the Forest
Zane Grey

© 1st World Library – Literary Society, 2004
PO Box 2211
Fairfield, IA 52556
www.1stworldlibrary.org
First Edition

LCCN: 2003195168

ISBN: 1-59540-541-0

Purchase *"The Man of The Forest"*
as a traditional bound book at:
www.1stWorldLibrary.org/purchase.asp?ISBN=1-59540-541-0

1st World Library Literary Society is a nonprofit organization dedicated to promoting literacy by:

- Creating a free internet library accessible from any computer worldwide.
- Hosting writing competitions and offering book publishing scholarships.

Readers interested in supporting literacy through sponsorship, donations or membership please contact:
literacy@1stworldlibrary.org
Check us out at: www.1stworldlibrary.org

The Man of the Forest
contributed by the Charles Family
in support of
1st World Library - Literary Society

CHAPTER I

At sunset hour the forest was still, lonely, sweet with tang of fir and spruce, blazing in gold and red and green; and the man who glided on under the great trees seemed to blend with the colors and, disappearing, to have become a part of the wild woodland.

Old Baldy, highest of the White Mountains, stood up round and bare, rimmed bright gold in the last glow of the setting sun. Then, as the fire dropped behind the domed peak, a change, a cold and darkening blight, passed down the black spear-pointed slopes over all that mountain world.

It was a wild, richly timbered, and abundantly watered region of dark forests and grassy parks, ten thousand feet above sea-level, isolated on all sides by the southern Arizona desert - the virgin home of elk and deer, of bear and lion, of wolf and fox, and the birthplace as well as the hiding-place of the fierce Apache.

September in that latitude was marked by the sudden cool night breeze following shortly after sundown. Twilight appeared to come on its wings, as did faint sounds, not distinguishable before in the stillness.

Milt Dale, man of the forest, halted at the edge of a timbered ridge, to listen and to watch. Beneath him lay a narrow valley, open and grassy, from which rose a faint murmur of running water. Its music was pierced by the wild staccato yelp of a hunting coyote. From overhead in the giant fir came a twittering and rustling of grouse settling for the night; and from across the valley drifted the last low calls of wild turkeys going to roost.

To Dale's keen ear these sounds were all they should have been, betokening an unchanged serenity of forestland. He was glad, for he had expected to hear the clipclop of white men's horses - which to hear up in those fastnesses was hateful to him. He and the Indian were friends. That fierce foe had no enmity toward the lone hunter. But there hid somewhere in the forest a gang of bad men, sheep-thieves, whom Dale did not want to meet.

As he started out upon the slope, a sudden flaring of the afterglow of sunset flooded down from Old Baldy, filling the valley with lights and shadows, yellow and blue, like the radiance of the sky. The pools in the curves of the brook shone darkly bright. Dale's gaze swept up and down the valley, and then tried to pierce the black shadows across the brook where the wall of spruce stood up, its speared and spiked crest against the pale clouds. The wind began to moan in the trees and there was a feeling of rain in the air. Dale, striking a trail, turned his back to the fading afterglow and strode down the valley.

With night at hand and a rain-storm brewing, he did not head for his own camp, some miles distant, but directed his steps toward an old log cabin. When he reached it darkness had almost set in. He approached with caution. This cabin, like the few others scattered in the valleys, might harbor Indians or a bear or a panther. Nothing, however, appeared to be there. Then Dale studied the clouds driving across the sky, and he felt the cool dampness of a fine, misty rain on his face. It would rain off and on during the night. Whereupon he entered the cabin.

And the next moment he heard quick hoof-beats of trotting horses. Peering out, he saw dim, moving forms in the darkness, quite close at hand. They had approached against the wind so that sound had been deadened. Five horses with riders, Dale made out - saw them loom close. Then he heard rough voices. Quickly he turned to feel in the dark for a ladder he knew led to a loft; and finding it, he quickly mounted, taking care not to make a noise with his rifle, and lay down upon the floor of brush and poles. Scarcely had he done so when heavy steps, with accompaniment of clinking spurs, passed through the door below into the cabin.

"Wal, Beasley, are you here?" queried a loud voice.

There was no reply. The man below growled under his breath, and again the spurs jingled.

"Fellars, Beasley ain't here yet," he called. "Put the hosses under the shed. We'll wait."

"Wait, huh!" came a harsh reply. "Mebbe all night - an' we got nuthin' to eat."

"Shut up, Moze. Reckon you're no good for anythin' but eatin'. Put them hosses away an' some of you rustle fire-wood in here."

Low, muttered curses, then mingled with dull thuds of

hoofs and strain of leather and heaves of tired horses.

Another shuffling, clinking footstep entered the cabin.

"Snake, it'd been sense to fetch a pack along," drawled this newcomer.

"Reckon so, Jim. But we didn't, an' what's the use hollerin'? Beasley won't keep us waitin' long."

Dale, lying still and prone, felt a slow start in all his blood - a thrilling wave. That deep-voiced man below was Snake Anson, the worst and most dangerous character of the region; and the others, undoubtedly, composed his gang, long notorious in that sparsely settle country. And the Beasley mentioned - he was one of the two biggest ranchers and sheep-raisers of the White Mountain ranges. What was the meaning of a rendezvous between Snake Anson and Beasley? Milt Dale answered that question to Beasley's discredit; and many strange matters pertaining to sheep and herders, always a mystery to the little village of Pine, now became as clear as daylight.

Other men entered the cabin.

"It ain't a-goin' to rain much," said one. Then came a crash of wood thrown to the ground.

"Jim, hyar's a chunk of pine log, dry as punk," said another.

Rustlings and slow footsteps, and then heavy thuds attested to the probability that Jim was knocking the end of a log upon the ground to split off a corner whereby a handful of dry splinters could be procured.

"Snake, lemme your pipe, an' I'll hev a fire in a jiffy."

"Wal, I want my terbacco an' I ain't carin' about no fire," replied Snake.

"Reckon you're the meanest cuss in these woods," drawled Jim.

Sharp click of steel on flint - many times - and then a sound of hard blowing and sputtering told of Jim's efforts to start a fire. Presently the pitchy blackness of the cabin changed; there came a little crackling of wood and the rustle of flame, and then a steady growing roar.

As it chanced, Dale lay face down upon the floor of the loft, and right near his eyes there were cracks between the boughs. When the fire blazed up he was fairly well able to see the men below. The only one he had ever seen was Jim Wilson, who had been well known at Pine before Snake Anson had ever been heard of. Jim was the best of a bad lot, and he had friends among the honest people. It was rumored that he and Snake did not pull well together.

"Fire feels good," said the burly Moze, who appeared as broad as he was black-visaged. "Fall's sure a-comin'. . . Now if only we had some grub!"

"Moze, there's a hunk of deer meat in my saddle-bag, an' if you git it you can have half," spoke up another voice.

Moze shuffled out with alacrity.

In the firelight Snake Anson's face looked lean and

serpent-like, his eyes glittered, and his long neck and all of his long length carried out the analogy of his name.

"Snake, what's this here deal with Beasley?" inquired Jim.

"Reckon you'll l'arn when I do," replied the leader. He appeared tired and thoughtful.

"Ain't we done away with enough of them poor greaser herders - for nothin'?" queried the youngest of the gang, a boy in years, whose hard, bitter lips and hungry eyes somehow set him apart from his comrades.

"You're dead right, Burt - an' that's my stand," replied the man who had sent Moze out. "Snake, snow 'll be flyin' round these woods before long," said Jim Wilson. "Are we goin' to winter down in the Tonto Basin or over on the Gila?"

"Reckon we'll do some tall ridin' before we strike south," replied Snake, gruffly.

At the juncture Moze returned.

"Boss, I heerd a hoss comin' up the trail," he said.

Snake rose and stood at the door, listening. Outside the wind moaned fitfully and scattering raindrops pattered upon the cabin.

"A-huh!" exclaimed Snake, in relief.

Silence ensued then for a moment, at the end of which interval Dale heard a rapid clip-clop on the rocky trail outside. The men below shuffled uneasily, but none of the spoke. The fire cracked cheerily. Snake Anson stepped back from before the door with an action that expressed both doubt and caution.

The trotting horse had halted out there somewhere.

"Ho there, inside!" called a voice from the darkness.

"Ho yourself!" replied Anson.

"That you, Snake?" quickly followed the query.

"Reckon so," returned Anson, showing himself.

The newcomer entered. He was a large man, wearing a slicker that shone wet in the firelight. His sombrero, pulled well down, shadowed his face, so that the upper half of his features might as well have been masked. He had a black, drooping mustache, and a chin like a rock. A potential force, matured and powerful, seemed to be wrapped in his movements.

"Hullo, Snake! Hullo, Wilson!" he said. "I've backed out on the other deal. Sent for you on - on another little matter ...particular private."

Here he indicated with a significant gesture that Snake's men were to leave the cabin.

"A-huh! ejaculated Anson, dubiously. Then he turned abruptly. Moze, you an' Shady an' Burt go wait outside. Reckon this ain't the deal I expected.... An' you can saddle the hosses."

The three members of the gang filed out, all glancing

keenly at the stranger, who had moved back into the shadow.

"All right now, Beasley," said Anson, low-voiced. "What's your game? Jim, here, is in on my deals."

Then Beasley came forward to the fire, stretching his hands to the blaze.

"Nothin' to do with sheep," replied he.

"Wal, I reckoned not," assented the other. "An' say - whatever your game is, I ain't likin' the way you kept me waitin' an' ridin' around. We waited near all day at Big Spring. Then thet greaser rode up an' sent us here. We're a long way from camp with no grub an' no blankets"

"I won't keep you long," said Beasley. "But even if I did you'd not mind - when I tell you this deal concerns Al Auchincloss - the man who made an outlaw of you!"

Anson's sudden action then seemed a leap of his whole frame. Wilson, likewise, bent forward eagerly. Beasley glanced at the door - then began to whisper.

"Old Auchincloss is on his last legs. He's goin' to croak. He's sent back to Missouri for a niece - a young girl - an' he means to leave his ranches an' sheep - all his stock to her. Seems he has no one else. . . . Them ranches - an' all them sheep an' hosses! You know me an' Al were pardners in sheep-raisin' for years. He swore I cheated him an' he threw me out. An' all these years I've been swearin' he did me dirt - owed me sheep an' money. I've got as many friends in Pine - an' all the way down the trail - as Auchincloss has. . . . An' Snake, see here -"

He paused to draw a deep breath and his big hands trembled over the blaze. Anson leaned forward, like a serpent ready to strike, and Jim Wilson was as tense with his divination of the plot at hand.

"See here," panted Beasley. "The girl's due to arrive at Magdalena on the sixteenth. That's a week from to-morrow. She'll take the stage to Snowdrop, where some of Auchincloss's men will meet her with a team."

"A-huh!" grunted Anson as Beasley halted again. "An' what of all thet?"

"She mustn't never get as far as Snowdrop!"

"You want me to hold up the stage - an' get the girl?"

"Exactly."

"Wal - an' what then?

Make off with her. . . . She disappears. That's your affair. . . . I'll press my claims on Auchincloss - hound him - an' be ready when he croaks to take over his property. Then the girl can come back, for all I care. . . You an' Wilson fix up the deal between you. If you have to let the gang in on it don't give them any hunch as to who an' what. This 'll make you a rich stake. An' providin', when it's paid, you strike for new territory."

"Thet might be wise," muttered Snake Anson. "Beasley, the weak point in your game is the uncertainty of life. Old Al is tough. He may fool you."

"Auchincloss is a dyin' man," declared Beasley, with such positiveness that it could not be doubted.

"Wal, he sure wasn't plumb hearty when I last seen him. . . . Beasley, in case I play your game - how'm I to know that girl?"

"Her name's Helen Rayner," replied Beasley, eagerly. "She's twenty years old. All of them Auchinclosses was handsome an' they say she's the handsomest."

"A-huh! . . . Beasley, this 's sure a bigger deal - an' one I ain't fancyin'. . . . But I never doubted your word. . . . Come on - an' talk out. What's in it for me?"

"Don't let any one in on this. You two can hold up the stage. Why, it was never held up. . . . But you want to mask. . . . How about ten thousand sheep - or what they bring at Phenix in gold?"

Jim Wilson whistled low.

"An' leave for new territory?" repeated Snake Anson, under his breath.

"You've said it."

"Wal, I ain't fancyin' the girl end of this deal, but you can count on me. . . . September sixteenth at Magdalena - an' her name's Helen - an' she's handsome?"

"Yes. My herders will begin drivin' south in about two weeks. Later, if the weather holds good, send me word by one of them an' I'll meet you."

Beasley spread his hands once more over the blaze, pulled on his gloves and pulled down his sombrero, and with an abrupt word of parting strode out into the night.

"Jim, what do you make of him?" queried Snake Anson.

"Pard, he's got us beat two ways for Sunday," replied Wilson.

"A-huh! . . . Wal, let's get back to camp." And he led the way out.

Low voices drifted into the cabin, then came snorts of horses and striking hoofs, and after that a steady trot, gradually ceasing. Once more the moan of wind and soft patter of rain filled the forest stillness.

CHAPTER II

Milt Dale quietly sat up to gaze, with thoughtful eyes, into the gloom.

He was thirty years old. As a boy of fourteen he had run off from his school and home in Iowa and, joining a wagon-train of pioneers, he was one of the first to see log cabins built on the slopes of the White Mountains. But he had not taken kindly to farming or sheep-raising or monotonous home toil, and for twelve years he had lived in the forest, with only infrequent visits to Pine and Show Down and Snowdrop. This wandering forest life of his did not indicate that he did not care for the villagers, for he did care, and he was welcome everywhere, but that he loved wild life and solitude and beauty with the primitive instinctive force of a savage.

And on this night he had stumbled upon a dark plot against the only one of all the honest white people in that region whom he could not call a friend.

"That man Beasley!" he soliloquized. "Beasley - in cahoots with Snake Anson! . . . Well, he was right. Al Auchincloss is on his last legs. Poor old man! When I tell him he'll never believe me, that's sure!"

Discovery of the plot meant to Dale that he must hurry down to Pine.

"A girl - Helen Rayner - twenty years old," he mused. "Beasley wants her made off with. . . . That means - worse than killed!"

Dale accepted facts of life with that equanimity and fatality acquired by one long versed in the cruel annals of forest lore. Bad men worked their evil just as savage wolves relayed a deer. He had shot wolves for that trick. With men, good or bad, he had not clashed. Old women and children appealed to him, but he had never had any interest in girls. The image, then, of this Helen Rayner came strangely to Dale; and he suddenly realized that he had meant somehow to circumvent Beasley, not to befriend old Al Auchincloss, but for the sake of the girl. Probably she was already on her way West, alone, eager, hopeful of a future home. How little people guessed what awaited them at a journey's end! Many trails ended abruptly in the forest - and only trained woodsmen could read the tragedy.

"Strange how I cut across country to-day from Spruce Swamp," reflected Dale. Circumstances, movements, usually were not strange to him. His methods and habits were seldom changed by chance. The matter, then, of his turning off a course out of his way for no apparent reason, and of his having overheard a plot singularly involving a young girl, was indeed an adventure to provoke thought. It provoked more, for Dale grew conscious of an unfamiliar smoldering heat along his veins. He who had little to do with the strife of men, and nothing to do with anger, felt his blood grow hot at the cowardly trap laid for an innocent girl.

"Old Al won't listen to me," pondered Dale. "An' even if he did, he wouldn't believe me. Maybe nobody will . . . . All the same, Snake Anson won't get that girl."

With these last words Dale satisfied himself of his own position, and his pondering ceased. Taking his rifle, he descended from the loft and peered out of the door. The night had grown darker, windier, cooler; broken clouds were scudding across the sky; only a few stars showed; fine rain was blowing from the northwest; and the forest seemed full of a low, dull roar.

"Reckon I'd better hang up here," he said, and turned to the fire. The coals were red now. From the depths of his hunting-coat he procured a little bag of salt and some strips of dried meat. These strips he laid for a moment on the hot embers, until they began to sizzle and curl; then with a sharpened stick he removed them and ate like a hungry hunter grateful for little.

He sat on a block of wood with his palms spread to the dying warmth of the fire and his eyes fixed upon the changing, glowing, golden embers. Outside, the wind continued to rise and the moan of the forest increased to a roar. Dale felt the comfortable warmth stealing over him, drowsily lulling; and he heard the storm-wind in the trees, now like a waterfall, and anon like a retreating army, and again low and sad; and he saw pictures in the glowing embers, strange as dreams.

Presently he rose and, climbing to the loft, he stretched himself out, and soon fell asleep.

When the gray dawn broke he was on his way, 'cross-country, to the village of Pine.

During the night the wind had shifted and the rain had ceased. A suspicion of frost shone on the grass in open places. All was gray - the parks, the glades - and deeper, darker gray marked the aisles of the forest.

Shadows lurked under the trees and the silence seemed consistent with spectral forms. Then the east kindled, the gray lightened, the dreaming woodland awoke to the far-reaching rays of a bursting red sun.

This was always the happiest moment of Dale's lonely days, as sunset was his saddest. He responded, and there was something in his blood that answered the whistle of a stag from a near-by ridge. His strides were long, noiseless, and they left dark trace where his feet brushed the dew-laden grass.

Dale pursued a zigzag course over the ridges to escape the hardest climbing, but the "senacas" - those parklike meadows so named by Mexican sheep-herders - were as round and level as if they had been made by man in beautiful contrast to the dark-green, rough, and rugged ridges. Both open senaca and dense wooded ridge showed to his quick eye an abundance of game. The cracking of twigs and disappearing flash of gray among the spruces, a round black lumbering object, a twittering in the brush, and stealthy steps, were all easy signs for Dale to read. Once, as he noiselessly emerged into a little glade, he espied a red fox stalking some quarry, which, as he advanced, proved to be a flock of partridges. They whirred up, brushing the branches, and the fox trotted away. In every senaca Dale encountered wild turkeys feeding on the seeds of the high grass.

It had always been his custom, on his visits to Pine, to kill and pack fresh meat down to several old friends, who were glad to give him lodging. And, hurried though he was now, he did not intend to make an exception of this trip.

At length he got down into the pine belt, where the great, gnarled, yellow trees soared aloft, stately, and aloof from one another, and the ground was a brown, odorous, springy mat of pine-needles, level as a floor. Squirrels watched him from all around, scurrying away at his near approach - tiny, brown, light-striped squirrels, and larger ones, russet-colored, and the splendid dark-grays with their white bushy tails and plumed ears.

This belt of pine ended abruptly upon wide, gray, rolling, open land, almost like a prairie, with foot-hills lifting near and far, and the red-gold blaze of aspen thickets catching the morning sun. Here Dale flushed a flock of wild turkeys, upward of forty in number, and their subdued color of gray flecked with white, and graceful, sleek build, showed them to be hens. There was not a gobbler in the flock. They began to run pell-mell out into the grass, until only their heads appeared bobbing along, and finally disappeared. Dale caught a glimpse of skulking coyotes that evidently had been stalking the turkeys, and as they saw him and darted into the timber he took a quick shot at the hindmost. His bullet struck low, as he had meant it to, but too low, and the coyote got only a dusting of earth and pine-needles thrown up into his face. This frightened him so that he leaped aside blindly to butt into a tree, rolled over, gained his feet, and then the cover of the forest. Dale was amused at this. His hand was against all the predatory beasts of the forest, though he had learned that lion and bear and wolf and fox were all as necessary to the great scheme of nature as were the gentle, beautiful wild creatures upon which they preyed. But some he loved better than others, and so he deplored the inexplicable cruelty.

He crossed the wide, grassy plain and struck another gradual descent where aspens and pines crowded a shallow ravine and warm, sun-lighted glades bordered along a sparkling brook. Here be heard a turkey gobble, and that was a signal for him to change his course and make a crouching, silent detour around a clump of aspens. In a sunny patch of grass a dozen or more big gobblers stood, all suspiciously facing in his direction, heads erect, with that wild aspect peculiar to their species. Old wild turkey gobblers were the most difficult game to stalk. Dale shot two of them. The others began to run like ostriches, thudding over the ground, spreading their wings, and with that running start launched their heavy bodies into whirring flight. They flew low, at about the height of a man from the grass, and vanished in the woods.

Dale threw the two turkeys over his shoulder and went on his way. Soon he came to a break in the forest level, from which he gazed down a league-long slope of pine and cedar, out upon the bare, glistening desert, stretching away, endlessly rolling out to the dim, dark horizon line.

The little hamlet of Pine lay on the last level of sparsely timbered forest. A road, running parallel with a dark-watered, swift-flowing stream, divided the cluster of log cabins from which columns of blue smoke drifted lazily aloft. Fields of corn and fields of oats, yellow in the sunlight, surrounded the village; and green pastures, dotted with horses and cattle, reached away to the denser woodland. This site appeared to be a natural clearing, for there was no evidence of cut timber. The scene was rather too wild to be pastoral, but it was serene, tranquil, giving the impression of a remote community, prosperous and happy, drifting along the peaceful tenor of sequestered lives.

Dale halted before a neat little log cabin and a little patch of garden bordered with sunflowers. His call was answered by an old woman, gray and bent, but remarkably spry, who appeared at the door.

"Why, land's sakes, if it ain't Milt Dale!" she exclaimed, in welcome.

"Reckon it's me, Mrs. Cass," he replied. "An, I've brought you a turkey."

"Milt, you're that good boy who never forgits old Widow Cass. . . . What a gobbler! First one I've seen this fall. My man Tom used to fetch home gobblers like that. . . . An' mebbe he'll come home again sometime."

Her husband, Tom Cass, had gone into the forest years before and had never returned. But the old woman always looked for him and never gave up hope.

"Men have been lost in the forest an' yet come back," replied Dale, as he had said to her many a time.

"Come right in. You air hungry, I know. Now, son, when last did you eat a fresh egg or a flapjack?"

"You should remember," he answered, laughing, as he followed her into a small, clean kitchen.

"Laws-a'-me! An' thet's months ago," she replied, shaking her gray head. "Milt, you should give up that wild life - an' marry - an' have a home."

"You always tell me that."

"Yes, an' I'll see you do it yet. . . . Now you set there, an' pretty soon I'll give you thet to eat which 'll make your mouth water."

"What's the news, Auntie?" he asked.

"Nary news in this dead place. Why, nobody's been to Snowdrop in two weeks! . . . Sary Jones died, poor old soul - she's better off - an' one of my cows run away. Milt, she's wild when she gits loose in the woods. An' you'll have to track her, 'cause nobody else can. An' John Dakker's heifer was killed by a lion, an' Lem Harden's fast hoss - you know his favorite - was stole by hoss-thieves. Lem is jest crazy. An' that reminds me, Milt, where's your big ranger, thet you'd never sell or lend?"

"My horses are up in the woods, Auntie; safe, I reckon, from horse-thieves."

"Well, that's a blessin'. We've had some stock stole this summer, Milt, an' no mistake."

Thus, while preparing a meal for Dale, the old woman went on recounting all that had happened in the little village since his last visit. Dale enjoyed her gossip and quaint philosophy, and it was exceedingly good to sit at her table. In his opinion, nowhere else could there have been such butter and cream, such ham and eggs. Besides, she always had apple pie, it seemed, at any time he happened in; and apple pie was one of Dale's few regrets while up in the lonely forest.

"How's old Al Auchincloss?" presently inquired Dale.

"Poorly - poorly," sighed Mrs. Cass. "But he tramps an' rides around same as ever. Al's not long for this world. . . . An', Milt, that reminds me - there's the biggest news you ever heard."

"You don't say so!" exclaimed Dale, to encourage the excited old woman.

"Al has sent back to Saint Joe for his niece, Helen Rayner. She's to inherit all his property. We've heard much of her - a purty lass, they say. . . . Now, Milt Dale, here's your chance. Stay out of the woods an' go to work. . . . You can marry that girl!"

"No chance for me, Auntie," replied Dale, smiling.

The old woman snorted. "Much you know! Any girl would have you, Milt Dale, if you'd only throw a kerchief."

"Me! . . . An' why, Auntie?" he queried, half amused, half thoughtful. When he got back to civilization he always had to adjust his thoughts to the ideas of people.

"Why? I declare, Milt, you live so in the woods you're like a boy of ten - an' then sometimes as old as the hills. . . .There's no young man to compare with you, hereabouts. An' this girl - she'll have all the spunk of the Auchinclosses."

"Then maybe she'd not be such a catch, after all," replied Dale.

"Wal, you've no cause to love them, that's sure. But, Milt, the Auchincloss women are always good wives."

"Dear Auntie, you're dreamin'," said Dale, soberly. "I want no wife. I'm happy in the woods."

"Air you goin' to live like an Injun all your days, Milt Dale?" she queried, sharply.

"I hope so."

"You ought to be ashamed. But some lass will change you, boy, an' mebbe it'll be this Helen Rayner. I hope an' pray so to thet."

"Auntie, supposin' she did change me. She'd never change old Al. He hates me, you know."

"Wal, I ain't so sure, Milt. I met Al the other day. He inquired for you, an' said you was wild, but he reckoned men like you was good for pioneer settlements. Lord knows the good turns you've done this village! Milt, old Al doesn't approve of your wild life, but he never had no hard feelin's till thet tame lion of yours killed so many of his sheep."

"Auntie, I don't believe Tom ever killed Al's sheep," declared Dale, positively.

"Wal, Al thinks so, an' many other people," replied Mrs. Cass, shaking her gray head doubtfully. "You never swore he didn't. An' there was them two sheep-herders who did swear they seen him."

"They only saw a cougar. An' they were so scared they ran."

"Who wouldn't? Thet big beast is enough to scare any one. For land's sakes, don't ever fetch him down here again! I'll never forgit the time you did. All the folks an' children an' hosses in Pine broke an' run thet day."

"Yes; but Tom wasn't to blame. Auntie, he's the tamest of my pets. Didn't he try to put his head on your lap an' lick your hand?"

"Wal, Milt, I ain't gainsayin' your cougar pet didn't act better 'n a lot of people I know. Fer he did. But the looks of him an' what's been said was enough for me."

"An' what's all that, Auntie?"

"They say he's wild when out of your sight. An' thet he'd trail an' kill anythin' you put him after."

"I trained him to be just that way."

"Wal, leave Tom to home up in the woods-when you visit us."

Dale finished his hearty meal, and listened awhile longer to the old woman's talk; then, taking his rifle and the other turkey, he bade her good-by. She followed him out.

"Now, Milt, you'll come soon again, won't you - jest to see Al's niece - who'll be here in a week?"

"I reckon I'll drop in some day. . . . Auntie, have you seen my friends, the Mormon boys?"

"No, I 'ain't seen them an' don't want to," she retorted. "Milt Dale, if any one ever corrals you it'll be Mormons."

"Don't worry, Auntie. I like those boys. They often see me up in the woods an' ask me to help them track a hoss or help kill some fresh meat."

"They're workin' for Beasley now."

"Is that so?" rejoined Dale, with a sudden start. "An' what doin'?"

"Beasley is gettin' so rich he's buildin' a fence, an' didn't have enough help, so I hear."

"Beasley gettin' rich!" repeated Dale, thoughtfully. "More sheep an' horses an' cattle than ever, I reckon?"

"Laws-a'-me! Why, Milt, Beasley 'ain't any idea what he owns. Yes, he's the biggest man in these parts, since poor old Al's took to failin'. I reckon Al's health ain't none improved by Beasley's success. They've had some bitter quarrels lately - so I hear. Al ain't what he was."

Dale bade good-by again to his old friend and strode away, thoughtful and serious. Beasley would not only be difficult to circumvent, but he would be dangerous to oppose. There did not appear much doubt of his driving his way rough-shod to the dominance of affairs there in Pine. Dale, passing down the road, began to meet acquaintances who had hearty welcome for his presence and interest in his doings, so that his pondering was interrupted for the time being. He carried the turkey to another old friend, and when he left her house he went on to the village store. This was a large log cabin, roughly covered with clapboards, with a wide plank platform in front and a hitching-rail in the road. Several horses were standing there, and a group of lazy, shirt-sleeved loungers.

"I'll be doggoned if it ain't Milt Dale!" exclaimed one.

"Howdy, Milt, old buckskin! Right down glad to see you," greeted another.

"Hello, Dale! You air shore good for sore eyes," drawled still another.

After a long period of absence Dale always experienced a singular warmth of feeling when he met these acquaintances. It faded quickly when he got back to the intimacy of his woodland, and that was because the people of Pine, with few exceptions - though they liked him and greatly admired his outdoor wisdom - regarded him as a sort of nonentity. Because he loved the wild and preferred it to village and range life, they had classed him as not one of them. Some believed him lazy; others believed him shiftless; others thought him an Indian in mind and habits; and there were many who called him slow-witted. Then there was another side to their regard for him, which always afforded him good-natured amusement. Two of this group asked him to bring in some turkey or venison; another wanted to hunt with him. Lem Harden came out of the store and appealed to Dale to recover his stolen horse. Lem's brother wanted a wild-running mare tracked and brought home. Jesse Lyons wanted a colt broken, and broken with patience, not violence, as was the method of the hard-riding boys at Pine. So one and all they besieged Dale with their selfish needs, all unconscious of the flattering nature of these overtures. And on the moment there happened by two women whose remarks, as they entered the store, bore strong testimony to Dale's personality.

"If there ain't Milt Dale!" exclaimed the older of the two. "How lucky! My cow's sick, an' the men are no good doctorin'. I'll jest ask Milt over."

"No one like Milt!" responded the other woman, heartily.

"Good day there - you Milt Dale!" called the first speaker. "When you git away from these lazy men come over."

Dale never refused a service, and that was why his infrequent visits to Pine were wont to be prolonged beyond his own pleasure.

Presently Beasley strode down the street, and when about to enter the store he espied Dale.

"Hullo there, Milt!" he called, cordially, as he came forward with extended hand. His greeting was sincere, but the lightning glance he shot over Dale was not born of his pleasure. Seen in daylight, Beasley was a big, bold, bluff man, with strong, dark features. His aggressive presence suggested that he was a good friend and a bad enemy.

Dale shook hands with him.

"How are you, Beasley?"

"Ain't complainin', Milt, though I got more work than I can rustle. Reckon you wouldn't take a job bossin' my sheep-herders?"

"Reckon I wouldn't," replied Dale. "Thanks all the same."

"What's goin' on up in the woods?"

"Plenty of turkey an' deer. Lots of bear, too. The Indians have worked back on the south side early this fall. But I reckon winter will come late an' be mild."

"Good! An' where 're you headin' from?"

"'Cross-country from my camp," replied Dale, rather evasively.

"Your camp! Nobody ever found that yet," declared Beasley, gruffly.

"It's up there," said Dale.

"Reckon you've got that cougar chained in your cabin door?" queried Beasley, and there was a barely distinguishable shudder of his muscular frame. Also the pupils dilated in his hard brown eyes.

"Tom ain't chained. An' I haven't no cabin, Beasley."

"You mean to tell me that big brute stays in your camp without bein' hog-tied or corralled!" demanded Beasley.

"Sure he does."

"Beats me! But, then, I'm queer on cougars. Have had many a cougar trail me at night. Ain't sayin' I was scared. But I don't care for that brand of varmint. . . . Milt, you goin' to stay down awhile?"

"Yes, I'll hang around some."

"Come over to the ranch. Glad to see you any time. Some old huntin' pards of yours are workin' for me."

"Thanks, Beasley. I reckon I'll come over."

Beasley turned away and took a step, and then, as if with an after-thought, he wheeled again.

"Suppose you've heard about old Al Auchincloss bein' near petered out?" queried Beasley. A strong, ponderous cast of thought seemed to emanate from his features. Dale divined that Beasley's next step would be to further his advancement by some word or hint.

"Widow Cass was tellin' me all the news. Too bad about old Al," replied Dale.

"Sure is. He's done for. An' I'm sorry - though Al's never been square -"

"Beasley," interrupted Dale, quickly, "you can't say that to me. Al Auchincloss always was the whitest an' squarest man in this sheep country."

Beasley gave Dale a fleeting, dark glance.

"Dale, what you think ain't goin' to influence feelin' on this range," returned Beasley, deliberately. "You live in the woods an' -"

"Reckon livin' in the woods I might think - an' know a whole lot," interposed Dale, just as deliberately. The group of men exchanged surprised glances. This was Milt Dale in different aspect. And Beasley did not conceal a puzzled surprise.

"About what - now?" he asked, bluntly.

"Why, about what's goin' on in Pine," replied Dale.

Some of the men laughed.

"Shore lots goin' on - an' no mistake," put in Lem Harden.

Probably the keen Beasley had never before considered Milt Dale as a responsible person; certainly never one in any way to cross his trail. But on the instant, perhaps, some instinct was born, or he divined an antagonism in Dale that was both surprising and perplexing.

"Dale, I've differences with Al Auchincloss - have had them for years," said Beasley. "Much of what he owns is mine. An' it's goin' to come to me. Now I reckon people will be takin' sides - some for me an' some for Al. Most are for me. . . . Where do you stand? Al Auchincloss never had no use for you, an' besides he's a dyin' man. Are you goin' on his side?"

"Yes, I reckon I am."

"Wal, I'm glad you've declared yourself," rejoined Beasley, shortly, and he strode away with the ponderous gait of a man who would brush any obstacle from his path.

"Milt, thet's bad - makin' Beasley sore at you," said Lem Harden. "He's on the way to boss this outfit."

"He's sure goin' to step into Al's boots," said another.

"Thet was white of Milt to stick up fer poor old Al," declared Lem's brother.

Dale broke away from them and wended a thoughtful way down the road. The burden of what he knew about Beasley weighed less heavily upon him, and the close-lipped course be had decided upon appeared wisest. He needed to think before undertaking to call upon old Al Auchincloss; and to that end he sought an hour's seclusion under the pines.

CHAPTER III

In the afternoon, Dale, having accomplished some tasks imposed upon him by his old friends at Pine, directed slow steps toward the Auchincloss ranch.

The flat, square stone and log cabin of unusually large size stood upon a little hill half a mile out of the village. A home as well as a fort, it had been the first structure erected in that region, and the process of building had more than once been interrupted by Indian attacks. The Apaches had for some time, however, confined their fierce raids to points south of the White Mountain range. Auchincloss's house looked down upon barns and sheds and corrals of all sizes and shapes, and hundreds of acres of well-cultivated soil. Fields of oats waved gray and yellow in the afternoon sun; an immense green pasture was divided by a willow-bordered brook, and here were droves of horses, and out on the rolling bare flats were straggling herds of cattle.

The whole ranch showed many years of toil and the perseverance of man. The brook irrigated the verdant valley between the ranch and the village. Water for the house, however, came down from the high, wooded slope of the mountain, and had been brought there by a simple expedient. Pine logs of uniform size had been laid end to end, with a deep trough cut in them, and they made a shining line down the slope, across the valley, and up the little hill to the Auchincloss home. Near the house the hollowed halves of logs had been bound together, making a crude pipe. Water ran uphill in this case, one of the facts that made the ranch famous, as it had always been a wonder and delight to the small boys of Pine. The two good women who managed Auchincloss's large household were often shocked by the strange things that floated into their kitchen with the ever-flowing stream of clear, cold mountain water.

As it happened this day Dale encountered Al Auchincloss sitting in the shade of a porch, talking to some of his sheep-herders and stockmen. Auchincloss was a short man of extremely powerful build and great width of shoulder. He had no gray hairs, and he did not look old, yet there was in his face a certain weariness, something that resembled sloping lines of distress, dim and pale, that told of age and the ebb-tide of vitality. His features, cast in large mold, were clean-cut and comely, and he had frank blue eyes, somewhat sad, yet still full of spirit.

Dale had no idea how his visit would be taken, and he certainly would not have been surprised to be ordered off the place. He had not set foot there for years. Therefore it was with surprise that he saw Auchincloss wave away the herders and take his entrance without any particular expression.

"Howdy, Al! How are you?" greeted Dale, easily, as he leaned his rifle against the log wall.

Auchincloss did not rise, but he offered his hand.

"Wal, Milt Dale, I reckon this is the first time I ever

seen you that I couldn't lay you flat on your back," replied the rancher. His tone was both testy and full of pathos.

"I take it you mean you ain't very well," replied Dale. "I'm sorry, Al."

"No, it ain't thet. Never was sick in my life. I'm just played out, like a hoss thet had been strong an' willin', an' did too much. . . .Wal, you don't look a day older, Milt. Livin' in the woods rolls over a man's head."

"Yes, I'm feelin' fine, an' time never bothers me."

"Wal, mebbe you ain't such a fool, after all. I've wondered lately - since I had time to think. . . . But, Milt, you don't git no richer."

"Al, I have all I want an' need."

"Wal, then, you don't support anybody; you don't do any good in the world."

"We don't agree, Al," replied Dale, with his slow smile.

"Reckon we never did. . . . An' you jest come over to pay your respects to me, eh?"

"Not altogether," answered Dale, ponderingly. "First off, I'd like to say I'll pay back them sheep you always claimed my tame cougar killed."

"You will! An' how'd you go about that?"

"Wasn't very many sheep, was there?

"A matter of fifty head."

"So many! Al, do you still think old Tom killed them sheep?"

"Humph! Milt, I know damn well he did."

"Al, now how could you know somethin' I don't? Be reasonable, now. Let's don't fall out about this again. I'll pay back the sheep. Work it out -"

"Milt Dale, you'll come down here an' work out that fifty head of sheep!" ejaculated the old rancher, incredulously.

"Sure."

"Wal, I'll be damned!" He sat back and gazed with shrewd eyes at Dale. "What's got into you, Milt? Hev you heard about my niece thet's comin', an' think you'll shine up to her?"

"Yes, Al, her comin' has a good deal to do with my deal," replied Dale, soberly. "But I never thought to shine up to her, as you hint."

"Haw! Haw! You're just like all the other colts hereabouts. Reckon it's a good sign, too. It'll take a woman to fetch you out of the woods. But, boy, this niece of mine, Helen Rayner, will stand you on your head. I never seen her. They say she's jest like her mother. An' Nell Auchincloss - what a girl she was!"

Dale felt his face grow red. Indeed, this was strange conversation for him.

"Honest, Al -" he began.

"Son, don't lie to an old man."

"Lie! I wouldn't lie to any one. Al, it's only men who live in towns an' are always makin' deals. I live in the forest, where there's nothin' to make me lie."

"Wal, no offense meant, I'm sure," responded Auchincloss. "An' mebbe there's somethin' in what you say . . . We was talkin' about them sheep your big cat killed. Wal, Milt, I can't prove it, that's sure. An' mebbe you'll think me doddery when I tell you my reason. It wasn't what them greaser herders said about seein' a cougar in the herd."

"What was it, then?" queried Dale, much interested.

"Wal, thet day a year ago I seen your pet. He was lyin' in front of the store an' you was inside tradin', fer supplies, I reckon. It was like meetin' an enemy face to face. Because, damn me if I didn't know that cougar was guilty when he looked in my eyes! There!"

The old rancher expected to be laughed at. But Dale was grave.

"Al, I know how you felt," he replied, as if they were discussing an action of a human being. "Sure I'd hate to doubt old Tom. But he's a cougar. An' the ways of animals are strange . . . Anyway, Al, I'll make good the loss of your sheep."

"No, you won't," rejoined Auchincloss, quickly. "We'll call it off . I'm takin' it square of you to make the offer.

Thet's enough. So forget your worry about work, if you had any."

"There's somethin' else, Al, I wanted to say," began Dale, with hesitation. "An' it's about Beasley."

Auchincloss started violently, and a flame of red shot into his face. Then he raised a big hand that shook. Dale saw in a flash how the old man's nerves had gone.

"Don't mention - thet - thet greaser - to me!" burst out the rancher. "It makes me see - red. . . . Dale, I ain't overlookin' that you spoke up fer me to-day - stood fer my side. Lem Harden told me. I was glad. An' thet's why - to-day - I forgot our old quarrel. . . . But not a word about thet sheep-thief - or I'll drive you off the place!"

"But, Al - be reasonable," remonstrated Dale. "It's necessary thet I speak of - of Beasley."

"It ain't. Not to me. I won't listen."

"Reckon you'll have to, Al," returned Dale. "Beasley's after your property. He's made a deal -"

"By Heaven! I know that!" shouted Auchincloss, tottering up, with his face now black-red. "Do you think thet's new to me? Shut up, Dale! I can't stand it."

"But Al - there's worse," went on Dale, hurriedly. "Worse! Your life's threatened - an' your niece, Helen - she's to be -"

"Shut up - an' clear out!" roared Auchincloss, waving his huge fists.

He seemed on the verge of a collapse as, shaking all over, he backed into the door. A few seconds of rage had transformed him into a pitiful old man.

"But, Al - I'm your friend -" began Dale, appealingly.

"Friend, hey?" returned the rancher, with grim, bitter passion. "Then you're the only one. . . . Milt Dale, I'm rich an' I'm a dyin' man. I trust nobody . . . But, you wild hunter - if you're my friend - prove it! . . . Go kill thet greaser sheep-thief! Do somethin' - an' then come talk to me!"

With that he lurched, half falling, into the house, and slammed the door.

Dale stood there for a blank moment, and then, taking up his rifle, he strode away.

Toward sunset Dale located the camp of his four Mormon friends, and reached it in time for supper.

John, Roy, Joe, and Hal Beeman were sons of a pioneer Mormon who had settled the little community of Snowdrop. They were young men in years, but hard labor and hard life in the open had made them look matured. Only a year's difference in age stood between John and Roy, and between Roy and Joe, and likewise Joe and Hal. When it came to appearance they were difficult to distinguish from one another. Horsemen, sheep-herders, cattle-raisers, hunters - they all possessed long, wiry, powerful frames, lean, bronzed, still faces, and the quiet, keen eyes of men used to the open.

Their camp was situated beside a spring in a cove

surrounded by aspens, some three miles from Pine; and, though working for Beasley, near the village, they had ridden to and fro from camp, after the habit of seclusion peculiar to their kind.

Dale and the brothers had much in common, and a warm regard had sprang up. But their exchange of confidences had wholly concerned things pertaining to the forest. Dale ate supper with them, and talked as usual when he met them, without giving any hint of the purpose forming in his mind. After the meal he helped Joe round up the horses, hobble them for the night, and drive them into a grassy glade among the pines. Later, when the shadows stole through the forest on the cool wind, and the camp-fire glowed comfortably, Dale broached the subject that possessed him.

"An' so you're working for Beasley?" he queried, by way of starting conversation.

"We was," drawled John. "But to-day, bein' the end of our month, we got our pay an' quit. Beasley sure was sore."

"Why'd you knock off?"

John essayed no reply, and his brothers all had that quiet, suppressed look of knowledge under restraint.

"Listen to what I come to tell you, then you'll talk," went on Dale. And hurriedly he told of Beasley's plot to abduct Al Auchincloss's niece and claim the dying man's property.

When Dale ended, rather breathlessly, the Mormon boys sat without any show of surprise or feeling. John, the eldest, took up a stick and slowly poked the red embers of the fire, making the white sparks fly.

"Now, Milt, why'd you tell us thet?" he asked, guardedly.

"You're the only friends I've got," replied Dale. "It didn't seem safe for me to talk down in the village. I thought of you boys right off. I ain't goin' to let Snake Anson get that girl. An' I need help, so I come to you."

"Beasley's strong around Pine, an' old Al's weakenin'. Beasley will git the property, girl or no girl," said John.

"Things don't always turn out as they look. But no matter about that. The girl deal is what riled me. . . . She's to arrive at Magdalena on the sixteenth, an' take stage for Snowdrop. . . . Now what to do? If she travels on that stage I'll be on it, you bet. But she oughtn't to be in it at all. . . . Boys, somehow I'm goin' to save her. Will you help me? I reckon I've been in some tight corners for you. Sure, this 's different. But are you my friends? You know now what Beasley is. An' you're all lost at the hands of Snake Anson's gang. You've got fast hosses, eyes for trackin', an' you can handle a rifle. You're the kind of fellows I'd want in a tight pinch with a bad gang. Will you stand by me or see me go alone?"

Then John Beeman, silently, and with pale face, gave Dale's hand a powerful grip, and one by one the other brothers rose to do likewise. Their eyes flashed with hard glint and a strange bitterness hovered around their thin lips.

"Milt, mebbe we know what Beasley is better 'n you,"

said John, at length. "He ruined my father. He's cheated other Mormons. We boys have proved to ourselves thet he gets the sheep Anson's gang steals. . . An' drives the herds to Phenix! Our people won't let us accuse Beasley. So we've suffered in silence. My father always said, let some one else say the first word against Beasley, an' you've come to us!"

Roy Beeman put a hand on Dale's shoulder. He, perhaps, was the keenest of the brothers and the one to whom adventure and peril called most. He had been oftenest with Dale, on many a long trail, and he was the hardest rider and the most relentless tracker in all that range country.

"An' we're goin' with you," he said, in a strong and rolling voice.

They resumed their seats before the fire. John threw on more wood, and with a crackling and sparkling the blaze curled up, fanned by the wind. As twilight deepened into night the moan in the pines increased to a roar. A pack of coyotes commenced to pierce the air in staccato cries.

The five young men conversed long and earnestly, considering, planning, rejecting ideas advanced by each. Dale and Roy Beeman suggested most of what became acceptable to all. Hunters of their type resembled explorers in slow and deliberate attention to details. What they had to deal with here was a situation of unlimited possibilities; the horses and outfit needed; a long detour to reach Magdalena unobserved; the rescue of a strange girl who would no doubt be self-willed and determined to ride on the stage - the rescue forcible, if necessary; the fight and the inevitable pursuit; the flight into the forest, and the safe delivery of the girl to Auchincloss.

"Then, Milt, will we go after Beasley?" queried Roy Beeman, significantly.

Dale was silent and thoughtful.

"Sufficient unto the day!" said John. "An, fellars, let's go to bed."

They rolled out their tarpaulins, Dale sharing Roy's blankets, and soon were asleep, while the red embers slowly faded, and the great roar of wind died down, and the forest stillness set in.

CHAPTER IV

Helen Rayner had been on the westbound overland train fully twenty-four hours before she made an alarming discovery.

Accompanied by her sister Bo, a precocious girl of sixteen, Helen had left St. Joseph with a heart saddened by farewells to loved ones at home, yet full of thrilling and vivid anticipations of the strange life in the Far West. All her people had the pioneer spirit; love of change, action, adventure, was in her blood. Then duty to a widowed mother with a large and growing family had called to Helen to accept this rich uncle's offer. She had taught school and also her little brothers and sisters; she had helped along in other ways. And now, though the tearing up of the roots of old loved ties was hard, this opportunity was irresistible in its call. The prayer of her dreams had been answered. To bring good fortune to her family; to take care of this beautiful, wild little sister; to leave the yellow, sordid, humdrum towns for the great, rolling, boundless open; to live on a wonderful ranch that was some day to be her own; to have fulfilled a deep, instinctive, and undeveloped love of horses, cattle, sheep, of desert and mountain, of trees and brooks and wild flowers - all this was the sum of her most passionate longings, now in some marvelous, fairylike way to come true.

A check to her happy anticipations, a blank, sickening dash of cold water upon her warm and intimate dreams, had been the discovery that Harve Riggs was on the train. His presence could mean only one thing - that he had followed her. Riggs had been the worst of many sore trials back there in St. Joseph. He had possessed some claim or influence upon her mother, who favored his offer of marriage to Helen; he was neither attractive, nor good, nor industrious, nor anything that interested her; he was the boastful, strutting adventurer, not genuinely Western, and he affected long hair and guns and notoriety. Helen had suspected the veracity of the many fights he claimed had been his, and also she suspected that he was not really big enough to be bad - as Western men were bad. But on the train, in the station at La Junta, one glimpse of him, manifestly spying upon her while trying to keep out of her sight, warned Helen that she now might have a problem on her hands.

The recognition sobered her. All was not to be a road of roses to this new home in the West. Riggs would follow her, if he could not accompany her, and to gain his own ends he would stoop to anything. Helen felt the startling realization of being cast upon her own resources, and then a numbing discouragement and loneliness and helplessness. But these feelings did not long persist in the quick pride and flash of her temper. Opportunity knocked at her door and she meant to be at home to it. She would not have been Al Auchincloss's niece if she had faltered. And, when temper was succeeded by genuine anger, she could have laughed to scorn this Harve Riggs and his schemes, whatever they were. Once and for all she dismissed fear of him. When she left St. Joseph she had faced the West with a beating heart and a high resolve to be worthy of that West. Homes had to be made out there in that far country, so Uncle Al had written, and women were needed to make homes. She meant to be one of these women and to make of her sister another. And with the thought that she would know definitely what to say to Riggs when he approached her, sooner or later, Helen dismissed him from mind.

While the train was in motion, enabling Helen to watch the ever-changing scenery, and resting her from the strenuous task of keeping Bo well in hand at stations, she lapsed again into dreamy gaze at the pine forests and the red, rocky gullies and the dim, bold mountains. She saw the sun set over distant ranges of New Mexico - a golden blaze of glory, as new to her as the strange fancics born in her, thrilling and fleeting by. Bo's raptures were not silent, and the instant the sun sank and the color faded she just as rapturously importuned Helen to get out the huge basket of food they bad brought from home.

They had two seats, facing each other, at the end of the coach, and piled there, with the basket on top, was luggage that constituted all the girls owned in the world. Indeed, it was very much more than they had ever owned before, because their mother, in her care for them and desire to have them look well in the eyes of this rich uncle, had spent money and pains to give them pretty and serviceable clothes.

The girls sat together, with the heavy basket on their knees, and ate while they gazed out at the cool, dark ridges. The train clattered slowly on, apparently over a road that was all curves. And it was supper-time for everybody in that crowded coach. If Helen had not been so absorbed by the great, wild mountain-land she would have had more interest in the passengers. As it was she saw them, and was amused and thoughtful at the men and women and a few children in the car, all middle-class people, poor and hopeful, traveling out there to the New West to find homes. It was splendid and beautiful, this fact, yet it inspired a brief and inexplicable sadness. From the train window, that world of forest and crag, with its long bare reaches between, seemed so lonely, so wild, so unlivable. How endless the distance! For hours and miles upon miles no house, no hut, no Indian tepee! It was amazing, the length and breadth of this beautiful land. And Helen, who loved brooks and running streams, saw no water at all.

Then darkness settled down over the slow-moving panorama; a cool night wind blew in at the window; white stars began to blink out of the blue. The sisters, with hands clasped and heads nestled together, went to sleep under a heavy cloak.

Early the next morning, while the girls were again delving into their apparently bottomless basket, the train stopped at Las Vegas.

"Look! Look!" cried Bo, in thrilling voice. "Cowboys! Oh, Nell, look!"

Helen, laughing, looked first at her sister, and thought how most of all she was good to look at. Bo was little, instinct with pulsating life, and she had chestnut hair and dark-blue eyes. These eyes were flashing, roguish, and they drew like magnets.

Outside on the rude station platform were railroad

men, Mexicans, and a group of lounging cowboys. Long, lean, bow-legged fellows they were, with young, frank faces and intent eyes. One of them seemed particularly attractive with his superb build, his red-bronze face and bright-red scarf, his swinging gun, and the huge, long, curved spurs. Evidently he caught Bo's admiring gaze, for, with a word to his companions, he sauntered toward the window where the girls sat. His gait was singular, almost awkward, as if he was not accustomed to walking. The long spurs jingled musically. He removed his sombrero and stood at ease, frank, cool, smiling. Helen liked him on sight, and, looking to see what effect he had upon Bo, she found that young lady staring, frightened stiff.

"Good mawnin'," drawled the cowboy, with slow, good-humored smile. "Now where might you-all be travelin'?"

The sound of his voice, the clean-cut and droll geniality; seemed new and delightful to Helen.

"We go to Magdalena - then take stage for the White Mountains," replied Helen.

The cowboy's still, intent eyes showed surprise.

"Apache country, miss," he said. "I reckon I'm sorry. Thet's shore no place for you-all . . . Beggin' your pawdin - you ain't Mormons?"

"No. We're nieces of Al Auchincloss," rejoined Helen.

"Wal, you don't say! I've been down Magdalena way an' heerd of Al. . . . Reckon you're goin' a-visitin'?"

"It's to be home for us."

"Shore thet's fine. The West needs girls. . . . Yes, I've heerd of Al. An old Arizona cattle-man in a sheep country! Thet's bad. . . . Now I'm wonderin' - if I'd drift down there an' ask him for a job ridin' for him - would I get it?"

His lazy smile was infectious and his meaning was as clear as crystal water. The gaze he bent upon Bo somehow pleased Helen. The last year or two, since Bo had grown prettier all the time, she had been a magnet for admiring glances. This one of the cowboy's inspired respect and liking, as well as amusement. It certainly was not lost upon Bo.

"My uncle once said in a letter that he never had enough men to run his ranch," replied Helen, smiling.

"Shore I'll go. I reckon I'd jest naturally drift that way - now."

He seemed so laconic, so easy, so nice, that he could not have been taken seriously, yet Helen's quick perceptions registered a daring, a something that was both sudden and inevitable in him. His last word was as clear as the soft look he fixed upon Bo.

Helen had a mischievous trait, which, subdue it as she would, occasionally cropped out; and Bo, who once in her wilful life had been rendered speechless, offered such a temptation.

"Maybe my little sister will put in a good word for you - to Uncle Al," said Helen. Just then the train jerked, and started slowly.

The cowboy took two long strides beside the car, his heated boyish face almost on a level with the window, his eyes, now shy and a little wistful, yet bold, too, fixed upon Bo.

"Good-by - Sweetheart!" he called.

He halted - was lost to view.

"Well!" ejaculated Helen, contritely, half sorry, half amused. "What a sudden young gentleman!"

Bo had blushed beautifully.

"Nell, wasn't he glorious!" she burst out, with eyes shining.

"I'd hardly call him that, but he was-nice," replied Helen, much relieved that Bo had apparently not taken offense at her.

It appeared plain that Bo resisted a frantic desire to look out of the window and to wave her hand. But she only peeped out, manifestly to her disappointment.

"Do you think he - he'll come to Uncle Al's?" asked Bo.

"Child, he was only in fun."

"Nell, I'll bet you he comes. Oh, it'd be great! I'm going to love cowboys. They don't look like that Harve Riggs who ran after you so."

Helen sighed, partly because of the reminder of her odious suitor, and partly because Bo's future already called mysteriously to the child. Helen had to be at once a mother and a protector to a girl of intense and wilful spirit.

One of the trainmen directed the girls' attention to a green, sloping mountain rising to a bold, blunt bluff of bare rock; and, calling it Starvation Peak, be told a story of how Indians had once driven Spaniards up there and starved them. Bo was intensely interested, and thereafter she watched more keenly than ever, and always had a question for a passing trainman. The adobe houses of the Mexicans pleased her, and, then the train got out into Indian country, where pueblos appeared near the track and Indians with their bright colors and shaggy wild mustangs - then she was enraptured.

"But these Indians are peaceful!" she exclaimed once, regretfully.

"Gracious, child! You don't want to see hostile Indians, do you?" queried Helen.

"I do, you bet," was the frank rejoinder.

"Well, I'll bet that I'll be sorry I didn't leave you with mother."

"Nell - you never will!"

They reached Albuquerque about noon, and this important station, where they had to change trains, had been the first dreaded anticipation of the journey. It certainly was a busy place - full of jabbering Mexicans, stalking, red-faced, wicked-looking cow-boys, lolling Indians. In the confusion Helen would have been hard put to it to preserve calmness, with Bo to watch, and all that baggage to carry, and the other train to find; but the kindly brakeman who had been attentive to them now helped them off the train into the other - a service for which Helen was very grateful.

"Albuquerque's a hard place," confided the trainman. "Better stay in the car - and don't hang out the windows. . . . Good luck to you!"

Only a few passengers were in the car and they were Mexicans at the forward end. This branch train consisted of one passenger-coach, with a baggage-car, attached to a string of freight-cars. Helen told herself, somewhat grimly, that soon she would know surely whether or not her suspicions of Harve Riggs had warrant. If he was going on to Magdalena on that day he must go in this coach. Presently Bo, who was not obeying admonitions, drew her head out of the window. Her eyes were wide in amaze, her mouth open.

"Nell! I saw that man Riggs!" she whispered. "He's going to get on this train."

"Bo, I saw him yesterday," replied Helen, soberly. "He's followed you - the - the - "

"Now, Bo, don't get excited," remonstrated Helen. "We've left home now. We've got to take things as they come. Never mind if Riggs has followed me. I'll settle him."

"Oh! Then you won't speak - have anything to do with him?"

"I won't if I can help it."

Other passengers boarded the train, dusty, uncouth, ragged men, and some hard-featured, poorly clad women, marked by toil, and several more Mexicans. With bustle and loud talk they found their several seats.

Then Helen saw Harve Riggs enter, burdened with much luggage. He was a man of about medium height, of dark, flashy appearance, cultivating long black mustache and hair. His apparel was striking, as it consisted of black frock-coat, black trousers stuffed in high, fancy-topped boots, an embroidered vest, and flowing tie, and a black sombrero. His belt and gun were prominent. It was significant that he excited comment among the other passengers.

When he had deposited his pieces of baggage he seemed to square himself, and, turning abruptly, approached the seat occupied by the girls. When he reached it he sat down upon the arm of the one opposite, took off his sombrero, and deliberately looked at Helen. His eyes were light, glinting, with hard, restless quiver, and his mouth was coarse and arrogant. Helen had never seen him detached from her home surroundings, and now the difference struck cold upon her heart.

"Hello, Nell!" he said. "Surprised to see me?"

"No," she replied, coldly.

"I'll gamble you are."

"Harve Riggs, I told you the day before I left home that

nothing you could do or say mattered to me."

"Reckon that ain't so, Nell. Any woman I keep track of has reason to think. An' you know it."

"Then you followed me - out here?" demanded Helen, and her voice, despite her control, quivered with anger

"I sure did," he replied, and there was as much thought of himself in the act as there was of her.

"Why? Why? It's useless - hopeless."

"I swore I'd have you, or nobody else would," he replied, and here, in the passion of his voice there sounded egotism rather than hunger for a woman's love. "But I reckon I'd have struck West anyhow, sooner or later."

"You're not going to - all the way - to Pine?" faltered Helen, momentarily weakening.

"Nell, I'll camp on your trail from now on," he declared.

Then Bo sat bolt-upright, with pale face and flashing eyes.

"Harve Riggs, you leave Nell alone," she burst out, in ringing, brave young voice. "I'll tell you what - I'll bet - if you follow her and nag her any more, my uncle Al or some cowboy will run you out of the country."

"Hello, Pepper!" replied Riggs, coolly. "I see your manners haven't improved an' you're still wild about cowboys."

"People don't have good manners with - with -"

"Bo, hush!" admonished Helen. It was difficult to reprove Bo just then, for that young lady had not the slightest fear of Riggs. Indeed, she looked as if she could slap his face. And Helen realized that however her intelligence had grasped the possibilities of leaving home for a wild country, and whatever her determination to be brave, the actual beginning of self-reliance had left her spirit weak. She would rise out of that. But just now this flashing-eyed little sister seemed a protector. Bo would readily adapt herself to the West, Helen thought, because she was so young, primitive, elemental.

Whereupon Bo turned her back to Riggs and looked out of the window. The man laughed. Then he stood up and leaned over Helen.

"Nell, I'm goin' wherever you go," he said, steadily. "You can take that friendly or not, just as it pleases you. But if you've got any sense you'll not give these people out here a hunch against me. I might hurt somebody. . . . An' wouldn't it be better - to act friends? For I'm goin' to look after you, whether you like it or not."

Helen had considered this man an annoyance, and later a menace, and now she must declare open enmity with him. However disgusting the idea that he considered himself a factor in her new life, it was the truth. He existed, he had control over his movements. She could not change that. She hated the need of thinking so much about him; and suddenly, with a hot, bursting anger, she hated the man.

"You'll not look after me. I'll take care of myself," she said, and she turned her back upon him. She heard him mutter under his breath and slowly move away down the car. Then Bo slipped a hand in hers.

"Never mind, Nell," she whispered. "You know what old Sheriff Haines said about Harve Riggs. 'A four-flush would-be gun-fighter! If he ever strikes a real Western town he'll get run out of it.' I just wish my red-faced cowboy had got on this train!"

Helen felt a rush of gladness that she had yielded to Bo's wild importunities to take her West. The spirit which had made Bo incorrigible at home probably would make her react happily to life out in this free country. Yet Helen, with all her warmth and gratefulness, had to laugh at her sister.

"Your red-faced cowboy! Why, Bo, you were scared stiff. And now you claim him!"

"I certainly could love that fellow," replied Bo, dreamily.

"Child, you've been saying that about fellows for a long time. And you've never looked twice at any of them yet."

"He was different. . . . Nell, I'll bet he comes to Pine."

"I hope he does. I wish he was on this train. I liked his looks, Bo."

"Well, Nell dear, he looked at me first and last - so don't get your hopes up. . . . Oh, the train's starting! . . . Good-by,

Albu-ker - what's that awful name? . . . Nell, let's eat dinner. I'm starved."

Then Helen forgot her troubles and the uncertain future, and what with listening to Bo's chatter, and partaking again of the endless good things to eat in the huge basket, and watching the noble mountains, she drew once more into happy mood.

The valley of the Rio Grande opened to view, wide near at hand in a great gray-green gap between the bare black mountains, narrow in the distance, where the yellow river wound away, glistening under a hot sun. Bo squealed in glee at sight of naked little Mexican children that darted into adobe huts as the train clattered by, and she exclaimed her pleasure in the Indians, and the mustangs, and particularly in a group of cowboys riding into town on spirited horses. Helen saw all Bo pointed out, but it was to the wonderful rolling valley that her gaze clung longest, and to the dim purple distance that seemed to hold something from her. She had never before experienced any feeling like that; she had never seen a tenth so far. And the sight awoke something strange in her. The sun was burning hot, as she could tell when she put a hand outside the window, and a strong wind blew sheets of dry dust at the train. She gathered at once what tremendous factors in the Southwest were the sun and the dust and the wind. And her realization made her love them. It was there; the open, the wild, the beautiful, the lonely land; and she felt the poignant call of blood in her - to seek, to strive, to find, to live. One look down that yellow valley, endless between its dark iron ramparts, had given her understanding of her uncle. She must be like him in spirit, as it was claimed she resembled him otherwise.

At length Bo grew tired of watching scenery that contained no life, and, with her bright head on the faded cloak, she went to sleep. But Helen kept steady, farseeing gaze out upon that land of rock and plain; and during the long hours, as she watched through clouds of dust and veils of heat, some strong and doubtful and restless sentiment seemed to change and then to fix. It was her physical acceptance - her eyes and her senses taking the West as she had already taken it in spirit.

A woman should love her home wherever fate placed her, Helen believed, and not so much from duty as from delight and romance and living. How could life ever be tedious or monotonous out here in this tremendous vastness of bare earth and open sky, where the need to achieve made thinking and pondering superficial?

It was with regret that she saw the last of the valley of the Rio Grande, and then of its paralleled mountain ranges. But the miles brought compensation in other valleys, other bold, black upheavals of rock, and then again bare, boundless yellow plains, and sparsely cedared ridges, and white dry washes, ghastly in the sunlight, and dazzling beds of alkali, and then a desert space where golden and blue flowers bloomed.

She noted, too, that the whites and yellows of earth and rock had begun to shade to red - and this she knew meant an approach to Arizona. Arizona, the wild, the lonely, the red desert, the green plateau - Arizona with its thundering rivers, its unknown spaces, its pasture-lands and timber-lands, its wild horses, cowboys, outlaws, wolves and lions and savages! As to a boy, that name stirred and thrilled and sang to her of nameless, sweet, intangible things, mysterious and all of adventure. But she, being a girl of twenty, who had accepted responsibilities, must conceal the depths of her heart and that which her mother had complained was her misfortune in not being born a boy.

Time passed, while Helen watched and learned and dreamed. The train stopped, at long intervals, at wayside stations where there seemed nothing but adobe sheds and lazy Mexicans, and dust and heat. Bo awoke and began to chatter, and to dig into the basket. She learned from the conductor that Magdalena was only two stations on. And she was full of conjectures as to who would meet them, what would happen. So Helen was drawn back to sober realities, in which there was considerable zest. Assuredly she did not know what was going to happen. Twice Riggs passed up and down the aisle, his dark face and light eyes and sardonic smile deliberately forced upon her sight. But again Helen fought a growing dread with contemptuous scorn. This fellow was not half a man. It was not conceivable what he could do, except annoy her, until she arrived at Pine. Her uncle was to meet her or send for her at Snowdrop, which place, Helen knew, was distant a good long ride by stage from Magdalena. This stage-ride was the climax and the dread of all the long journey, in Helen's considerations.

"Oh, Nell!" cried Bo, with delight. "We're nearly there! Next station, the conductor said."

"I wonder if the stage travels at night," said Helen, thoughtfully.

"Sure it does!" replied the irrepressible Bo.

The train, though it clattered along as usual, seemed to Helen to fly. There the sun was setting over bleak New Mexican bluffs, Magdalena was at hand, and night, and adventure. Helen's heart beat fast. She watched the yellow plains where the cattle grazed; their presence, and irrigation ditches and cottonwood-trees told her that the railroad part of the journey was nearly ended. Then, at Bo's little scream, she looked across the car and out of the window to see a line of low, flat, red-adobe houses. The train began to slow down. Helen saw children run, white children and Mexican together; then more houses, and high upon a hill an immense adobe church, crude and glaring, yet somehow beautiful.

Helen told Bo to put on her bonnet, and, performing a like office for herself, she was ashamed of the trembling of her fingers. There were bustle and talk in the car.

The train stopped. Helen peered out to see a straggling crowd of Mexicans and Indians, all motionless and stolid, as if trains or nothing else mattered. Next Helen saw a white man, and that was a relief. He stood out in front of the others. Tall and broad, somehow striking, he drew a second glance that showed him to be a hunter clad in gray-fringed buckskin, and carrying a rifle.

CHAPTER V

Here, there was no kindly brakeman to help the sisters with their luggage. Helen bade Bo take her share; thus burdened, they made an awkward and laborious shift to get off the train.

Upon the platform of the car a strong hand seized Helen's heavy bag, with which she was straining, and a loud voice called out:

"Girls, we're here - sure out in the wild an' woolly West!"

The speaker was Riggs, and he had possessed himself of part of her baggage with action and speech meant more to impress the curious crowd than to be really kind. In the excitement of arriving Helen had forgotten him. The manner of sudden reminder - the insincerity of it - made her temper flash. She almost fell, encumbered as she was, in her hurry to descend the steps. She saw the tall hunter in gray step forward close to her as she reached for the bag Riggs held.

"Mr. Riggs, I'll carry my bag," she said.

"Let me lug this. You help Bo with hers," he replied, familiarly.

"But I want it," she rejoined, quietly, with sharp

determination. No little force was needed to pull the bag away from Riggs.

"See here, Helen, you ain't goin' any farther with that joke, are you?" he queried, deprccatingly, and he still spoke quite loud.

"It's no joke to me," replied Helen. "I told you I didn't want your attention."

"Sure. But that was temper. I'm your friend - from your home town. An' I ain't goin' to let a quarrel keep me from lookin' after you till you're safe at your uncle's."

Helen turned her back upon him. The tall hunter had just helped Bo off the car. Then Helen looked up into a smooth bronzed face and piercing gray eyes.

"Are you Helen Rayner?" he asked.

"Yes."

"My name's Dale. I've come to meet you."

"Ah! My uncle sent you?" added Helen, in quick relief.

"No; I can't say Al sent me," began the man, "but I reckon -"

He was interrupted by Riggs, who, grasping Helen by the arm, pulled her back a step.

"Say, mister, did Auchincloss send you to meet my young friends here?" he demanded, arrogantly.

Dale's glance turned from Helen to Riggs. She could

not read this quiet gray gaze, but it thrilled her.

"No. I come on my own hook," he answered.

"You'll understand, then - they're in my charge," added Riggs.

This time the steady light-gray eyes met Helen's, and if there was not a smile in them or behind them she was still further baffled.

"Helen, I reckon you said you didn't want this fellow's attention."

"I certainly said that," replied Helen, quickly. Just then Bo slipped close to her and gave her arm a little squeeze. Probably Bo's thought was like hers - here was a real Western man. That was her first impression, and following swiftly upon it was a sensation of eased nerves.

Riggs swaggered closer to Dale.

"Say, Buckskin, I hail from Texas -"

"You're wastin' our time an' we've need to hurry," interrupted Dale. His tone seemed friendly. "An' if you ever lived long in Texas you wouldn't pester a lady an' you sure wouldn't talk like you do."

"What!" shouted Riggs, hotly. He dropped his right hand significantly to his hip.

"Don't throw your gun. It might go off," said Dale.

Whatever Riggs's intention had been - and it was

probably just what Dale evidently had read it - he now flushed an angry red and jerked at his gun.

Dale's hand flashed too swiftly for Helen's eye to follow it. But she heard the thud as it struck. The gun went flying to the platform and scattered a group of Indians and Mexicans.

"You'll hurt yourself some day," said Dale.

Helen had never heard a slow, cool voice like this hunter's. Without excitement or emotion or hurry, it yet seemed full and significant of things the words did not mean. Bo uttered a strange little exultant cry.

Riggs's arm had dropped limp. No doubt it was numb. He stared, and his predominating expression was surprise. As the shuffling crowd began to snicker and whisper, Riggs gave Dale a malignant glance, shifted it to Helen, and then lurched away in the direction of his gun.

Dale did not pay any more attention to him. Gathering up Helen's baggage, he said, "Come on," and shouldered a lane through the gaping crowd. The girls followed close at his heels.

"Nell! what 'd I tell you?" whispered Bo. "Oh, you're all atremble!"

Helen was aware of her unsteadiness; anger and fear and relief in quick succession had left her rather weak. Once through the motley crowd of loungers, she saw an old gray stage-coach and four lean horses. A grizzled, sunburned man sat on the driver's seat, whip and reins in hand. Beside him was a younger man with rifle across his knees. Another man, young, tall, lean, dark, stood holding the coach door open. He touched his sombrero to the girls. His eyes were sharp as he addressed Dale.

"Milt, wasn't you held up?"

"No. But some long-haired galoot was tryin' to hold up the girls. Wanted to throw his gun on me. I was sure scared," replied Dale, as he deposited the luggage.

Bo laughed. Her eyes, resting upon Dale, were warm and bright. The young man at the coach door took a second look at her, and then a smile changed the dark hardness of his face.

Dale helped the girls up the high step into the stage, and then, placing the lighter luggage, in with them, he threw the heavier pieces on top

"Joe, climb up," he said.

"Wal, Milt," drawled the driver," let's ooze along."

Dale hesitated, with his hand on the door. He glanced at the crowd, now edging close again, and then at Helen.

"I reckon I ought to tell you," he said, and indecision appeared to concern him.

"What?" exclaimed Helen.

"Bad news. But talkin' takes time. An' we mustn't lose any."

"There's need of hurry?" queried Helen, sitting up sharply.

"I reckon."

"Is this the stage to Snowdrop?

"No. That leaves in the mornin'. We rustled this old trap to get a start to-night."

"The sooner the better. But I - I don't understand," said Helen, bewildered.

"It'll not be safe for you to ride on the mornin' stage," returned Dale.

"Safe! Oh, what do you mean?" exclaimed Helen. Apprehensively she gazed at him and then back at Bo.

"Explainin' will take time. An' facts may change your mind. But if you can't trust me -"

"Trust you!" interposed Helen, blankly. "You mean to take us to Snowdrop? "

"I reckon we'd better go roundabout an' not hit Snowdrop," he replied, shortly.

"Then to Pine - to my uncle - Al Auchincloss?

"Yes, I'm goin' to try hard."

Helen caught her breath. She divined that some peril menaced her. She looked steadily, with all a woman's keenness, into this man's face. The moment was one of the fateful decisions she knew the West had in store for her. Her future and that of Bo's were now to be dependent upon her judgments. It was a hard moment and, though she shivered inwardly, she welcomed the initial and inevitable step. This man Dale, by his dress of buckskin, must be either scout or hunter. His size, his action, the tone of his voice had been reassuring. But Helen must decide from what she saw in his face whether or not to trust him. And that face was clear bronze, unlined, unshadowed, like a tranquil mask, clean-cut, strong-jawed, with eyes of wonderful transparent gray.

"Yes, I'll trust you," she said. "Get in, and let us hurry. Then you can explain."

"All ready, Bill. Send 'em along," called Dale.

He had to stoop to enter the stage, and, once in, he appeared to fill that side upon which he sat. Then the driver cracked his whip; the stage lurched and began to roll; the motley crowd was left bchind. Helen awakened to the reality, as she saw Bo staring with big eyes at the hunter, that a stranger adventure than she had ever dreamed of had began with the rattling roll of that old stage-coach.

Dale laid off his sombrero and leaned forward, holding his rifle between his knees. The light shone better upon his features now that he was bareheaded. Helen had never seen a face like that, which at first glance appeared darkly bronzed and hard, and then became clear, cold, aloof, still, intense. She wished she might see a smile upon it. And now that the die was cast she could not tell why she had trusted it. There was singular force in it, but she did not recognize what kind of force. One instant she thought it was stern, and the next that it was sweet, and again that it was neither.

"I'm glad you've got your sister," he said, presently.

"How did you know she's my sister?"

"I reckon she looks like you."

"No one else ever thought so," replied Helen, trying to smile.

Bo had no difficulty in smiling, as she said, "Wish I was half as pretty as Nell."

"Nell. Isn't your name Helen?" queried Dale.

"Yes. But my - some few call me Nell."

"I like Nell better than Helen. An' what's yours?" went on Dale, looking at Bo.

"Mine's Bo. just plain B-o. Isn't it silly? But I wasn't asked when they gave it to me," she replied.

"Bo. It's nice an' short. Never heard it before. But I haven't met many people for years."

"Oh! we've left the town!" cried Bo. "Look, Nell! How bare! It's just like desert."

"It is desert. We've forty miles of that before we come to a hill or a tree."

Helen glanced out. A flat, dull-green expanse waved away from the road on and on to a bright, dark horizon-line, where the sun was setting rayless in a clear sky. Open, desolate, and lonely, the scene gave her a cold thrill.

"Did your uncle Al ever write anythin' about a man named Beasley?" asked Dale.

"Indeed he did," replied Helen, with a start of surprise.

"Beasley! That name is familiar to us - and detestable. My uncle complained of this man for years. Then he grew bitter - accused Beasley. But the last year or so not a word!"

"Well, now," began the hunter, earnestly, "let's get the bad news over. I'm sorry you must be worried. But you must learn to take the West as it is. There's good an' bad, maybe more bad. That's because the country's young. . . . So to come right out with it - this Beasley hired a gang of outlaws to meet the stage you was goin' in to Snowdrop - to-morrow - an' to make off with you."

"Make off with me?" ejaculated Helen, bewildered.

"Kidnap you! Which, in that gang, would be worse than killing you!" declared Dale, grimly, and he closed a huge fist on his knee.

Helen was utterly astounded.

"How hor-rible!" she gasped out. "Make off with me! . . . What in Heaven's name for?"

Bo gave vent to a fierce little utterance.

"For reasons you ought to guess," replied Dale, and he

leaned forward again. Neither his voice nor face changed in the least, but yet there was a something about him that fascinated Helen. "I'm a hunter. I live in the woods. A few nights ago I happened to be caught out in a storm an' I took to an old log cabin. Soon as I got there I heard horses. I hid up in the loft. Some men rode up an' come in. It was dark. They couldn't see me. An' they talked. It turned out they were Snake Anson an' his gang of sheep-thieves. They expected to meet Beasley there. Pretty soon he came. He told Anson how old Al, your uncle, was on his last legs - how he had sent for you to have his property when he died. Beasley swore he had claims on Al. An' he made a deal with Anson to get you out of the way. He named the day you were to reach Magdalena. With Al dead an' you not there, Beasley could get the property. An' then he wouldn't care if you did come to claim it. It 'd be too late. . . . Well, they rode away that night. An' next day I rustled down to Pine. They're all my friends at Pine, except old Al. But they think I'm queer. I didn't want to confide. in many people. Beasley is strong in Pine, an' for that matter I suspect Snake Anson has other friends there besides Beasley. So I went to see your uncle. He never had any use for me because he thought I was lazy like an Indian. Old Al hates lazy men. Then we fell out - or he fell out - because he believed a tame lion of mine had killed some of his sheep. An' now I reckon that Tom might have done it. I tried to lead up to this deal of Beasley's about you, but old Al wouldn't listen. He's cross - very cross. An' when I tried to tell him, why, he went right out of his head. Sent me off the ranch. Now I reckon you begin to see what a pickle I was in. Finally I went to four friends I could trust. They're Mormon boys - brothers.

That's Joe out on top, with the driver. I told them all

about Beasley's deal an' asked them to help me. So we planned to beat Anson an' his gang to Magdalena. It happens that Beasley is as strong in Magdalena as he is in Pine. An' we had to go careful. But the boys had a couple of friends here - Mormons, too, who agreed to help us. They had this old stage. . . . An' here you are." Dale spread out his big hands and looked gravely at Helen and then at Bo.

"You're perfectly splendid!" cried Bo, ringingly. She was white; her fingers were clenched; her eyes blazed.

Dale appeared startled out of his gravity, and surprised, then pleased. A smile made his face like a boy's. Helen felt her body all rigid, yet slightly trembling. Her hands were cold. The horror of this revelation held her speechless. But in her heart she echoed Bo's exclamation of admiration and gratitude.

"So far, then," resumed Dale, with a heavy breath of relief. "No wonder you're upset. I've a blunt way of talkin'. . . . Now we've thirty miles to ride on this Snowdrop road before we can turn off. To-day sometime the rest of the boys - Roy, John, an' Hal - were to leave Show Down, which's a town farther on from Snowdrop. They have my horses an' packs besides their own. Somewhere on the road we'll meet them - to-night, maybe - or tomorrow. I hope not to-night, because that 'd mean Anson's gang was ridin' in to Magdalena."

Helen wrung her hands helplessly.

"Oh, have I no courage?" she whispered.

"Nell, I'm as scared as you are," said Bo, consolingly,

embracing her sister.

"I reckon that's natural," said Dale, as if excusing
them. "But, scared or not, you both brace up. It's a bad
job. But I've done my best. An' you'll be safer with me
an' the Beeman boys than you'd be in Magdalena, or
anywhere else, except your uncle's."

"Mr. - Mr. Dale," faltered Helen, with her tears falling,
"don't think me a coward - or - or ungrateful. I'm
neither. It's only I'm so - so shocked. After all we
hoped and expected - this - this - is such a - a terrible
surprise."

"Never mind, Nell dear. Let's take what comes,"
murmured Bo.

"That's the talk," said Dale. "You see, I've come right
out with the worst. Maybe we'll get through easy.
When we meet the boys we'll take to the horses an' the
trails. Can you ride?"

"Bo has been used to horses all her life and I ride fairly
well," responded Helen. The idea of riding quickened
her spirit.

"Good! We may have some hard ridin' before I get you
up to Pine. Hello! What's that?"

Above the creaking, rattling, rolling roar of the stage
Helen heard a rapid beat of hoofs. A horse flashed by,
galloping hard.

Dale opened the door and peered out. The stage rolled
to a halt. He stepped down and gazed ahead.

"Joe, who was that?" he queried.

"Nary me. An' Bill didn't know him, either," replied Joe. "I seen him 'way back. He was ridin' some. An' he slowed up goin' past us. Now he's runnin' again."

Dale shook his head as if he did not like the circumstances.

"Milt, he'll never get by Roy on this road," said Joe.

Maybe he'll get by before Roy strikes in on the road."

"It ain't likely."

Helen could not restrain her fears. "Mr. Dale, you think he was a messenger - going ahead to post that - that Anson gang?"

"He might be," replied Dale, simply.

Then the young man called Joe leaned out from the seat above and called: "Miss Helen, don't you worry. Thet fellar is more liable to stop lead than anythin' else."

His words, meant to be kind and reassuring, were almost as sinister to Helen as the menace to her own life. Long had she known how cheap life was held in the West, but she had only known it abstractly, and she had never let the fact remain before her consciousness. This cheerful young man spoke calmly of spilling blood in her behalf. The thought it roused was tragic - for bloodshed was insupportable to her - and then the thrills which followed were so new, strange, bold, and tingling that they were revolting. Helen grew conscious of unplumbed depths, of instincts at which she was amazed and ashamed.

"Joe, hand down that basket of grub - the small one with the canteen," said Dale, reaching out a long arm. Presently he placed a cloth-covered basket inside the stage. "Girls, eat all you want an' then some."

"We have a basket half full yet," replied Helen.

"You'll need it all before we get to Pine. . . . Now, I'll ride up on top with the boys an' eat my supper. It'll be dark, presently, an' we'll stop often to listen. But don't be scared."

With that he took his rifle and, closing the door, clambered up to the driver's seat. Then the stage lurched again and began to roll along.

Not the least thing to wonder at of this eventful evening was the way Bo reached for the basket of food. Helen simply stared at her.

"Bo, you can't eat!" she exclaimed.

"I should smile I can," replied that practical young lady. "And you're going to if I have to stuff things in your mouth. Where's your wits, Nell? He said we must eat. That means our strength is going to have some pretty severe trials. . . . Gee! it's all great - just like a story! The unexpected - why, he looks like a prince turned hunter! - long, dark, stage journey - held up - fight - escape - wild ride on horses - woods and camps and wild places - pursued - hidden in the forest - more hard rides - then safe at the ranch. And of course he falls madly in love with me - no, you, for I'll be true to my Las Vegas lover -"

"Hush, silly! Bo, tell me, aren't you scared?"

"Scared! I'm scared stiff. But if Western girls stand such things, we can. No Western girl is going to beat me!"

That brought Helen to a realization of the brave place she had given herself in dreams, and she was at once ashamed of herself and wildly proud of this little sister.

"Bo, thank Heaven I brought you with me!" exclaimed Helen, fervently. "I'll eat if it chokes me."

Whereupon she found herself actually hungry, and while she ate she glanced out of the stage, first from one side and then from the other. These windows had no glass and they let the cool night air blow in. The sun had long since sunk. Out to the west, where a bold, black horizon-line swept away endlessly, the sky was clear gold, shading to yellow and blue above. Stars were out, pale and wan, but growing brighter. The earth appeared bare and heaving, like a calm sea. The wind bore a fragrance new to Helen, acridly sweet and clean, and it was so cold it made her fingers numb.

"I heard some animal yelp," said Bo, suddenly, and she listened with head poised.

But Helen heard nothing save the steady clip-clop of hoofs, the clink of chains, the creak and rattle of the old stage, and occasionally the low voices of the men above.

When the girls had satisfied hunger and thirst, night

had settled down black. They pulled the cloaks up over them, and close together leaned back in a corner of the seat and talked in whispers. Helen did not have much to say, but Bo was talkative.

"This beats me!" she said once, after an interval. "Where are we, Nell? Those men up there are Mormons. Maybe they are abducting us!"

"Mr. Dale isn't a Mormon," replied Helen.

"How do you know?"

"I could tell by the way he spoke of his friends."

"Well, I wish it wasn't so dark. I'm not afraid of men in daylight. . . . Nell, did you ever see such a wonderful looking fellow? What'd they call him? Milt - Milt Dale. He said he lived in the woods. If I hadn't fallen in love with that cowboy who called me - well, I'd be a goner now."

After an interval of silence Bo whispered, startlingly, "Wonder if Harve Riggs is following us now?"

"Of course he is," replied Helen, hopelessly.

"He'd better look out. Why, Nell, he never saw - he never - what did Uncle Al used to call it? - sav - savvied - that's it. Riggs never savvied that hunter. But I did, you bet."

"Savvied! What do you mean, Bo?"

"I mean that long-haired galoot never saw his real danger. But I felt it. Something went light inside me.

Dale never took him seriously at all."

"Riggs will turn up at Uncle Al's, sure as I'm born," said Helen.

"Let him turn," replied Bo, contemptuously. "Nell, don't you ever bother your head again about him. I'll bet they're all men out here. And I wouldn't be in Harve Riggs's boots for a lot."

After that Bo talked of her uncle and his fatal illness, and from that she drifted back to the loved ones at home, now seemingly at the other side of the world, and then she broke down and cried, after which she fell asleep on Helen's shoulder.

But Helen could not have fallen asleep if she had wanted to.

She had always, since she could remember, longed for a moving, active life; and 'or want of a better idea she had chosen to dream of gipsies. And now it struck her grimly that, if these first few hours of her advent in the West were forecasts of the future, she was destined to have her longings more than fulfilled.

Presently the stage rolled slower and slower, until it came to a halt. Then the horses heaved, the harnesses clinked, the men whispered. Otherwise there was an intense quiet. She looked out, expecting to find it pitch-dark. It was black, yet a transparent blackness. To her surprise she could see a long way. A shooting-star electrified her. The men were listening. She listened, too, but beyond the slight sounds about the stage she heard nothing. Presently the driver clucked to his horses, and travel was resumed.

For a while the stage rolled on rapidly, evidently downhill, swaying from side to side, and rattling as if about to fall to pieces. Then it slowed on a level, and again it halted for a few moments, and once more in motion it began a laborsome climb. Helen imagined miles had been covered. The desert appeared to heave into billows, growing rougher, and dark, round bushes dimly stood out. The road grew uneven and rocky, and when the stage began another descent its violent rocking jolted Bo out of her sleep and in fact almost out of Helen's arms.

"Where am I?" asked Bo, dazedly.

"Bo, you're having your heart's desire, but I can't tell you where you are," replied Helen.

Bo awakened thoroughly, which fact was now no wonder, considering the jostling of the old stage.

"Hold on to me, Nell! . . . Is it a runaway?"

"We've come about a thousand miles like this, I think," replied Helen. "I've not a whole bone in my body."

Bo peered out of the window.

"Oh, how dark and lonesome! But it'd be nice if it wasn't so cold. I'm freezing."

"I thought you loved cold air," taunted Helen.

"Say, Nell, you begin to talk like yourself," responded Bo.

It was difficult to hold on to the stage and each other

and the cloak all at once, but they succeeded, except in the roughest places, when from time to time they were bounced around. Bo sustained a sharp rap on the head.

"Oooooo!" she moaned. "Nell Rayner, I'll never forgive you for fetching me on this awful trip."

"Just think of your handsome Las Vegas cowboy," replied Helen.

Either this remark subdued Bo or the suggestion sufficed to reconcile her to the hardships of the ride.

Meanwhile, as they talked and maintained silence and tried to sleep, the driver of the stage kept at his task after the manner of Western men who knew how to get the best out of horses and bad roads and distance.

By and by the stage halted again and remained at a standstill for so long, with the men whispering on top, that Helen and Bo were roused to apprehension.

Suddenly a sharp whistle came from the darkness ahead.

"Thet's Roy," said Joe Beeman, in a low voice.

"I reckon. An' meetin' us so quick looks bad," replied Dale. "Drive on, Bill."

"Mebbe it seems quick to you," muttered the driver, but if we hain't come thirty mile, an' if thet ridge thar hain't your turnin'-off place, why, I don't know nothin'."

The stage rolled on a little farther, while Helen and Bo

sat clasping each other tight, wondering with bated breath what was to be the next thing to happen.

Then once more they were at a standstill. Helen heard the thud of boots striking the ground, and the snorts of horses.

"Nell, I see horses," whispered Bo, excitedly. "There, to the side of the road . . . and here comes a man. . . . Oh, if he shouldn't be the one they're expecting!"

Helen peered out to see a tall, dark form, moving silently, and beyond it a vague outline of horses, and then pale gleams of what must have been pack-loads.

Dale loomed up, and met the stranger in the road.

"Howdy, Milt? You got the girl sure, or you wouldn't be here," said a low voice.

"Roy, I've got two girls - sisters," replied Dale.

The man Roy whistled softly under his breath. Then another lean, rangy form strode out of the darkness, and was met by Dale.

"Now, boys - how about Anson's gang?" queried Dale.

"At Snowdrop, drinkin' an' quarrelin'. Reckon they'll leave there about daybreak," replied Roy.

"How long have you been here?"

"Mebbe a couple of hours."

"Any horse go by?"

"No."

"Roy, a strange rider passed us before dark. He was hittin' the road. An' he's got by here before you came."

"I don't like thet news," replied Roy, tersely. "Let's rustle. With girls on hossback you'll need all the start you can get. Hey, John?"

"Snake Anson shore can foller hoss tracks," replied the third man.

"Milt, say the word," went on Roy, as he looked up at the stars. "Daylight not far away. Here's the forks of the road, an' your hosses, an' our outfit. You can be in the pines by sunup."

In the silence that ensued Helen heard the throb of her heart and the panting little breaths of her sister. They both peered out, hands clenched together, watching and listening in strained attention.

"It's possible that rider last night wasn't a messenger to Anson," said Dale. "In that case Anson won't make anythin' of our wheel tracks or horse tracks. He'll go right on to meet the regular stage. Bill, can you go back an' meet the stage comin' before Anson does?"

"Wal, I reckon so - an' take it easy at thet," replied Bill.

"All right," continued Dale, instantly. "John, you an' Joe an' Hal ride back to meet the regular stage. An' when you meet it get on an' be on it when Anson holds it up."

"Thet's shore agreeable to me," drawled John.

"I'd like to be on it, too," said Roy, grimly.

"No. I'll need you till I'm safe in the woods. Bill, hand down the bags. An' you, Roy, help me pack them. Did you get all the supplies I wanted?"

"Shore did. If the young ladies ain't powerful particular you can feed them well for a couple of months."

Dale wheeled and, striding to the stage, he opened the door.

"Girls, you're not asleep? Come," he called.

Bo stepped down first.

"I was asleep till this - this vehicle fell off the road back a ways," she replied.

Roy Beeman's low laugh was significant. He took off his sombrero and stood silent. The old driver smothered a loud guffaw.

"Veehicle! Wal, I'll be doggoned! Joe, did you hear thet? All the spunky gurls ain't born out West."

As Helen followed with cloak and bag Roy assisted her, and she encountered keen eyes upon her face. He seemed both gentle and respectful, and she felt his solicitude. His heavy gun, swinging low, struck her as she stepped down.

Dale reached into the stage and hauled out baskets and bags. These he set down on the ground.

"Turn around, Bill, an' go along with you. John an' Hal

will follow presently," ordered Dale.

"Wal, gurls," said, looking down upon them, "I was shore powerful glad to meet you-all. An' I'm ashamed of my country - offerin' two sich purty gurls insults an' low-down tricks. But shore you'll go through safe now. You couldn't be in better company fer ridin' or huntin' or marryin' or gittin' religion -"

"Shut up, you old grizzly!" broke in Dale, sharply.

"Haw! Haw! Good-by, gurls, an' good luck!" ended Bill, as he began to whip the reins.

Bo said good-by quite distinctly, but Helen could only murmur hers. The old driver seemed a friend.

Then the horses wheeled and stamped, the stage careened and creaked, presently to roll out of sight in the gloom.

"You're shiverin'," said Dale, suddenly, looking down upon Helen. She felt his big, hard hand clasp hers. "Cold as ice!"

"I am c-cold," replied Helen. "I guess we're not warmly dressed."

"Nell, we roasted all day, and now we're freezing," declared Bo. "I didn't know it was winter at night out here."

"Miss, haven't you some warm gloves an' a coat?" asked Roy, anxiously. "It 'ain't begun to get cold yet."

"Nell, we've heavy gloves, riding-suits and boots - all

fine and new - in this black bag," said Bo, enthusiastically kicking a bag at her feet.

"Yes, so we have. But a lot of good they'll do us, to-night," returned Helen.

"Miss, you'd do well to change right here," said Roy, earnestly. "It'll save time in the long run an' a lot of sufferin' before sunup."

Helen stared at the young man, absolutely amazed with his simplicity. She was advised to change her traveling-dress for a riding-suit - out somewhere in a cold, windy desert - in the middle of the night - among strange young man!

"Bo, which bag is it?" asked Dale, as if she were his sister. And when she indicated the one, he picked it up. "Come off the road."

Bo followed him, and Helen found herself mechanically at their heels. Dale led them a few paces off the road behind some low bushes.

"Hurry an' change here," he said. "We'll make a pack of your outfit an' leave room for this bag."

Then he stalked away and in a few strides disappeared.

Bo sat down to begin unlacing her shoes. Helen could just see her pale, pretty face and big, gleaming eyes by the light of the stars. It struck her then that Bo was going to make eminently more of a success of Western life than she was.

"Nell, those fellows are n-nice," said Bo, reflectively.

"Aren't you c-cold? Say, he said hurry!"

It was beyond Helen's comprehension how she ever began to disrobe out there in that open, windy desert, but after she had gotten launched on the task she found that it required more fortitude than courage. The cold wind pierced right through her. Almost she could have laughed at the way Bo made things fly.

"G-g-g-gee!" chattered Bo. "I n-never w-was so c-c-cold in all my life. Nell Rayner, m-may the g-good Lord forgive y-you!"

Helen was too intent on her own troubles to take breath to talk. She was a strong, healthy girl, swift and efficient with her hands, yet this, the hardest physical ordeal she had ever experienced, almost overcame her. Bo outdistanced her by moments, helped her with buttons, and laced one whole boot for her. Then, with hands that stung, Helen packed the traveling-suits in the bag.

"There! But what an awful mess!" exclaimed Helen. "Oh, Bo, our pretty traveling-dresses!"

"We'll press them t-to-morrow - on a l-log," replied Bo, and she giggled.

They started for the road. Bo, strange to note, did not carry her share of the burden, and she seemed unsteady on her feet.

The men were waiting beside a group of horses, one of which carried a pack.

"Nothin' slow about you," said Dale, relieving Helen of

the grip. "Roy, put them up while I sling on this bag."

Roy led out two of the horses.

"Get up," he said, indicating Bo. "The stirrups are short on this saddle."

Bo was an adept at mounting, but she made such awkward and slow work of it in this instance that Helen could not believe her eyes.

"Haw 're the stirrups?" asked Roy. "Stand in them. Guess they're about right. . . . Careful now! Thet hoss is skittish. Hold him in."

Bo was not living up to the reputation with which Helen had credited her.

"Now, miss, you get up," said Roy to Helen. And in another instant she found herself astride a black, spirited horse. Numb with cold as she was, she yet felt the coursing thrills along her veins.

Roy was at the stirrups with swift hands.

"You're taller 'n I guessed," he said. "Stay up, but lift your foot. . . . Shore now, I'm glad you have them thick, soft boots. Mebbe we'll ride all over the White Mountains."

"Bo, do you hear that?" called Helen.

But Bo did not answer. She was leaning rather unnaturally in her saddle. Helen became anxious. Just then Dale strode back to them.

"All cinched up, Roy?"

"Jest ready," replied Roy.

Then Dale stood beside Helen. How tall he was! His wide shoulders seemed on a level with the pommel of her saddle. He put an affectionate hand on the horse.

"His name's Ranger an' he's the fastest an' finest horse in this country."

"I reckon he shore is - along with my bay," corroborated Roy.

"Roy, if you rode Ranger he'd beat your pet," said Dale. "We can start now. Roy, you drive the pack-horses."

He took another look at Helen's saddle and then moved to do likewise with Bo's.

"Are you - all right?" he asked, quickly.

Bo reeled in her seat.

"I'm n-near froze," she replied, in a faint voice. Her face shone white in the starlight. Helen recognized that Bo was more than cold.

"Oh, Bo!" she called, in distress.

"Nell, don't you worry, now."

"Let me carry you," suggested Dale.

"No. I'll s-s-stick on this horse or d-die," fiercely retorted Bo.

The two men looked up at her white face and then at each other. Then Roy walked away toward the dark bunch of horses off the road and Dale swung astride the one horse left.

"Keep close to me," he said.

Bo fell in line and Helen brought up the rear.

Helen imagined she was near the end of a dream. Presently she would awaken with a start and see the pale walls of her little room at home, and hear the cherry branches brushing her window, and the old clarion-voiced cock proclaim the hour of dawn.

CHAPTER VI

The horses trotted. And the exercise soon warmed Helen, until she was fairly comfortable except in her fingers. In mind, however, she grew more miserable as she more fully realized her situation. The night now became so dark that, although the head of her horse was alongside the flank of Bo's, she could scarcely see Bo. From time to time Helen's anxious query brought from her sister the answer that she was all right.

Helen had not ridden a horse for more than a year, and for several years she had not ridden with any regularity. Despite her thrills upon mounting, she had entertained misgivings. But she was agreeably surprised, for the horse, Ranger, had an easy gait, and she found she had not forgotten how to ride. Bo, having been used to riding on a farm near home, might be expected to acquit herself admirably. It occurred to Helen what a plight they would have been in but for the thick, comfortable riding outfits.

Dark as the night was, Helen could dimly make out the road underneath. It was rocky, and apparently little used. When Dale turned off the road into the low brush or sage of what seemed a level plain, the traveling was harder, rougher, and yet no slower. The horses kept to the gait of the leaders. Helen, discovering it unnecessary, ceased attempting to guide Ranger. There were dim shapes in the gloom ahead, and always they gave Helen uneasiness, until closer approach proved them to be rocks or low, scrubby trees. These increased in both size and number as the horses progressed. Often Helen looked back into the gloom behind. This act was involuntary and occasioned her sensations of dread. Dale expected to be pursued. And Helen experienced, along with the dread, flashes of unfamiliar resentment. Not only was there an attempt afoot to rob her of her heritage, but even her personal liberty. Then she shuddered at the significance of Dale's words regarding her possible abduction by this hired gang. It seemed monstrous, impossible. Yet, manifestly it was true enough to Dale and his allies. The West, then, in reality was raw, hard, inevitable.

Suddenly her horse stopped. He had come up alongside Bo's horse. Dale had halted ahead, and apparently was listening. Roy and the pack-train were out of sight in the gloom.

"What is it?" whispered Helen.

"Reckon I heard a wolf," replied Dale.

"Was that cry a wolf's?" asked Bo. "I heard. It was wild."

"We're gettin' up close to the foot-hills," said Dale. "Feel how much colder the air is."

"I'm warm now," replied Bo. "I guess being near froze was what ailed me. . . . Nell, how 're you?"

"I'm warm, too, but -" Helen answered.

"If you had your choice of being here or back home,

snug in bed - which would you take?" asked Bo.

"Bo!" exclaimed Helen, aghast.

"Well, I'd choose to be right here on this horse," rejoined Bo.

Dale heard her, for he turned an instant, then slapped his horse and started on.

Helen now rode beside Bo, and for a long time they climbed steadily in silence. Helen knew when that dark hour before dawn had passed, and she welcomed an almost imperceptible lightening in the east. Then the stars paled. Gradually a grayness absorbed all but the larger stars. The great white morning star, wonderful as Helen had never seen it, lost its brilliance and life and seemed to retreat into the dimming blue.

Daylight came gradually, so that the gray desert became distinguishable by degrees. Rolling bare hills, half obscured by the gray lifting mantle of night, rose in the foreground, and behind was gray space, slowly taking form and substance. In the east there was a kindling of pale rose and silver that lengthened and brightened along a horizon growing visibly rugged.

"Reckon we'd better catch up with Roy," said Dale, and he spurred his horse.

Ranger and Bo's mount needed no other urging, and they swung into a canter. Far ahead the pack-animals showed with Roy driving them. The cold wind was so keen in Helen's face that tears blurred her eyes and froze her cheeks. And riding Ranger at that pace was like riding in a rocking-chair. That ride, invigorating and exciting, seemed all too short.

"Oh, Nell, I don't care - what becomes of - me!" exclaimed Bo, breathlessly.

Her face was white and red, fresh as a rose, her eyes glanced darkly blue, her hair blew out in bright, unruly strands. Helen knew she felt some of the physical stimulation that had so roused Bo, and seemed so irresistible, but somber thought was not deflected thereby.

It was clear daylight when Roy led off round a knoll from which patches of scrubby trees - cedars, Dale called them - straggled up on the side of the foot-hills.

"They grow on the north slopes, where the snow stays longest," said Dale.

They descended into a valley that looked shallow, but proved to be deep and wide, and then began to climb another foot-hill. Upon surmounting it Helen saw the rising sun, and so glorious a view confronted her that she was unable to answer Bo's wild exclamations.

Bare, yellow, cedar-dotted slopes, apparently level, so gradual was the ascent, stretched away to a dense ragged line of forest that rose black over range after range, at last to fail near the bare summit of a magnificent mountain, sunrise-flushed against the blue sky.

"Oh, beautiful!" cried Bo. "But they ought to be called Black Mountains."

"Old Baldy, there, is white half the year," replied Dale.

"Look back an' see what you say," suggested Roy.

The girls turned to gaze silently. Helen imagined she looked down upon the whole wide world. How vastly different was the desert! Verily it yawned away from her, red and gold near at hand, growing softly flushed with purple far away, a barren void, borderless and immense, where dark-green patches and black lines and upheaved ridges only served to emphasize distance and space.

"See thet little green spot," said Roy, pointing. "Thet's Snowdrop. An' the other one - 'way to the right - thet's Show Down."

"Where is Pine?" queried Helen, eagerly.

"Farther still, up over the foot-hills at the edge of the woods."

"Then we're riding away from it."

"Yes. If we'd gone straight for Pine thet gang could overtake us. Pine is four days' ride. An' by takin' to the mountains Milt can hide his tracks. An' when he's thrown Anson off the scent, then he'll circle down to Pine."

"Mr. Dale, do you think you'll get us there safely - and soon?" asked Helen, wistfully.

"I won't promise soon, but I promise safe. An' I don't like bein' called Mister," he replied.

"Are we ever going to eat?" inquired Bo, demurely.

At this query Roy Beeman turned with a laugh to look at Bo. Helen saw his face fully in the light, and it was thin and hard, darkly bronzed, with eyes like those of a hawk, and with square chin and lean jaws showing scant, light beard.

"We shore are," he replied. "Soon as we reach the timber. Thet won't be long."

"Reckon we can rustle some an' then take a good rest," said Dale, and he urged his horse into a jog-trot.

During a steady trot for a long hour, Helen's roving eyes were everywhere, taking note of the things from near to far - the scant sage that soon gave place to as scanty a grass, and the dark blots that proved to be dwarf cedars, and the ravines opening out as if by magic from what had appeared level ground, to wind away widening between gray stone walls, and farther on, patches of lonely pine-trees, two and three together, and then a straggling clump of yellow aspens, and up beyond the fringed border of forest, growing nearer all the while, the black sweeping benches rising to the noble dome of the dominant mountain of the range.

No birds or animals were seen in that long ride up toward the timber, which fact seemed strange to Helen. The air lost something of its cold, cutting edge as the sun rose higher, and it gained sweeter tang of forest-land. The first faint suggestion of that fragrance was utterly new to Helen, yet it brought a vague sensation of familiarity and with it an emotion as strange. It was as if she had smelled that keen, pungent tang long ago, and her physical sense caught it before her memory.

The yellow plain had only appeared to be level. Roy led down into a shallow ravine, where a tiny stream meandered, and he followed this around to the left, coming at length to a point where cedars and dwarf pines formed a little grove. Here, as the others rode up, he sat cross-legged in his saddle, and waited.

"We'll hang up awhile," he said. "Reckon you're tired?"

"I'm hungry, but not tired yet," replied Bo.

Helen dismounted, to find that walking was something she had apparently lost the power to do. Bo laughed at her, but she, too, was awkward when once more upon the ground.

Then Roy got down. Helen was surprised to find him lame. He caught her quick glance.

"A hoss threw me once an' rolled on me. Only broke my collar-bone, five ribs, one arm, an' my bow-legs in two places!"

Notwithstanding this evidence that he was a cripple, as he stood there tall and lithe in his homespun, ragged garments, he looked singularly powerful and capable.

"Reckon walkin' around would be good for you girls," advised Dale. "If you ain't stiff yet, you'll be soon. An' walkin' will help. Don't go far. I'll call when breakfast's ready."

A little while later the girls were whistled in from their walk and found camp-fire and meal awaiting them. Roy was sitting cross-legged, like an Indian, in front of a tarpaulin, upon which was spread a homely but substantial fare. Helen's quick eye detected a cleanliness and thoroughness she had scarcely expected to find in the camp cooking of men of the wilds. Moreover, the fare was good. She ate heartily, and as for Bo's appetite, she was inclined to be as much ashamed of that as amused at it. The young men were all eyes, assiduous in their service to the girls, but speaking seldom. It was not lost upon Helen how Dale's gray gaze went often down across the open country. She divined apprehension from it rather than saw much expression in it.

"I - declare," burst out Bo, when she could not eat any more, "this isn't believable. I'm dreaming. . . . Nell, the black horse you rode is the prettiest I ever saw."

Ranger, with the other animals, was grazing along the little brook. Packs and saddles had been removed. The men ate leisurely. There was little evidence of hurried flight. Yet Helen could not cast off uneasiness. Roy might have been deep, and careless, with a motive to spare the girls' anxiety, but Dale seemed incapable of anything he did not absolutely mean.

"Rest or walk," he advised the girls. "We've got forty miles to ride before dark."

Helen preferred to rest, but Bo walked about, petting the horses and prying into the packs. She was curious and eager.

Dale and Roy talked in low tones while they cleaned up the utensils and packed them away in a heavy canvas bag.

"You really expect Anson 'll strike my trail this mornin'?" Dale was asking.

"I shore do," replied Roy.

"An' how do you figure that so soon?"

"How'd you figure it - if you was Snake Anson?" queried Roy, in reply.

"Depends on that rider from Magdalena," Said Dale, soberly. "Although it's likely I'd seen them wheel tracks an' hoss tracks made where we turned off. But supposin' he does."

"Milt, listen. I told you Snake met us boys face to face day before yesterday in Show Down. An' he was plumb curious."

"But he missed seein' or hearin' about me," replied Dale.

"Mebbe he did an' mebbe he didn't. Anyway, what's the difference whether he finds out this mornin' or this evenin'?"

"Then you ain't expectin' a fight if Anson holds up the stage?"

"Wal, he'd have to shoot first, which ain't likely. John an' Hal, since thet shootin'-scrape a year ago, have been sort of gun-shy. Joe might get riled. But I reckon the best we can be shore of is a delay. An' it'd be sense not to count on thet."

"Then you hang up here an' keep watch for Anson's

gang - say long enough so's to be sure they'd be in sight if they find our tracks this mornin'. Makin' sure one way or another, you ride 'cross-country to Big Spring, where I'll camp to-night."

Roy nodded approval of that suggestion. Then without more words both men picked up ropes and went after the horses. Helen was watching Dale, so that when Bo cried out in great excitement Helen turned to see a savage yellow little mustang standing straight up on his hind legs and pawing the air. Roy had roped him and was now dragging him into camp.

"Nell, look at that for a wild pony!" exclaimed Bo.

Helen busied herself getting well out of the way of the infuriated mustang. Roy dragged him to a cedar near by.

"Come now, Buckskin," said Roy, soothingly, and he slowly approached the quivering animal. He went closer, hand over hand, on the lasso. Buckskin showed the whites of his eyes and also his white teeth. But he stood while Roy loosened the loop and, slipping it down over his head, fastened it in a complicated knot round his nose.

"Thet's a hackamore," he said, indicating the knot. He's never had a bridle, an' never will have one, I reckon."

"You don't ride him?" queried Helen.

"Sometimes I do," replied Roy, with a smile. "Would you girls like to try him?"

"Excuse me," answered Helen.

"Gee!" ejaculated Bo. "He looks like a devil. But I'd tackle him - if you think I could."

The wild leaven of the West had found quick root in Bo Rayner.

"Wal, I'm sorry, but I reckon I'll not let you - for a spell," replied Roy, dryly.

"He pitches somethin' powerful bad."

"Pitches. You mean bucks?"

"I reckon."

In the next half-hour Helen saw more and learned more about how horses of the open range were handled than she had ever heard of. Excepting Ranger, and Roy's bay, and the white pony Bo rode, the rest of the horses had actually to be roped and hauled into camp to be saddled and packed. It was a job for fearless, strong men, and one that called for patience as well as arms of iron. So that for Helen Rayner the thing succeeding the confidence she had placed in these men was respect. To an observing woman that half-hour told much.

When all was in readiness for a start Dale mounted, and said, significantly: "Roy, I'll look for you about sundown. I hope no sooner."

"Wal, it'd be bad if I had to rustle along soon with bad news. Let's hope for the best. We've been shore lucky so far. Now you take to the pine-mats in the woods an' hide your trail."

Dale turned away. Then the girls bade Roy good-by,

and followed. Soon Roy and his buckskin-colored mustang were lost to sight round a clump of trees.

The unhampered horses led the way; the pack-animals trotted after them; the riders were close behind. All traveled at a jog-trot. And this gait made the packs bob up and down and from side to side. The sun felt warm at Helen's back and the wind lost its frosty coldness, that almost appeared damp, for a dry, sweet fragrance. Dale drove up the shallow valley that showed timber on the levels above and a black border of timber some few miles ahead. It did not take long to reach the edge of the forest.

Helen wondered why the big pines grew so far on that plain and no farther. Probably the growth had to do with snow, but, as the ground was level, she could not see why the edge of the woods should come just there.

They rode into the forest.

To Helen it seemed a strange, critical entrance into another world, which she was destined to know and to love. The pines were big, brown-barked, seamed, and knotted, with no typical conformation except a majesty and beauty. They grew far apart. Few small pines and little underbrush flourished beneath them. The floor of this forest appeared remarkable in that it consisted of patches of high silvery grass and wide brown areas of pine-needles. These manifestly were what Roy had meant by pine-mats. Here and there a fallen monarch lay riven or rotting. Helen was presently struck with the silence of the forest and the strange fact that the horses seldom made any sound at all, and when they did it was a cracking of dead twig or thud of hoof on log. Likewise she became aware of a springy nature of the ground. And then she saw that the pine-mats gave like rubber cushions under the hoofs of the horses, and after they had passed sprang back to place again, leaving no track. Helen could not see a sign of a trail they left behind. Indeed, it would take a sharp eye to follow Dale through that forest. This knowledge was infinitely comforting to Helen, and for the first time since the flight had begun she felt a lessening of the weight upon mind and heart. It left her free for some of the appreciation she might have had in this wonderful ride under happier circumstances.

Bo, however, seemed too young, too wild, too intense to mind what the circumstances were. She responded to reality. Helen began to suspect that the girl would welcome any adventure, and Helen knew surely now that Bo was a true Auchincloss. For three long days Helen had felt a constraint with which heretofore she had been unfamiliar; for the last hours it had been submerged under dread. But it must be, she concluded, blood like her sister's, pounding at her veins to be set free to race and to burn.

Bo loved action. She had an eye for beauty, but she was not contemplative. She was now helping Dale drive the horses and hold them in rather close formation. She rode well, and as yet showed no symptoms of fatigue or pain. Helen began to be aware of both, but not enough yet to limit her interest.

A wonderful forest without birds did not seem real to her. Of all living creatures in nature Helen liked birds best, and she knew many and could imitate the songs of a few. But here under the stately pines there were no birds. Squirrels, however, began to be seen here and there, and in the course of an hour's travel became abundant. The only one with which she was familiar was the chipmunk. All the others, from the slim bright blacks to the striped russets and the white-tailed grays, were totally new to her. They appeared tame and curious. The reds barked and scolded at the passing cavalcade; the blacks glided to some safe branch, there to watch; the grays paid no especial heed to this invasion of their domain.

Once Dale, halting his horse, pointed with long arm, and Helen, following the direction, descried several gray deer standing in a glade, motionless, with long ears up. They made a wild and beautiful picture. Suddenly they bounded away with remarkable springy strides.

The forest on the whole held to the level, open character, but there were swales and stream-beds breaking up its regular conformity. Toward noon, however, it gradually changed, a fact that Helen believed she might have observed sooner had she been more keen. The general lay of the land began to ascend, and the trees to grow denser.

She made another discovery. Ever since she had entered the forest she had become aware of a fullness in her head and a something affecting her nostrils. She imagined, with regret, that she had taken cold. But presently her head cleared somewhat and she realized that the thick pine odor of the forest had clogged her nostrils as if with a sweet pitch. The smell was overpowering and disagreeable because of its strength. Also her throat and lungs seemed to burn.

When she began to lose interest in the forest and her surroundings it was because of aches and pains which would no longer be denied recognition. Thereafter she was not permitted to forget them and they grew worse. One, especially, was a pain beyond all her experience. It lay in the muscles of her side, above her hip, and it grew to be a treacherous thing, for it was not persistent. It came and went. After it did come, with a terrible flash, it could be borne by shifting or easing the body. But it gave no warning. When she expected it she was mistaken; when she dared to breathe again, then, with piercing swiftness, it returned like a blade in her side. This, then, was one of the riding-pains that made a victim of a tenderfoot on a long ride. It was almost too much to be borne. The beauty of the forest, the living creatures to be seen scurrying away, the time, distance - everything faded before that stablike pain. To her infinite relief she found that it was the trot that caused this torture. When Ranger walked she did not have to suffer it. Therefore she held him to a walk as long as she dared or until Dale and Bo were almost out of sight; then she loped him ahead until he had caught up.

So the hours passed, the sun got around low, sending golden shafts under the trees, and the forest gradually changed to a brighter, but a thicker, color. This slowly darkened. Sunset was not far away.

She heard the horses splashing in water, and soon she rode up to see the tiny streams of crystal water running swiftly over beds of green moss. She crossed a number of these and followed along the last one into a more open place in the forest where the pines were huge, towering, and far apart. A low, gray bluff of stone rose to the right, perhaps one-third as high as the trees. From somewhere came the rushing sound of running water.

"Big Spring," announced Dale. "We camp here. You girls have done well."

Another glance proved to Helen that all those little streams poured from under this gray bluff.

"I'm dying for a drink," cried Bo. with her customary hyperbole.

"I reckon you'll never forget your first drink here," remarked Dale.

Bo essayed to dismount, and finally fell off, and when she did get to the ground her legs appeared to refuse their natural function, and she fell flat. Dale helped her up.

"What's wrong with me, anyhow?" she demanded, in great amaze.

"Just stiff, I reckon," replied Dale, as he led her a few awkward steps.

"Bo, have you any hurts?" queried Helen, who still sat her horse, loath to try dismounting, yet wanting to beyond all words.

Bo gave her an eloquent glance.

"Nell, did you have one in your side, like a wicked, long darning-needle, punching deep when you weren't ready?"

"That one I'll never get over!" exclaimed Helen, softly. Then, profiting by Bo's experience, she dismounted cautiously, and managed to keep upright. Her legs felt like wooden things.

Presently the girls went toward the spring.

"Drink slow," called out Dale.

Big Spring had its source somewhere deep under the gray, weathered bluff, from which came a hollow subterranean gurgle and roar of water. Its fountainhead must have been a great well rushing up through the cold stone.

Helen and Bo lay flat on a mossy bank, seeing their faces as they bent over, and they sipped a mouthful, by Dale's advice, and because they were so hot and parched and burning they wanted to tarry a moment with a precious opportunity.

The water was so cold that it sent a shock over Helen, made her teeth ache, and a singular, revivifying current steal all through her, wonderful in its cool absorption of that dry heat of flesh, irresistible in its appeal to thirst. Helen raised her head to look at this water. It was colorless as she had found it tasteless.

"Nell - drink!" panted Bo. "Think of our - old spring - in the orchard - full of pollywogs!"

And then Helen drank thirstily, with closed eyes, while a memory of home stirred from Bo's gift of poignant speech.

CHAPTER VII

The first camp duty Dale performed was to throw a pack off one of the horses, and, opening it, he took out tarpaulin and blankets, which he arranged on the ground under a pine-tree.

"You girls rest," he said, briefly.

"Can't we help?" asked Helen, though she could scarcely stand.

"You'll be welcome to do all you like after you're broke in."

"Broke in!" ejaculated Bo, with a little laugh. "I'm all broke up now."

"Bo, it looks as if Mr. Dale expects us to have quite a stay with him in the woods."

"It does," replied Bo, as slowly she sat down upon the blankets, stretched out with a long sigh, and laid her head on a saddle. "Nell, didn't he say not to call him Mister?"

Dale was throwing the packs off the other horses.

Helen lay down beside Bo, and then for once in her life she experienced the sweetness of rest.

"Well, sister, what do you intend to call him?" queried Helen, curiously.

"Milt, of course," replied Bo.

Helen had to laugh despite her weariness and aches.

"I suppose, then, when your Las Vegas cowboy comes along you will call him what he called you."

Bo blushed, which was a rather unusual thing for her.

"I will if I like," she retorted. "Nell, ever since I could remember you've raved about the West. Now you're out West, right in it good and deep. So wake up!"

That was Bo's blunt and characteristic way of advising the elimination of Helen's superficialities. It sank deep. Helen had no retort. Her ambition, as far as the West was concerned, had most assuredly not been for such a wild, unheard-of jaunt as this. But possibly the West - a living from day to day - was one succession of adventures, trials, tests, troubles, and achievements. To make a place for others to live comfortably some day! That might be Bo's meaning, embodied in her forceful hint. But Helen was too tired to think it out then. She found it interesting and vaguely pleasant to watch Dale.

He hobbled the horses and turned them loose. Then with ax in hand he approached a short, dead tree, standing among a few white-barked aspens. Dale appeared to advantage swinging the ax. With his coat off, displaying his wide shoulders, straight back, and long, powerful arms, he looked a young giant. He was lithe and supple, brawny but not bulky. The ax rang on the hard wood, reverberating through the forest. A few strokes sufficed to bring down the stub. Then he split it up. Helen was curious to see how he kindled a fire. First he ripped splinters out of the heart of the log, and laid them with coarser pieces on the ground. Then from a saddlebag which hung on a near-by branch he took flint and steel and a piece of what Helen supposed was rag or buckskin, upon which powder had been rubbed. At any rate, the first strike of the steel brought sparks, a blaze, and burning splinters. Instantly the flame leaped a foot high. He put on larger pieces of wood crosswise, and the fire roared.

That done, he stood erect, and, facing the north, he listened. Helen remembered now that she had seen him do the same thing twice before since the arrival at Big Spring. It was Roy for whom he was listening and watching. The sun had set and across the open space the tips of the pines were losing their brightness.

The camp utensils, which the hunter emptied out of a sack, gave forth a jangle of iron and tin. Next he unrolled a large pack, the contents of which appeared to be numerous sacks of all sizes. These evidently contained food supplies. The bucket looked as if a horse had rolled over it, pack and all. Dale filled it at the spring. Upon returning to the camp-fire he poured water into a washbasin, and, getting down to his knees, proceeded to wash his hands thoroughly. The act seemed a habit, for Helen saw that while he was doing it he gazed off into the woods and listened. Then he dried his hands over the fire, and, turning to the spread-out pack, he began preparations for the meal.

Suddenly Helen thought of the man and all that his actions implied. At Magdalena, on the stage-ride, and last night, she had trusted this stranger, a hunter of the White Mountains, who appeared ready to befriend her. And she had felt an exceeding gratitude. Still, she had looked at him impersonally. But it began to dawn upon her that chance had thrown her in the company of a remarkable man. That impression baffled her. It did not spring from the fact that he was brave and kind to help a young woman in peril, or that he appeared deft and quick at camp-fire chores. Most Western men were brave, her uncle had told her, and many were roughly kind, and all of them could cook. This hunter was physically a wonderful specimen of manhood, with something leonine about his stature. But that did not give rise to her impression. Helen had been a school-teacher and used to boys, and she sensed a boyish simplicity or vigor or freshness in this hunter. She believed, however, that it was a mental and spiritual force in Dale which had drawn her to think of it.

"Nell, I've spoken to you three times," protested Bo, petulantly. "What 're you mooning over?"

"I'm pretty tired - and far away, Bo," replied Helen. "What did you say?"

"I said I had an e-normous appetite."

"Really. That's not remarkable for you. I'm too tired to eat. And afraid to shut my eyes. They'd never come open. When did we sleep last, Bo?"

"Second night before we left home," declared Bo.

"Four nights! Oh, we've slept some."

"I'll bet I make mine up in this woods. Do you suppose

we'll sleep right here - under this tree - with no covering?"

"It looks so," replied Helen, dubiously.

"How perfectly lovely!" exclaimed Bo, in delight. "We'll see the stars through the pines."

"Seems to be clouding over. Wouldn't it be awful if we had a storm?"

"Why, I don't know," answered Bo, thoughtfully. "It must storm out West."

Again Helen felt a quality of inevitableness in Bo. It was something that had appeared only practical in the humdrum home life in St. Joseph. All of a sudden Helen received a flash of wondering thought - a thrilling consciousness that she and Bo had begun to develop in a new and wild environment. How strange, and fearful, perhaps, to watch that growth! Bo, being younger, more impressionable, with elemental rather than intellectual instincts, would grow stronger more swiftly. Helen wondered if she could yield to her own leaning to the primitive. But how could anyone with a thoughtful and grasping mind yield that way? It was the savage who did not think.

Helen saw Dale stand erect once more and gaze into the forest.

"Reckon Roy ain't comin'," he soliloquized. "An' that's good." Then he turned to the girls. "Supper's ready."

The girls responded with a spirit greater than their activity. And they ate like famished children that had been lost in the woods. Dale attended them with a pleasant light upon his still face.

"To-morrow night we'll have meat," he said.

"What kind?" asked Bo.

"Wild turkey or deer. Maybe both, if you like. But it's well to take wild meat slow. An' turkey - that 'll melt in your mouth."

"Uummm!" murmured Bo, greedily. "I've heard of wild turkey."

When they had finished Dale ate his meal, listening to the talk of the girls, and occasionally replying briefly to some query of Bo's. It was twilight when he began to wash the pots and pans, and almost dark by the time his duties appeared ended. Then he replenished the campfire and sat down on a log to gaze into the fire. The girls leaned comfortably propped against the saddles.

"Nell, I'll keel over in a minute," said Bo. "And I oughtn't - right on such a big supper."

"I don't see how I can sleep, and I know I can't stay awake," rejoined Helen.

Dale lifted his head alertly.

"Listen."

The girls grew tense and still. Helen could not hear a sound, unless it was a low thud of hoof out in the gloom. The forest seemed sleeping. She knew from

Bo's eyes, wide and shining in the camp-fire light, that she, too, had failed to catch whatever it was Dale meant.

"Bunch of coyotes comin'," he explained.

Suddenly the quietness split to a chorus of snappy, high-strung, strange barks. They sounded wild, yet they held something of a friendly or inquisitive note. Presently gray forms could be descried just at the edge of the circle of light. Soft rustlings of stealthy feet surrounded. the camp, and then barks and yelps broke out all around. It was a restless and sneaking pack of animals, thought Helen; she was glad after the chorus ended and with a few desultory, spiteful yelps the coyotes went away.

Silence again settled down. If it had not been for the anxiety always present in Helen's mind she would have thought this silence sweet and unfamiliarly beautiful.

"Ah! Listen to that fellow," spoke up Dale. His voice was thrilling.

Again the girls strained their ears. That was not necessary, for presently, clear and cold out of the silence, pealed a mournful howl, long drawn, strange and full and wild.

"Oh! What's that?" whispered Bo.

"That's a big gray wolf - a timber-wolf, or lofer, as he's sometimes called," replied Dale. "He's high on some rocky ridge back there. He scents us, an' he doesn't like it. . . . There he goes again. Listen! Ah, he's hungry."

While Helen listened to this exceedingly wild cry - so wild that it made her flesh creep and the most indescribable sensations of loneliness come over her - she kept her glance upon Dale.

"You love him?" she murmured involuntarily, quite without understanding the motive of her query.

Assuredly Dale had never had that question asked of him before, and it seemed to Helen, as he pondered, that he had never even asked it of himself.

"I reckon so," he replied, presently.

"But wolves kill deer, and little fawns, and everything helpless in the forest," expostulated Bo.

The hunter nodded his head.

"Why, then, can you love him?" repeated Helen.

"Come to think of it, I reckon it's because of lots of reasons," returned Dale. "He kills clean. He eats no carrion. He's no coward. He fights. He dies game. . . . An' he likes to be alone."

"Kills clean. What do you mean by that?"

"A cougar, now, he mangles a deer. An' a silvertip, when killin' a cow or colt, he makes a mess of it. But a wolf kills clean, with sharp snaps."

"What are a cougar and a silvertip?"

"Cougar means mountain-lion or panther, an' a silvertip is a grizzly bear."

"Oh, they're all cruel!" exclaimed Helen, shrinking.

"I reckon. Often I've shot wolves for relayin' a deer."

"What's that?"

"Sometimes two or more wolves will run a deer, an' while one of them rests the other will drive the deer around to his pardner, who'll, take up the chase. That way they run the deer down. Cruel it is, but nature, an' no worse than snow an' ice that starve deer, or a fox that kills turkey-chicks breakin' out of the egg, or ravens that pick the eyes out of new-born lambs an' wait till they die. An' for that matter, men are crueler than beasts of prey, for men add to nature, an' have more than instincts."

Helen was silenced, as well as shocked. She had not only learned a new and striking viewpoint in natural history, but a clear intimation to the reason why she had vaguely imagined or divined a remarkable character in this man. A hunter was one who killed animals for their fur, for their meat or horns, or for some lust for blood - that was Helen's definition of a hunter, and she believed it was held by the majority of people living in settled states. But the majority might be wrong. A hunter might be vastly different, and vastly more than a tracker and slayer of game. The mountain world of forest was a mystery to almost all men. Perhaps Dale knew its secrets, its life, its terror, its beauty, its sadness, and its joy; and if so, how full, how wonderful must be his mind! He spoke of men as no better than wolves. Could a lonely life in the wilderness teach a man that? Bitterness, envy, jealousy, spite, greed, and hate - these had no place in this hunter's heart. It was not Helen's shrewdness, but a woman's intuition, which divined that.

Dale rose to his feet and, turning his ear to the north, listened once more.

"Are you expecting Roy still?" inquired Helen.

"No, it ain't likely he'll turn up to-night," replied Dale, and then he strode over to put a hand on the pine-tree that soared above where the girls lay. His action, and the way he looked up at the tree-top and then at adjacent trees, held more of that significance which so interested Helen.

"I reckon he's stood there some five hundred years an' will stand through to-night," muttered Dale.

This pine was the monarch of that wide-spread group.

"Listen again," said Dale.

Bo was asleep. And Helen, listening, at once caught low, distant roar.

"Wind. It's goin' to storm," explained Dale. "You'll hear somethin' worth while. But don't be scared. Reckon we'll be safe. Pines blow down often. But this fellow will stand any fall wind that ever was. . . . Better slip under the blankets so I can pull the tarp up."

Helen slid down, just as she was, fully dressed except for boots, which she and Bo had removed; and she laid her head close to Bo's. Dale pulled the tarpaulin up and folded it back just below their heads.

"When it rains you'll wake, an' then just pull the tarp

up over you," he said.

"Will it rain?" Helen asked. But she was thinking that this moment was the strangest that had ever happened to her. By the light of the camp-fire she saw Dale's face, just as usual, still, darkly serene, expressing no thought. He was kind, but he was not thinking of these sisters as girls, alone with him in a pitch-black forest, helpless and defenseless. He did not seem to be thinking at all. But Helen had never before in her life been so keenly susceptible to experience.

"I'll be close by an' keep the fire goin' all night," he said.

She heard him stride off into the darkness. Presently there came a dragging, bumping sound, then a crash of a log dropped upon the fire. A cloud of sparks shot up, and many pattered down to hiss upon the damp ground. Smoke again curled upward along the great, seamed tree-trunk, and flames sputtered and crackled.

Helen listened again for the roar of wind. It seemed to come on a breath of air that fanned her cheek and softly blew Bo's curls, and it was stronger. But it died out presently, only to come again, and still stronger. Helen realized then that the sound was that of an approaching storm. Her heavy eyelids almost refused to stay open, and she knew if she let them close she would instantly drop to sleep. And she wanted to hear the storm-wind in the pines.

A few drops of cold rain fell upon her face, thrilling her with the proof that no roof stood between her and the elements. Then a breeze bore the smell of burnt wood into her face, and somehow her quick mind flew to girlhood days when she burned brush and leaves with her little brothers. The memory faded. The roar that had seemed distant was now back in the forest, coming swiftly, increasing in volume. Like a stream in flood it bore down. Helen grew amazed, startled. How rushing, oncoming, and heavy this storm-wind! She likened its approach to the tread of an army. Then the roar filled the forest, yet it was back there behind her. Not a pine-needle quivered in the light of the camp-fire. But the air seemed to be oppressed with a terrible charge. The roar augmented till it was no longer a roar, but an on-sweeping crash, like an ocean torrent engulfing the earth. Bo awoke to cling to Helen with fright. The deafening storm-blast was upon them. Helen felt the saddle-pillow move under her head. The giant pine had trembled to its very roots. That mighty fury of wind was all aloft, in the tree-tops. And for a long moment it bowed the forest under its tremendous power. Then the deafening crash passed to roar, and that swept on and on, lessening in volume, deepening in low detonation, at last to die in the distance.

No sooner had it died than back to the north another low roar rose and ceased and rose again. Helen lay there, whispering to Bo, and heard again the great wave of wind come and crash and cease. That was the way of this storm-wind of the mountain forest.

A soft patter of rain on the tarpaulin warned Helen to remember Dale's directions, and, pulling up the heavy covering, she arranged it hoodlike over the saddle. Then, with Bo close and warm beside her, she closed her eyes, and the sense of the black forest and the wind and rain faded. Last of all sensations was the smell of smoke that blew under the tarpaulin.

When she opened her eyes she remembered everything, as if only a moment had elapsed. But it was
daylight, though gray and cloudy. The pines were
dripping mist. A fire crackled cheerily and blue smoke
curled upward and a savory odor of hot coffee hung in
the air. Horses were standing near by, biting and
kicking at one another. Bo was sound asleep. Dale
appeared busy around the camp-fire. As Helen
watched the hunter she saw him pause in his task, turn
his ear to listen, and then look expectantly. And at that
juncture a shout pealed from the forest. Helen
recognized Roy's voice. Then she heard a splashing of
water, and hoof-beats coming closer. With that the
buckskin mustang trotted into camp, carrying Roy.

"Bad mornin' for ducks, but good for us," he called.

"Howdy, Roy!" greeted Dale, and his gladness was
unmistakable. "I was lookin' for you."

Roy appeared to slide off the mustang without effort,
and his swift hands slapped the straps as he unsaddled.
Buckskin was wet with sweat and foam mixed with
rain. He heaved. And steam rose from him.

"Must have rode hard," observed Dale.

"I shore did," replied Roy. Then he espied Helen, who
had sat up, with hands to her hair, and eyes staring at
him.

"Mornin', miss. It's good news."

"Thank Heaven!" murmured Helen, and then she shook
Bo. That young lady awoke, but was loath to give up
slumber. "Bo! Bo! Wake up! Mr. Roy is back."

Whereupon Bo sat up, disheveled and sleepy-eyed.

"Oh-h, but I ache!" she moaned. But her eyes took in the camp scene to the effect that she added, "Is breakfast ready?"

"Almost. An' flapjacks this mornin'," replied Dale.

Bo manifested active symptoms of health in the manner with which she laced her boots. Helen got their traveling-bag, and with this they repaired to a flat stone beside the spring, not, however, out of earshot of the men.

"How long are you goin' to hang around camp before tellin' me?" inquired Dale.

"Jest as I figgered, Milt," replied Roy. "Thet rider who passed you was a messenger to Anson. He an' his gang got on our trailquick. About ten o'clock I seen them comin'. Then I lit out for the woods. I stayed off in the woods close enough to see where they come in. An' shore they lost your trail. Then they spread through the woods, workin' off to the south, thinkin', of course, thet you would circle round to Pine on the south side of Old Baldy. There ain't a hoss-tracker in Snake Anson's gang, thet's shore. Wal, I follered them for an hour till they'd rustled some miles off our trail. Then I went back to where you struck into the woods. An' I waited there all afternoon till dark, expectin' mebbe they'd back-trail. But they didn't. I rode on a ways an' camped in the woods till jest before daylight."

"So far so good," declared Dale.

"Shore. There's rough country south of Baldy an' along

the two or three trails Anson an' his outfit will camp, you bet."

"It ain't to be thought of," muttered Dale, at some idea that had struck him.

"What ain't?"

"Goin' round the north side of Baldy."

"It shore ain't," rejoined Roy, bluntly.

"Then I've got to hide tracks certain - rustle to my camp an' stay there till you say it's safe to risk takin' the girls to Pine."

"Milt, you're talkin' the wisdom of the prophets."

"I ain't so sure we can hide tracks altogether. If Anson had any eyes for the woods he'd not have lost me so soon.

"No. But, you see, he's figgerin' to cross your trail."

"If I could get fifteen or twenty mile farther on an' hide tracks certain, I'd feel safe from pursuit, anyway," said the hunter, reflectively.

"Shore an' easy," responded Roy, quickly. "I jest met up with some greaser sheep-herders drivin' a big flock. They've come up from the south an' are goin' to fatten up at Turkey Senacas. Then they'll drive back south an' go on to Phenix. Wal, it's muddy weather. Now you break camp quick an' make a plain trail out to thet sheep trail, as if you was travelin' south. But, instead, you ride round ahead of thet flock of sheep. They'll keep to the open parks an' the trails through them necks of woods out here. An', passin' over your tracks, they'll hide 'em."

"But supposin' Anson circles an' hits this camp? He'll track me easy out to that sheep trail. What then?"

"Jest what you want. Goin' south thet sheep trail is downhill an' muddy. It's goin' to rain hard. Your tracks would get washed out even if you did go south. An' Anson would keep on thet way till he was clear off the scent. Leave it to me, Milt. You're a hunter. But I'm a hoss-tracker."

"All right. We'll rustle."

Then he called the girls to hurry.

CHAPTER VIII

Once astride the horse again, Helen had to congratulate herself upon not being so crippled as she had imagined. Indeed, Bo made all the audible complaints.

Both girls had long water-proof coats, brand-new, and of which they were considerably proud. New clothes had not been a common event in their lives.

"Reckon I'll have to slit these," Dale had said, whipping out a huge knife.

"What for?" had been Bo's feeble protest.

"They wasn't made for ridin'. An' you'll get wet enough even if I do cut them. An' if I don't, you'll get soaked."

"Go ahead," had been Helen's reluctant permission.

So their long new coats were slit half-way up the back. The exigency of the case was manifest to Helen, when she saw how they came down over the cantles of the saddles and to their boot-tops.

The morning was gray and cold. A fine, misty rain fell and the trees dripped steadily. Helen was surprised to see the open country again and that apparently they were to leave the forest behind for a while. The country was wide and flat on the right, and to the left it rolled and heaved along a black, scalloped timber-line. Above this bordering of the forest low, drifting clouds obscured the mountains. The wind was at Helen's back and seemed to be growing stronger. Dale and Roy were ahead, traveling at a good trot, with the pack-animals bunched before them. Helen and Bo had enough to do to keep up.

The first hour's ride brought little change in weather or scenery, but it gave Helen an inkling of what she must endure if they kept that up all day. She began to welcome the places where the horses walked, but she disliked the levels. As for the descents, she hated those. Ranger would not go down slowly and the shake-up she received was unpleasant. Moreover, the spirited black horse insisted on jumping the ditches and washes. He sailed over them like a bird. Helen could not acquire the knack of sitting the saddle properly, and so, not only was her person bruised on these occasions, but her feelings were hurt. Helen had never before been conscious of vanity. Still, she had never rejoiced in looking at a disadvantage, and her exhibitions here must have been frightful. Bo always would forge to the front, and she seldom looked back, for which Helen was grateful.

Before long they struck into a broad, muddy belt, full of innumerable small hoof tracks. This, then, was the sheep trail Roy had advised following. They rode on it for three or four miles, and at length, coming to a gray-green valley, they saw a huge flock of sheep. Soon the air was full of bleats and baas as well as the odor of sheep, and a low, soft roar of pattering hoofs. The flock held a compact formation, covering several acres, and grazed along rapidly. There were three herders on horses and. Several pack-burros. Dale engaged one of the Mexicans in conversation, and passed something to him, then pointed northward and down along the trail. The Mexican grinned from ear to ear, and Helen caught the quick "Si, señor! Gracias, señor!" It was a pretty sight, that flock of sheep, as it rolled along like a rounded woolly stream of grays and browns and here and there a black. They were keeping to a trail over the flats. Dale headed into this trail and, if anything, trotted a little faster.

Presently the clouds lifted and broke, showing blue sky and one streak of sunshine. But the augury was without warrant. The wind increased. A huge black pall bore down from the mountains and it brought rain that could be seen falling in sheets from above and approaching like a swiftly moving wall. Soon it enveloped the fugitives.

With head bowed, Helen rode along for what seemed ages in a cold, gray rain that blew almost on a level. Finally the heavy downpour passed, leaving a fine mist. The clouds scurried low and dark, hiding the mountains altogether and making the gray, wet plain a dreary sight. Helen's feet and knees were as wet as if she had waded in water. And they were cold. Her gloves, too, had not been intended for rain, and they were wet through. The cold bit at her fingers so that she had to beat her hands together. Ranger misunderstood this to mean that he was to trot faster, which event was worse for Helen than freezing.

She saw another black, scudding mass of clouds bearing down with its trailing sheets of rain, and this one appeared streaked with white. Snow! The wind was now piercingly cold. Helen's body kept warm, but her extremities and ears began to suffer exceedingly.

She gazed ahead grimly. There was no help; she had to go on. Dale and Roy were hunched down in their saddles, probably wet through, for they wore no rain-proof coats. Bo kept close behind them, and plain it was that she felt the cold.

This second storm was not so bad as the first, because there was less rain. Still, the icy keenness of the wind bit into the marrow. It lasted for an hour, during which the horses trotted on, trotted on. Again the gray torrent roared away, the fine mist blew, the clouds lifted and separated, and, closing again, darkened for another onslaught. This one brought sleet. The driving pellets stung Helen's neck and cheeks, and for a while they fell so thick and so hard upon her back that she was afraid she could not hold up under them. The bare places on the ground showed a sparkling coverlet of marbles of ice.

Thus, storm after storm rolled over Helen's head. Her feet grew numb and ceased to hurt. But her fingers, because of her ceaseless efforts to keep up the circulation, retained the stinging pain. And now the wind pierced right through her. She marveled at her endurance, and there were many times that she believed she could not ride farther. Yet she kept on. All the winters she had ever lived had not brought such a day as this. Hard and cold, wet and windy, at an increasing elevation - that was the explanation. The air did not have sufficient oxygen for her blood.

Still, during all those interminable hours, Helen watched where she was traveling, and if she ever returned over that trail she would recognize it. The afternoon appeared far advanced when Dale and Roy led down into an immense basin where a reedy lake spread over the flats. They rode along its margin, splashing up to the knees of the horses. Cranes and herons flew on with lumbering motion; flocks of ducks winged swift flight from one side to the other. Beyond this depression the land sloped rather abruptly; outcroppings of rock circled along the edge of the highest ground, and again a dark fringe of trees appeared.

How many miles! wondered Helen. They seemed as many and as long as the hours. But at last, just as another hard rain came, the pines were reached. They proved to be widely scattered and afforded little protection from the storm.

Helen sat her saddle, a dead weight. Whenever Ranger quickened his gait or crossed a ditch she held on to the pommel to keep from falling off. Her mind harbored only sensations of misery, and a persistent thought - why did she ever leave home for the West? Her solicitude for Bo had been forgotten. Nevertheless, any marked change in the topography of the country was registered, perhaps photographed on her memory by the torturing vividness of her experience.

The forest grew more level and denser. Shadows of twilight or gloom lay under the trees. Presently Dale and Roy, disappeared, going downhill, and likewise Bo. Then Helen's ears suddenly filled with a roar of rapid water. Ranger trotted faster. Soon Helen came to the edge of a great valley, black and gray, so full of obscurity that she could not see across or down into it. But she knew there was a rushing river at the bottom. The sound was deep, continuous, a heavy, murmuring roar, singularly musical. The trail was steep. Helen had not lost all feeling, as she had believed and hoped. Her poor, mistreated body still responded excruciatingly to concussions, jars, wrenches, and all the other horrible movements making up a horse-trot.

For long Helen did not look up. When she did so there lay a green, willow-bordered, treeless space at the bottom of the valley, through which a brown-white stream rushed with steady, ear-filling roar.

Dale and Roy drove the pack-animals across the stream, and followed, going deep to the flanks of their horses. Bo rode into the foaming water as if she had been used to it all her days. A slip, a fall, would have meant that Bo must drown in that mountain torrent.

Ranger trotted straight to the edge, and there, obedient to Helen's clutch on the bridle, he halted. The stream was fifty feet wide, shallow on the near side, deep on the opposite, with fast current and big waves. Helen was simply too frightened to follow.

"Let him come!" yelled Dale. "Stick on now! . . . Ranger!"

The big black plunged in, making the water fly. That stream was nothing for him, though it seemed impassable to Helen. She had not the strength left to lift her stirrups and the water surged over them. Ranger, in two more plunges, surmounted the bank, and then, trotting across the green to where the other horses stood steaming under some pines, he gave a great heave and halted.

Roy reached up to help her off.

"Thirty miles, Miss Helen," he said, and the way he

spoke was a compliment.

He had to lift her off and help her to the tree where Bo leaned. Dale had ripped off a saddle and was spreading saddle-blankets on the ground under the pine.

"Nell - you swore - you loved me!" was Bo's mournful greeting. The girl was pale, drawn, blue-lipped, and she could not stand up.

"Bo, I never did - or I'd never have brought you to this - wretch that I am!" cried Helen. "Oh, what a horrible ride!"

Rain was falling, the trees were dripping, the sky was lowering. All the ground was soaking wet, with pools and puddles everywhere. Helen could imagine nothing but a heartless, dreary, cold prospect. Just then home was vivid and poignant in her thoughts. Indeed, so utterly miserable was she that the exquisite relief of sitting down, of a cessation of movement, of a release from that infernal perpetual-trotting horse, seemed only a mockery. It could not be true that the time had come for rest.

Evidently this place had been a camp site for hunters or sheep-herders, for there were remains of a fire. Dale lifted the burnt end of a log and brought it down hard upon the ground, splitting off pieces. Several times he did this. It was amazing to see his strength, his facility, as he split off handfuls of splinters. He collected a bundle of them, and, laying them down, he bent over them. Roy wielded the ax on another log, and each stroke split off a long strip. Then a tiny column of smoke drifted up over Dale's shoulder as he leaned, bareheaded, sheltering the splinters with his hat. A blaze leaped up. Roy came with an armful of strips all white and dry, out of the inside of a log. Crosswise these were laid over the blaze, and it began to roar. Then piece by piece the men built up a frame upon which they added heavier woods, branches and stumps and logs, erecting a pyramid through which flames and smoke roared upward. It had not taken two minutes. Already Helen felt the warmth on her icy face. She held up her bare, numb hands.

Both Dale and Roy were wet through to the skin, yet they did not tarry beside the fire. They relieved the horses. A lasso went up between two pines, and a tarpaulin over it, V-shaped and pegged down at the four ends. The packs containing the baggage of the girls and the supplies and bedding were placed under this shelter.

Helen thought this might have taken five minutes more. In this short space of time the fire had leaped and flamed until it was huge and hot. Rain was falling steadily all around, but over and near that roaring blaze, ten feet high, no water fell. It evaporated. The ground began to steam and to dry. Helen suffered at first while the heat was driving out the cold. But presently the pain ceased.

"Nell, I never knew before how good a fire could feel," declared Bo.

And therein lay more food for Helen's reflection.

In ten minutes Helen was dry and hot. Darkness came down upon the dreary, sodden forest, but that great camp-fire made it a different world from the one Helen had anticipated. It blazed and roared, cracked like a pistol, hissed and sputtered, shot sparks everywhere, and sent aloft a dense, yellow, whirling column of smoke. It began to have a heart of gold.

Dale took a long pole and raked out a pile of red embers upon which the coffee-pot and oven soon began to steam.

"Roy, I promised the girls turkey to-night," said the hunter.

"Mebbe to-morrow, if the wind shifts. This 's turkey country."

"Roy, a potato will do me!" exclaimed Bo.

"Never again will I ask for cake and pie! I never appreciated good things to eat. And I've been a little pig, always. I never - never knew what it was to be hungry - until now."

Dale glanced up quickly.

"Lass, it's worth learnin'," he said.

Helen's thought was too deep for words. In such brief space had she been transformed from misery to comfort!

The rain kept on falling, though it appeared to grow softer as night settled down black. The wind died away and the forest was still, except for the steady roar of the stream. A folded tarpaulin was laid between the pine and the fire, well in the light and warmth, and upon it the men set steaming pots and plates and cups, the fragrance from which was strong and inviting.

"Fetch the saddle-blanket an' set with your backs to the fire," said Roy.

Later, when the girls were tucked away snugly in their blankets and sheltered from the rain, Helen remained awake after Bo had fallen asleep. The big blaze made the improvised tent as bright as day. She could see the smoke, the trunk of the big pine towering aloft, and a blank space of sky. The stream hummed a song, seemingly musical at times, and then discordant and dull, now low, now roaring, and always rushing, gurgling, babbling, flowing, chafing in its hurry.

Presently the hunter and his friend returned from hobbling the horses, and beside the fire they conversed in low tones.

"Wal, thet trail we made to-day will be hid, I reckon," said Roy, with satisfaction.

"What wasn't sheeped over would be washed out. We've had luck. An' now I ain't worryin'," returned Dale.

"Worryin'? Then it's the first I ever knowed you to do."

"Man, I never had a job like this," protested the hunter.

"Wal, thet's so."

"Now, Roy, when old Al Auchincloss finds out about this deal, as he's bound to when you or the boys get back to Pine, he's goin' to roar."

"Do you reckon folks will side with him against Beasley?"

"Some of them. But Al, like as not, will tell folks to go where it's hot. He'll bunch his men an' strike for the mountains to find his nieces."

"Wal, all you've got to do is to keep the girls hid till I can guide him up to your camp. Or, failin' thet, till you can slip the girls down to Pine."

"No one but you an' your brothers ever seen my senaca. But it could be found easy enough."

"Anson might blunder on it. But thet ain't likely."

"Why ain't it?"

"Because I'll stick to thet sheep-thief's tracks like a wolf after a bleedin' deer. An' if he ever gets near your camp I'll ride in ahead of him."

"Good!" declared Dale. "I was calculatin' you'd go down to Pine, sooner or later."

"Not unless Anson goes. I told John thet in case there was no fight on the stage to make a bee-line back to Pine. He was to tell Al an' offer his services along with Joe an' Hal."

"One way or another, then, there's bound to be blood spilled over this."

"Shore! An' high time. I jest hope I get a look down my old 'forty-four' at thet Beasley."

"In that case I hope you hold straighter than times I've seen you."

"Milt Dale, I'm a good shot," declared Roy, stoutly.

"You're no good on movin' targets."

"Wal, mebbe so. But I'm not lookin' for a movin' target when I meet up with Beasley. I'm a hossman, not a hunter. You're used to shootin' flies off deer's horns, jest for practice."

"Roy, can we make my camp by to-morrow night?" queried Dale, more seriously.

"We will, if each of us has to carry one of the girls. But they'll do it or die. Dale, did you ever see a gamer girl than thet kid Bo?"

"Me! Where'd I ever see any girls?" ejaculated Dale. "I remember some when I was a boy, but I was only fourteen then. Never had much use for girls."

"I'd like to have a wife like that Bo," declared Roy, fervidly.

There ensued a moment's silence.

"Roy, you're a Mormon an' you already got a wife," was Dale's reply.

"Now, Milt, have you lived so long in the woods thet you never heard of a Mormon with two wives?" returned Roy, and then he laughed heartily.

"I never could stomach what I did hear pertainin' to more than one wife for a man."

"Wal, my friend, you go an' get yourself one. An' see

then if you wouldn't like to have two."

"I reckon one 'd be more than enough for Milt Dale."

"Milt, old man, let me tell you thet I always envied you your freedom," said Roy, earnestly. "But it ain't life."

"You mean life is love of a woman?"

"No. Thet's only part. I mean a son - a boy thet's like you - thet you feel will go on with your life after you're gone."

"I've thought of that - thought it all out, watchin' the birds an' animals mate in the woods. . . . If I have no son I'll never live hereafter."

"Wal," replied Roy, hesitatingly, "I don't go in so deep as thet. I mean a son goes on with your blood an' your work."

"Exactly. . . An', Roy, I envy you what you ve got, because it's out of all bounds for Milt Dale."

Those words, sad and deep, ended the conversation. Again the rumbling, rushing stream dominated the forest. An owl hooted dismally. A horse trod thuddingly near by and from that direction came a cutting tear of teeth on grass.

A voice pierced Helen's deep dreams and, awaking, she found Bo shaking and calling her.

"Are you dead?" came the gay voice.

"Almost. Oh, my back's broken," replied Helen. The

desire to move seemed clamped in a vise, and even if that came she believed the effort would be impossible.

"Roy called us," said Bo. "He said hurry. I thought I'd die just sitting up, and I'd give you a million dollars to lace my boots. Wait, sister, till you try to pull on one of those stiff boots!"

With heroic and violent spirit Helen sat up to find that in the act her aches and pains appeared beyond number. Reaching for her boots, she found them cold and stiff. Helen unlaced one and, opening it wide, essayed to get her sore foot down into it. But her foot appeared swollen and the boot appeared shrunken. She could not get it half on, though she expended what little strength seemed left in her aching arms. She groaned.

Bo laughed wickedly. Her hair was tousled, her eyes dancing, her cheeks red.

"Be game!" she said. "Stand up like a real Western girl and pull your boot on."

Whether Bo's scorn or advice made the task easier did not occur to Helen, but the fact was that she got into her boots. Walking and moving a little appeared to loosen the stiff joints and ease that tired feeling. The water of the stream where the girls washed was colder than any ice Helen had ever felt. It almost paralyzed her hands. Bo mumbled, and blew like a porpoise. They had to run to the fire before being able to comb their hair. The air was wonderfully keen. The dawn was clear, bright, with a red glow in the east where the sun was about to rise.

"All ready, girls," called Roy. "Reckon you can help yourselves. Milt ain't comin' in very fast with the hosses. I'll rustle off to help him. We've got a hard day before us. Yesterday wasn't nowhere to what to-day 'll be."

"But the sun's going to shine?" implored Bo.

"Wal, you bet," rejoined Roy, as he strode off.

Helen and Bo ate breakfast and had the camp to themselves for perhaps half an hour; then the horses came thudding down, with Dale and Roy riding bareback.

By the time all was in readiness to start the sun was up, melting the frost and ice, so that a dazzling, bright mist, full of rainbows, shone under the trees.

Dale looked Ranger over, and tried the cinches of Bo's horse.

"What's your choice - a long ride behind the packs with me - or a short cut over the hills with Roy?" he asked.

"I choose the lesser of two rides," replied Helen, smiling. "Reckon that 'll be easier, but you'll know you've had a ride," said Dale, significantly.

"What was that we had yesterday?" asked Bo, archly.

"Only thirty miles, but cold an' wet. To-day will be fine for ridin'."

"Milt, I'll take a blanket an' some grub in case you don't meet us to-night," said Roy. "An' I reckon we'll split up here where I'll have to strike out on thet short cut."

Bo mounted without a helping hand, but Helen's limbs were so stiff that she could not get astride the high Ranger without assistance. The hunter headed up the slope of the cañon, which on that side was not steep. It was brown pine forest, with here and there a clump of dark, silver-pointed evergreens that Roy called spruce. By the time this slope was surmounted Helen's aches were not so bad. The saddle appeared to fit her better, and the gait of the horse was not so unfamiliar. She reflected, however, that she always had done pretty well uphill. Here it was beautiful forest-land, uneven and wilder. They rode for a time along the rim, with the white rushing stream in plain sight far below, with its melodious roar ever thrumming in the ear.

Dale reined in and peered down at the pine-mat.

"Fresh deer sign all along here," he said, pointing.

"Wal, I seen thet long ago," rejoined Roy.

Helen's scrutiny was rewarded by descrying several tiny depressions in the pine-needles, dark in color and sharply defined.

"We may never get a better chance," said Dale. "Those deer are workin' up our way. Get your rifle out."

Travel was resumed then, with Roy a little in advance of the pack-train. Presently he dismounted, threw his bridle, and cautiously peered ahead. Then, turning, he waved his sombrero. The pack-animals halted in a bunch. Dale beckoned for the girls to follow and rode up to Roy's horse. This point, Helen saw, was at the top of an intersecting cañon. Dale dismounted, without drawing his rifle from its saddle-sheath, and approached Roy.

"Buck an' two does," he said, low-voiced. "An' they've winded us, but don't see us yet. . . . Girls, ride up closer."

Following the directions indicated by Dale's long arm, Helen looked down the slope. It was open, with tall pines here and there, and clumps of silver spruce, and aspens shining like gold in the morning sunlight. Presently Bo exclaimed: "Oh, look! I see! I see!" Then Helen's roving glance passed something different from green and gold and brown. Shifting back to it she saw a magnificent stag, with noble spreading antlers, standing like a statue, his head up in alert and wild posture. His color was gray. Beside him grazed two deer of slighter and more graceful build, without horns.

"It's downhill," whispered Dale. "An' you're goin' to overshoot."

Then Helen saw that Roy had his rifle leveled.

"Oh, don't!" she cried.

Dale's remark evidently nettled Roy. He lowered the rifle.

"Milt, it's me lookin' over this gun. How can you stand there an' tell me I'm goin' to shoot high? I had a dead bead on him."

"Roy, you didn't allow for downhill . . . Hurry. He sees us now."

Roy leveled the rifle and, taking aim as before, he fired. The buck stood perfectly motionless, as if he had indeed been stone. The does, however, jumped with a start, and gazed in fright in every direction.

"Told you! I seen where your bullet hit thet pine - half a foot over his shoulder. Try again an' aim at his legs."

Roy now took a quicker aim and pulled trigger. A puff of dust right at the feet of the buck showed where Roy's lead had struck this time. With a single bound, wonderful to see, the big deer was out of sight behind trees and brush. The does leaped after him.

"Doggone the luck!" ejaculated Roy, red in the face, as he worked the lever of his rifle. "Never could shoot downhill, nohow!"

His rueful apology to the girls for missing brought a merry laugh from Bo.

"Not for worlds would I have had you kill that beautiful deer!" she exclaimed.

"We won't have venison steak off him, that's certain," remarked Dale, dryly. "An' maybe none off any deer, if Roy does the shootin'."

They resumed travel, sheering off to the right and keeping to the edge of the intersecting cañon. At length they rode down to the bottom, where a tiny brook babbled through willows, and they followed this for a mile or so down to where it flowed into the larger stream. A dim trail overgrown with grass showed at this point.

"Here's where we part," said Dale. "You'll beat me into my camp, but I'll get there sometime after dark."

"Hey, Milt, I forgot about thet darned pet cougar of yours an' the rest of your menagerie. Reckon they won't scare the girls? Especially old Tom?"

"You won't see Tom till I get home," replied Dale.

"Ain't he corralled or tied up?"

"No. He has the run of the place."

"Wal, good-by, then, an' rustle along."

Dale nodded to the girls, and, turning his horse, he drove the pack-train before him up the open space between the stream and the wooded slope.

Roy stepped off his horse with that single action which appeared such a feat to Helen.

"Guess I'd better cinch up," he said, as he threw a stirrup up over the pommel of his saddle. "You girls are goin' to see wild country."

"Who's old Tom?" queried Bo, curiously.

"Why, he's Milt's pet cougar."

"Cougar? That's a panther - a mountain-lion, didn't he say?"

"Shore is. Tom is a beauty. An' if he takes a likin' to you he'll love you, play with you, maul you half to death."

Bo was all eyes.

"Dale has other pets, too?" she questioned, eagerly.

"I never was up to his camp but what it was overrun with birds an' squirrels an' vermin of all kinds, as tame as tame as cows. Too darn tame, Milt says. But I can't figger thet. You girls will never want to leave thet senaca of his."

"What's a senaca?" asked Helen, as she shifted her foot to let him tighten the cinches on her saddle.

"Thet's Mexican for park, I guess," he replied. "These mountains are full of parks; an', say, I don't ever want to see no prettier place till I get to heaven. . . . There, Ranger, old boy, thet's tight."

He slapped the horse affectionately, and, turning to his own, he stepped and swung his long length up.

"It ain't deep crossin' here. Come on," he called, and spurred his bay.

The stream here was wide and it looked deep, but turned out to be deceptive.

"Wal, girls, here beginneth the second lesson," he drawled, cheerily. "Ride one behind the other - stick close to me - do what I do - an' holler when you want to rest or if somethin' goes bad."

With that he spurred into the thicket. Bo went next and Helen followed. The willows dragged at her so hard that she was unable to watch Roy, and the result was that a low-sweeping branch of a tree knocked her hard on the head. It hurt and startled her, and roused her mettle. Roy was keeping to the easy trot that covered ground so well, and he led up a slope to the open pine forest. Here the ride for several miles was straight, level, and open. Helen liked the forest to-day. It was brown and green, with patches of gold where the sun struck. She saw her first bird - big blue grouse that whirred up from under her horse, and little checkered gray quail that appeared awkward on the wing. Several times Roy pointed out deer flashing gray across some forest aisle, and often when he pointed Helen was not quick enough to see.

Helen realized that this ride would make up for the hideous one of yesterday. So far she had been only barely conscious of sore places and aching bones. These she would bear with. She loved the wild and the beautiful, both of which increased manifestly with every mile. The sun was warm, the air fragrant and cool, the sky blue as azure and so deep that she imagined that she could look far up into it.

Suddenly Roy reined in so sharply that he pulled the bay up short.

"Look!" he called, sharply.

Bo screamed.

"Not thet way! Here! Aw, he's gone!"

"Nell! It was a bear! I saw it! Oh! not like circus bears at all!" cried Bo.

Helen had missed her opportunity.

"Reckon he was a grizzly, an' I'm jest as well pleased thet he loped off," said Roy. Altering his course somewhat, he led to an old rotten log that the bear had been digging in. "After grubs. There, see his track. He was a whopper shore enough."

They rode on, out to a high point that overlooked cañon and range, gorge and ridge, green and black as far as Helen could see. The ranges were bold and long, climbing to the central uplift, where a number of fringed peaks raised their heads to the vast bare dome of Old Baldy. Far as vision could see, to the right lay one rolling forest of pine, beautiful and serene. Somewhere down beyond must have lain the desert, but it was not in sight.

"I see turkeys 'way down there," said Roy, backing away. "We'll go down and around an' mebbe I'll get a shot."

Descent beyond a rocky point was made through thick brush. This slope consisted of wide benches covered with copses and scattered pines and many oaks. Helen was delighted to see the familiar trees, although these were different from Missouri oaks. Rugged and gnarled, but not tall, these trees spread wide branches, the leaves of which were yellowing. Roy led into a grassy glade, and, leaping off his horse, rifle in hand, he prepared to shoot at something. Again Bo cried out, but this time it was in delight. Then Helen saw an immense flock of turkeys, apparently like the turkeys she knew at home, but these had bronze and checks of white, and they looked wild. There must have been a hundred in the flock, most of them hens. A few gobblers on the far side began the flight, running swiftly off. Helen plainly heard the thud of their feet. Roy shot once - twice - three times. Then rose a great commotion. and thumping, and a loud roar of many wings. Dust and leaves whirling in the air were left where the turkeys had been.

"Wal, I got two," said Roy, and he strode forward to pick up his game. Returning, he tied two shiny, plump gobblers back of his saddle and remounted his horse. "We'll have turkey to-night, if Milt gets to camp in time."

The ride was resumed. Helen never would have tired riding through those oak groves, brown and sear and yellow, with leaves and acorns falling.

"Bears have been workin' in here already," said Roy. "I see tracks all over. They eat acorns in the fall. An' mebbe we'll run into one yet."

The farther down he led the wilder and thicker grew the trees, so that dodging branches was no light task. Ranger did not seem to care how close he passed a tree or under a limb, so that he missed them himself; but Helen thereby got some additional bruises. Particularly hard was it, when passing a tree, to get her knee out of the way in time.

Roy halted next at what appeared a large green pond full of vegetation and in places covered with a thick scum. But it had a current and an outlet, proving it to be a huge, spring. Roy pointed down at a muddy place.

"Bear-wallow. He heard us comin'. Look at thet little track. Cub track. An' look at these scratches on this tree, higher 'n my head. An old she-bear stood up, an' scratched them."

Roy sat his saddle and reached up to touch fresh marks on the tree.

"Woods's full of big bears," he said, grinning. "An' I take it particular kind of this old she rustlin' off with her cub. She-bears with cubs are dangerous."

The next place to stir Helen to enthusiasm was the glen at the bottom of this cañon. Beech-trees, maples, aspens, overtopped by lofty pines, made dense shade over a brook where trout splashed on the brown, swirling current, and leaves drifted down, and stray flecks of golden sunlight lightened the gloom. Here was hard riding to and fro across the brook, between huge mossy boulders, and between aspens so close together that Helen could scarce squeeze her knees through.

Once more Roy climbed out of that cañon, over a ridge into another, down long wooded slopes and through scrub-oak thickets, on and on till the sun stood straight overhead. Then he halted for a short rest, unsaddled the horses to let them roll, and gave the girls some cold lunch that he had packed. He strolled off with his gun, and, upon returning, resaddled and gave the word to start.

That was the last of rest and easy traveling for the girls. The forest that he struck into seemed ribbed like a washboard with deep ravines so steep of slope as to make precarious travel. Mostly he kept to the bottom where dry washes afforded a kind of trail. But it was necessary to cross these ravines when they were too long to be headed, and this crossing was work.

The locust thickets characteristic of these slopes were thorny and close knit. They tore and scratched and stung both horses and riders. Ranger appeared to be the most intelligent of the horses and suffered less. Bo's white mustang dragged her through more than one brambly place. On the other hand, some of these steep slopes, were comparatively free of underbrush. Great firs and pines loomed up on all sides. The earth was soft and the hoofs sank deep. Toward the bottom of a descent Ranger would brace his front feet and then slide down on his haunches. This mode facilitated travel, but it frightened Helen. The climb out then on the other side had to be done on foot.

After half a dozen slopes surmounted in this way Helen's strength was spent and her breath was gone. She felt light-headed. She could not get enough air. Her feet felt like lead, and her riding-coat was a burden. A hundred times, hot and wet and throbbing, she was compelled to stop. Always she had been a splendid walker and climber. And here, to break up the long ride, she was glad to be on her feet. But she could only drag one foot up after the other. Then, when her nose began to bleed, she realized that it was the elevation which was causing all the trouble. Her heart, however, did not hurt her, though she was conscious of an oppression on her breast.

At last Roy led into a ravine so deep and wide and full of forest verdure that it appeared impossible to cross. Nevertheless, he started down, dismounting after a little way. Helen found that leading Ranger down was worse than riding him. He came fast and he would step right in her tracks. She was not quick enough to get, away from him. Twice he stepped on her foot, and again his broad chest hit her shoulder and threw her flat. When he began to slide, near the bottom, Helen had to run for her life.

"Oh, Nell! Isn't - this - great?" panted Bo, from somewhere ahead.

"Bo - your - mind's - gone," panted Helen, in reply.

Roy tried several places to climb out, and failed in each. Leading down the ravine for a hundred yards or more, he essayed another attempt. Here there had been a slide, and in part the earth was bare. When he had worked up this, he halted above, and called:

"Bad place! Keep on the up side of the hosses!"

This appeared easier said than done. Helen could not watch Bo, because Ranger would not wait. He pulled at the bridle and snorted.

"Faster you come the better," called Roy.

Helen could not see the sense of that, but she tried. Roy and Bo had dug a deep trail zigzag up that treacherous slide. Helen made the mistake of starting to follow in their tracks, and when she realized this Ranger was climbing fast, almost dragging her, and it was too late to get above. Helen began to labor. She slid down right in front of Ranger. The intelligent animal, with a snort, plunged out of the trail to keep from stepping on her. Then he was above her.

"Lookout down there," yelled Roy, in warning. "Get on the up side!"

But that did not appear possible. The earth began to slide under Ranger, and that impeded Helen's progress. He got in advance of her, straining on the bridle.

"Let go!" yelled Roy.

Helen dropped the bridle just as a heavy slide began to move with Ranger. He snorted fiercely, and, rearing high, in a mighty plunge he gained solid ground. Helen was buried to her knees, but, extricating herself, she crawled to a safe point and rested before climbing farther.

"Bad cave-in, thet," was Roy's comment, when at last she joined him and Bo at the top.

Roy appeared at a loss as to which way to go. He rode to high ground and looked in all directions. To Helen, one way appeared as wild and rough as another, and all was yellow, green, and black under the westering sun. Roy rode a short distance in one direction, then changed for another.

Presently he stopped.

"Wal, I'm shore turned round," he said.

"You're not lost?" cried Bo.

"Reckon I've been thet for a couple of hours," he replied, cheerfully. "Never did ride across here I had the direction, but I'm blamed now if I can tell which way thet was."

Helen gazed at him in consternation.

"Lost!" she echoed.

CHAPTER IX

A silence ensued, fraught with poignant fear for Helen, as she gazed into Bo's whitening face. She read her sister's mind. Bo was remembering tales of lost people who never were found.

"Me an' Milt get lost every day," said Roy. "You don't suppose any man can know all this big country. It's nothin' for us to be lost."

"Oh! . . . I was lost when I was little," said Bo.

"Wal, I reckon it'd been better not to tell you so offhand like," replied Roy, contritely. "Don't feel bad, now. All I need is a peek at Old Baldy. Then I'll have my bearin'. Come on."

Helen's confidence returned as Roy led off at a fast trot. He rode toward the westering sun, keeping to the ridge they had ascended, until once more he came out upon a promontory. Old Baldy loomed there, blacker and higher and closer. The dark forest showed round, yellow, bare spots like parks.

"Not so far off the track," said Roy, as he wheeled his horse. "We'll make camp in Milt's senaca to-night."

He led down off the ridge into a valley and then up to higher altitude, where the character of the forest changed. The trees were no longer pines, but firs and spruce, growing thin and exceedingly tall, with few branches below the topmost foliage. So dense was this forest that twilight seemed to have come.

Travel was arduous. Everywhere were windfalls that had to be avoided, and not a rod was there without a fallen tree. The horses, laboring slowly, sometimes sank knee-deep into the brown duff. Gray moss festooned the tree-trunks and an amber-green moss grew thick on the rotting logs.

Helen loved this forest primeval. It was so still, so dark, so gloomy, so full of shadows and shade, and a dank smell of rotting wood, and sweet fragrance of spruce. The great windfalls, where trees were jammed together in dozens, showed the savagery of the storms. Wherever a single monarch lay uprooted there had sprung up a number of ambitious sons, jealous of one another, fighting for place. Even the trees fought one another! The forest was a place of mystery, but its strife could be read by any eye. The lightnings had split firs clear to the roots, and others it had circled with ripping tear from top to trunk.

Time came, however, when the exceeding wildness of the forest, in density and fallen timber, made it imperative for Helen to put all her attention on the ground and trees in her immediate vicinity. So the pleasure of gazing ahead at the beautiful wilderness was denied her. Thereafter travel became toil and the hours endless.

Roy led on, and Ranger followed, while the shadows darkened under the trees. She was reeling in her saddle, half blind and sick, when Roy called out cheerily that they were almost there.

Whatever his idea was, to Helen it seemed many miles that she followed him farther, out of the heavy-timbered forest down upon slopes of low spruce, like evergreen, which descended sharply to another level, where dark, shallow streams flowed gently and the solemn stillness held a low murmur of falling water, and at last the wood ended upon a wonderful park full of a thick, rich, golden light of fast-fading sunset.

"Smell the smoke," said Roy. "By Solomon! if Milt ain't here ahead of me!"

He rode on. Helen's weary gaze took in the round senaca, the circling black slopes, leading up to craggy rims all gold and red in the last flare of the sun; then all the spirit left in her flashed up in thrilling wonder at this exquisite, wild, and colorful spot.

Horses were grazing out in the long grass and there were deer grazing with them. Roy led round a corner of the fringed, bordering woodland, and there, under lofty trees, shone a camp-fire. Huge gray rocks loomed beyond, and then cliffs rose step by step to a notch in the mountain wall, over which poured a thin, lacy waterfall. As Helen gazed in rapture the sunset gold faded to white and all the western slope of the amphitheater darkened.

Dale's tall form appeared.

"Reckon you're late," he said, as with a comprehensive flash of eye he took in the three.

"Milt, I got lost," replied Roy.

"I feared as much. . . . You girls look like you'd done better to ride with me," went on Dale, as he offered a hand to help Bo off. She took it, tried to get her foot out of the stirrups, and then she slid from the saddle into Dale's arms. He placed her on her feet and, supporting her, said, solicitously: "A hundred-mile ride in three days for a tenderfoot is somethin' your uncle Al won't believe. . . . Come, walk if it kills you!"

Whereupon he led Bo, very much as if he were teaching a child to walk. The fact that the voluble Bo had nothing to say was significant to Helen, who was following, with the assistance of Roy.

One of the huge rocks resembled a sea-shell in that it contained a hollow over which the wide-spreading shelf flared out. It reached toward branches of great pines. A spring burst from a crack in the solid rock. The campfire blazed under a pine, and the blue column of smoke rose just in front of the shelving rock. Packs were lying on the grass and some of them were open. There were no signs here of a permanent habitation of the hunter. But farther on were other huge rocks, leaning, cracked, and forming caverns, some of which perhaps he utilized.

"My camp is just back," said Dale, as if he had read Helen's mind. "To-morrow we'll fix up comfortable-like round here for you girls."

Helen and Bo were made as easy as blankets and saddles could make them, and the men went about their tasks.

"Nell - isn't this - a dream?" murmured Bo.

"No, child. It's real - terribly real," replied Helen. "Now that we're here - with that awful ride over - we can think."

"It's so pretty - here," yawned Bo. "I'd just as lief Uncle Al didn't find us very soon."

"Bo! He's a sick man. Think what the worry will be to him."

"I'll bet if he knows Dale he won't be so worried."

"Dale told us Uncle Al disliked him."

"Pooh! What difference does that make? . . . Oh, I don't know which I am - hungrier or tireder!"

"I couldn't eat to-night," said Helen, wearily.

When she stretched out she had a vague, delicious sensation that that was the end of Helen Rayner, and she was glad. Above her, through the lacy, fernlike pine-needles, she saw blue sky and a pale star just showing. Twilight was stealing down swiftly. The silence was beautiful, seemingly undisturbed by the soft, silky, dreamy fall of water. Helen closed her eyes, ready for sleep, with the physical commotion within her body gradually yielding. In some places her bones felt as if they had come out through her flesh; in others throbbed deep-seated aches; her muscles appeared slowly to subside, to relax, with the quivering twinges ceasing one by one; through muscle and bone, through all her body, pulsed a burning current.

Bo's head dropped on Helen's shoulder. Sense became vague to Helen. She lost the low murmur of the waterfall, and then the sound or feeling of some one at the campfire. And her last conscious thought was that she tried to open her eyes and could not.

When she awoke all was bright. The sun shone almost directly overhead. Helen was astounded. Bo lay wrapped in deep sleep, her face flushed, with beads of perspiration on her brow and the chestnut curls damp. Helen threw down the blankets, and then, gathering courage - for she felt as if her back was broken - she endeavored to sit up. In vain! Her spirit was willing, but her muscles refused to act. It must take a violent spasmodic effort. She tried it with shut eyes, and, succeeding, sat there trembling. The commotion she had made in the blankets awoke Bo, and she blinked her surprised blue eyes in the sunlight.

"Hello - Nell! do I have to - get up?" she asked, sleepily.

"Can you?" queried Helen.

"Can I what?" Bo was now thoroughly awake and lay there staring at her sister.

"Why - get up."

"I'd like to know why not," retorted Bo, as she made the effort. She got one arm and shoulder up, only to flop back like a crippled thing. And she uttered the most piteous little moan. "I'm dead! I know - I am!"

"Well, if you're going to be a Western girl you'd better have spunk enough to move."

"A-huh!" ejaculated Bo. Then she rolled over, not

without groans, and, once upon her face, she raised herself on her hands and turned to a sitting posture. "Where's everybody? . . . Oh, Nell, it's perfectly lovely here. Paradise!"

Helen looked around. A fire was smoldering. No one was in sight. Wonderful distant colors seemed to strike her glance as she tried to fix it upon near-by objects. A beautiful little green tent or shack had been erected out of spruce boughs. It had a slanting roof that sloped all the way from a ridge-pole to the ground; half of the opening in front was closed, as were the sides. The spruce boughs appeared all to be laid in the same direction, giving it a smooth, compact appearance, actually as if it had grown there.

"That lean-to wasn't there last night?" inquired Bo.

"I didn't see it. Lean-to? Where'd you get that name?"

"It's Western, my dear. I'll bet they put it up for us. . . . Sure, I see our bags inside. Let's get up. It must be late."

The girls had considerable fun as well as pain in getting up and keeping each other erect until their limbs would hold them firmly. They were delighted with the spruce lean-to. It faced the open and stood just under the wide-spreading shelf of rock. The tiny outlet from the spring flowed beside it and spilled its clear water over a stone, to fall into a little pool. The floor of this woodland habitation consisted of tips of spruce boughs to about a foot in depth, all laid one way, smooth and springy, and so sweetly odorous that the air seemed intoxicating. Helen and Bo opened their baggage, and what with use of the cold water, brush and comb, and clean blouses, they made themselves feel as comfortable as possible, considering the excruciating aches. Then they went out to the campfire.

Helen's eye was attracted by moving objects near at hand. Then simultaneously with Bo's cry of delight Helen saw a beautiful doe approaching under the trees. Dale walked beside it.

"You sure had a long sleep," was the hunter's greeting. "I reckon you both look better."

"Good morning. Or is it afternoon? We're just able to move about," said Helen.

"I could ride," declared Bo, stoutly. "Oh, Nell, look at the deer! It's coming to me."

The doe had hung back a little as Dale reached the camp-fire. It was a gray, slender creature, smooth as silk, with great dark eyes. It stood a moment, long ears erect, and then with a graceful little trot came up to Bo and reached a slim nose for her outstretched hand. All about it, except the beautiful soft eyes, seemed wild, and yet it was as tame as a kitten. Then, suddenly, as Bo fondled the long ears, it gave a start and, breaking away, ran back out of sight under the pines.

"What frightened it?" asked Bo.

Dale pointed up at the wall under the shelving roof of rock. There, twenty feet from the ground, curled up on a ledge, lay a huge tawny animal with a face like that of a cat.

"She's afraid of Tom," replied Dale. "Recognizes him as a hereditary foe, I guess. I can't make friends of them."

"Oh! So that's Tom - the pet lion!" exclaimed Bo. "Ugh! No wonder that deer ran off!"

"How long has he been up there?" queried Helen, gazing fascinated at Dale's famous pet.

"I couldn't say. Tom comes an' goes," replied Dale. "But I sent him up there last night."

"And he was there - perfectly free - right over us - while we slept!" burst out Bo.

"Yes. An' I reckon you slept the safer for that."

"Of all things! Nell, isn't he a monster? But he doesn't look like a lion - an African lion. He's a panther. I saw his like at the circus once."

"He's a cougar," said Dale. "The panther is long and slim. Tom is not only long, but thick an' round. I've had him four years. An' he was a kitten no bigger 'n my fist when I got him."

"Is he perfectly tame - safe?" asked Helen, anxiously.

"I've never told anybody that Tom was safe, but he is," replied Dale. "You can absolutely believe it. A wild cougar wouldn't attack a man unless cornered or starved. An' Tom is like a big kitten."

The beast raised his great catlike face, with its sleepy, half-shut eyes, and looked down upon them.

"Shall I call him down?" inquired Dale.

For once Bo did not find her voice.

"Let us - get a little more used to him - at a distance," replied Helen, with a little laugh.

"If he comes to you, just rub his head an' you'll see how tame he is," said Dale. "Reckon you're both hungry?"

"Not so very," returned Helen, aware of his penetrating gray gaze upon her.

"Well, I am," vouchsafed Bo.

"Soon as the turkey's done we'll eat. My camp is round between the rocks. I'll call you."

Not until his broad back was turned did Helen notice that the hunter looked different. Then she saw he wore a lighter, cleaner suit of buckskin, with no coat, and instead of the high-heeled horseman's boots he wore moccasins and leggings. The change made him appear more lithe.

"Nell, I don't know what you think, but I call him handsome," declared Bo.

Helen had no idea what she thought.

"Let's try to walk some," she suggested.

So they essayed that painful task and got as far as a pine log some few rods from their camp. This point was close to the edge of the park, from which there was an unobstructed view.

"My! What a place!" exclaimed Bo, with eyes wide and round.

"Oh, beautiful!" breathed Helen.

An unexpected blaze of color drew her gaze first. Out of the black spruce slopes shone patches of aspens, gloriously red and gold, and low down along the edge of timber troops of aspens ran out into the park, not yet so blazing as those above, but purple and yellow and white in the sunshine. Masses of silver spruce, like trees in moonlight, bordered the park, sending out here and there an isolated tree, sharp as a spear, with under-branches close to the ground. Long golden-green grass, resembling half-ripe wheat, covered the entire floor of the park, gently waving to the wind. Above sheered the black, gold-patched slopes, steep and unscalable, rising to buttresses of dark, iron-hued rock. And to the east circled the rows of cliff-bench, gray and old and fringed, splitting at the top in the notch where the lacy, slumberous waterfall, like white smoke, fell and vanished, to reappear in wider sheet of lace, only to fall and vanish again in the green depths.

It was a verdant valley, deep-set in the mountain walls, wild and sad and lonesome. The waterfall dominated the spirit of the place, dreamy and sleepy and tranquil; it murmured sweetly on one breath of wind, and lulled with another, and sometimes died out altogether, only to come again in soft, strange roar.

"Paradise Park!" whispered Bo to herself.

A call from Dale disturbed their raptures. Turning,

they hobbled with eager but painful steps in the direction of a larger camp-fire, situated to the right of the great rock that sheltered their lean-to. No hut or house showed there and none was needed. Hiding-places and homes for a hundred hunters were there in the sections of caverned cliffs, split off in bygone ages from the mountain wall above. A few stately pines stood out from the rocks, and a clump of silver spruce ran down to a brown brook. This camp was only a step from the lean-to, round the corner of a huge rock, yet it had been out of sight. Here indeed was evidence of a hunter's home - pelts and skins and antlers, a neat pile of split fire-wood, a long ledge of rock, well sheltered, and loaded with bags like a huge pantry-shelf, packs and ropes and saddles, tools and weapons, and a platform of dry brush as shelter for a fire around which hung on poles a various assortment of utensils for camp.

"Hyar - you git!" shouted Dale, and he threw a stick at something. A bear cub scampered away in haste. He was small and woolly and brown, and he grunted as he ran. Soon he halted.

"That's Bud," said Dale, as the girls came up. "Guess he near starved in my absence. An' now he wants everythin', especially the sugar. We don't have sugar often up here."

"Isn't he dear? Oh, I love him!" cried Bo. "Come back, Bud. Come, Buddie."

The cub, however, kept his distance, watching Dale with bright little eyes.

"Where's Mr. Roy?" asked Helen.

"Roy's gone. He was sorry not to say good-by. But it's important he gets down in the pines on Anson's trail. He'll hang to Anson, an' in case they get near Pine he'll ride in to see where your uncle is."

"What do you expect?" questioned Helen, gravely.

"'Most anythin'," he replied. "Al, I reckon, knows now. Maybe he's rustlin' into the mountains by this time. If he meets up with Anson, well an' good, for Roy won't be far off. An' sure if he runs across Roy, why they'll soon be here. But if I were you I wouldn't count on seein' your uncle very soon. I'm sorry. I've done my best. It sure is a bad deal."

"Don't think me ungracious," replied Helen, hastily. How plainly he had intimated that it must be privation and annoyance for her to be compelled to accept his hospitality! "You are good - kind. I owe you much. I'll be eternally grateful."

Dale straightened as he looked at her. His glance was intent, piercing. He seemed to be receiving a strange or unusual portent. No need for him to say he had never before been spoken to like that!

"You may have to stay here with me - for weeks - maybe months - if we've the bad luck to get snowed in," he said, slowly, as if startled at this deduction. "You're safe here. No sheep-thief could ever find this camp. I'll take risks to get you safe into Al's hands. But I'm goin' to be pretty sure about what I'm doin'. . . . So - there's plenty to eat an' it's a pretty place."

"Pretty! Why, it's grand!" exclaimed Bo. "I've called it Paradise Park."

"Paradise Park," he repeated, weighing the words. "You've named it an' also the creek. Paradise Creek! I've been here twelve years with no fit name for my home till you said that."

"Oh, that pleases me!" returned Bo, with shining eyes.

"Eat now," said Dale. "An' I reckon you'll like that turkey."

There was a clean tarpaulin upon which were spread steaming, fragrant pans - roast turkey, hot biscuits and gravy, mashed potatoes as white as if prepared at home, stewed dried apples, and butter and coffee. This bounteous repast surprised and delighted the girls; when they had once tasted the roast wild turkey, then Milt Dale had occasion to blush at their encomiums.

"I hope - Uncle Al - doesn't come for a month," declared Bo, as she tried to get her breath. There was a brown spot on her nose and one on each cheek, suspiciously close to her mouth.

Dale laughed. It was pleasant to hear him, for his laugh seemed unused and deep, as if it came from tranquil depths.

"Won't you eat with us?" asked Helen.

"Reckon I will," he said. "it'll save time, an' hot grub tastes better."

Quite an interval of silence ensued, which presently was broken by Dale.

"Here comes Tom."

Helen observed with a thrill that the cougar was magnificent, seen erect on all-fours, approaching with slow, sinuous grace. His color was tawny, with spots of whitish gray. He had bow-legs, big and round and furry, and a huge head with great tawny eyes. No matter how tame he was said to be, he looked wild. Like a dog he walked right up, and it so happened that he was directly behind Bo, within reach of her when she turned.

"Oh, Lord!" cried Bo, and up went both of her hands, in one of which was a huge piece of turkey. Tom took it, not viciously, but nevertheless with a snap that made Helen jump. As if by magic the turkey vanished. And Tom took a closer step toward Bo. Her expression of fright changed to consternation.

"He stole my turkey!"

"Tom, come here," ordered Dale, sharply. The cougar glided round rather sheepishly. "Now lie down an' behave."

Tom crouched on all-fours, his head resting on his paws, with his beautiful tawny eyes, light and piercing, fixed upon the hunter.

"Don't grab," said Dale, holding out a piece of turkey. Whereupon Tom took it less voraciously.

As it happened, the little bear cub saw this transaction, and he plainly indicated his opinion of the preference shown to Tom.

"Oh, the dear!" exclaimed Bo. "He means it's not fair . . . . Come, Bud - come on."

But Bud would not approach the group until called by Dale. Then he scrambled to them with every manifestation of delight. Bo almost forgot her own needs in feeding him and getting acquainted with him. Tom plainly showed his jealousy of Bud, and Bud likewise showed his fear of the great cat.

Helen could not believe the evidence of her eyes - that she was in the woods calmly and hungrily partaking of sweet, wild-flavored meat - that a full-grown mountain lion lay on one side of her and a baby brown bear sat on the other - that a strange hunter, a man of the forest, there in his lonely and isolated fastness, appealed to the romance in her and interested her as no one else she had ever met.

When the wonderful meal was at last finished Bo enticed the bear cub around to the camp of the girls, and there soon became great comrades with him. Helen, watching Bo play, was inclined to envy her. No matter where Bo was placed, she always got something out of it. She adapted herself. She, who could have a good time with almost any one or anything, would find the hours sweet and fleeting in this beautiful park of wild wonders.

But merely objective actions - merely physical movements, had never yet contented Helen. She could run and climb and ride and play with hearty and healthy abandon, but those things would not suffice long for her, and her mind needed food. Helen was a thinker. One reason she had desired to make her home in the West was that by taking up a life of the open, of action, she might think and dream and brood less. And here she was in the wild West, after the three most strenuously active days of her career, and still the same old giant revolved her mind and turned it upon herself and upon all she saw.

"What can I do?" she asked Bo, almost helplessly.

"Why, rest, you silly!" retorted Bo. "You walk like an old, crippled woman with only one leg."

Helen hoped the comparison was undeserved, but the advice was sound. The blankets spread out on the grass looked inviting and they felt comfortably warm in the sunshine. The breeze was slow, languorous, fragrant, and it brought the low hum of the murmuring waterfall, like a melody of bees. Helen made a pillow and lay down to rest. The green pine-needles, so thin and fine in their crisscross network, showed clearly against the blue sky. She looked in vain for birds. Then her gaze went. Wonderingly to the lofty fringed rim of the great amphitheater, and as she studied it she began to grasp its remoteness, how far away it was in the rarefied atmosphere. A black eagle, sweeping along, looked of tiny size, and yet he was far under the heights above. How pleasant she fancied it to be up there! And drowsy fancy lulled her to sleep.

Helen slept all afternoon, and upon awakening, toward sunset, found Bo curled beside her. Dale had thoughtfully covered them with a blanket; also he had built a camp-fire. The air was growing keen and cold.

Later, when they had put their coats on and made comfortable seats beside the fire, Dale came over, apparently to visit them.

"I reckon you can't sleep all the time," he said. "An' bein' city girls, you'll get lonesome."

"Lonesome!" echoed Helen. The idea of her being lonesome here had not occurred to her.

"I've thought that all out," went on Dale, as he sat down, Indian fashion, before the blaze. "It's natural you'd find time drag up here, bein' used to lots of people an' goin's-on, an' work, an' all girls like."

"I'd never be lonesome here," replied Helen, with her direct force.

Dale did not betray surprise, but he showed that his mistake was something to ponder over.

"Excuse me," he said, presently, as his gray eyes held hers. "That's how I had it. As I remember girls - an' it doesn't seem long since I left home - most of them would die of lonesomeness up here." Then he addressed himself to Bo. "How about you? You see, I figured you'd be the one that liked it, an' your sister the one who wouldn't."

"I won't get lonesome very soon," replied Bo.

"I'm glad. It worried me some - not ever havin' girls as company before. An' in a day or so, when you're rested, I'll help you pass the time."

Bo's eyes were full of flashing interest, and Helen asked him, "How?"

It was a sincere expression of her curiosity and not doubtful or ironic challenge of an educated woman to a man of the forest. But as a challenge he took it.

"How!" he repeated, and a strange smile flitted across

his face. "Why, by givin' you rides an' climbs to beautiful places. An' then, if you're interested,' to show you how little so-called civilized people know of nature."

Helen realized then that whatever his calling, hunter or wanderer or hermit, he was not uneducated, even if he appeared illiterate.

"I'll be happy to learn from you," she said.

"Me, too!" chimed in Bo. "You can't tell too much to any one from Missouri."

He smiled, and that warmed Helen to him, for then he seemed less removed from other people. About this hunter there began to be something of the very nature of which he spoke - a stillness, aloofness, an unbreakable tranquillity, a cold, clear spirit like that in the mountain air, a physical something not unlike the tamed wildness of his pets or the strength of the pines.

"I'll bet I can tell you more 'n you'll ever remember," he said.

"What 'll you bet?" retorted Bo.

"Well, more roast turkey against - say somethin' nice when you're safe an' home to your uncle Al's, runnin' his ranch."

"Agreed. Nell, you hear?"

Helen nodded her head.

"All right. We'll leave it to Nell," began Dale, half

seriously. "Now I'll tell you, first, for the fun of passin' time we'll ride an' race my horses out in the park. An' we'll fish in the brooks an' hunt in the woods. There's an old silvertip around that you can see me kill. An' we'll climb to the peaks an' see wonderful sights. . . . So much for that. Now, if you really want to learn - or if you only want me to tell you - well, that's no matter. Only I'll win the bet! . . . You'll see how this park lies in the crater of a volcano an' was once full of water - an' how the snow blows in on one side in winter, a hundred feet deep, when there's none on the other. An' the trees - how they grow an' live an' fight one another an' depend on one another, an' protect the forest from storm-winds. An' how they hold the water that is the fountains of the great rivers. An' how the creatures an' things that live in them or on them are good for them, an' neither could live without the other. An' then I'll show you my pets tame an' untamed, an' tell you how it's man that makes any creature wild - how easy they are to tame - an' how they learn to love you. An' there's the life of the forest, the strife of it - how the bear lives, an' the cats, an' the wolves, an' the deer. You'll see how cruel nature is how savage an' wild the wolf or cougar tears down the deer - how a wolf loves fresh, hot blood, an' how a cougar unrolls the skin of a deer back from his neck. An' you'll see that this cruelty of nature - this work of the wolf an' cougar - is what makes the deer so beautiful an' healthy an' swift an' sensitive. Without his deadly foes the deer would deteriorate an' die out. An' you'll see how this principle works out among all creatures of the forest. Strife! It's the meanin' of all creation, an' the salvation. If you're quick to see, you'll learn that the nature here in the wilds is the same as that of men - only men are no longer cannibals. Trees fight to live - birds fight - animals fight - men fight. They all live off one another.

An' it's this fightin' that brings them all closer an' closer to bein' perfect. But nothin' will ever be perfect."

"But how about religion?" interrupted Helen, earnestly.

"Nature has a religion, an' it's to live - to grow - to reproduce, each of its kind."

"But that is not God or the immortality of the soul," declared Helen.

"Well, it's as close to God an' immortality as nature ever gets."

"Oh, you would rob me of my religion!"

"No, I just talk as I see life," replied Dale, reflectively, as he poked a stick into the red embers of the fire. "Maybe I have a religion. I don't know. But it's not the kind you have - not the Bible kind. That kind doesn't keep the men in Pine an' Snowdrop an' all over - sheepmen an' ranchers an' farmers an' travelers, such as I've known - the religion they profess doesn't keep them from lyin', cheatin', stealin', an' killin'. I reckon no man who lives as I do - which perhaps is my religion - will lie or cheat or steal or kill, unless it's to kill in self-defense or like I'd do if Snake Anson would ride up here now. My religion, maybe, is love of life - wild life as it was in the beginnin' - an' the wind that blows secrets from everywhere, an' the water that sings all day an' night, an' the stars that shine constant, an' the trees that speak somehow, an' the rocks that aren't dead. I'm never alone here or on the trails. There's somethin' unseen, but always with me. An' that's It! Call it God if you like.

But what stalls me is - where was that Spirit when this earth was a ball of fiery gas? Where will that Spirit be when all life is frozen out or burned out on this globe an' it hangs dead in space like the moon? That time will come. There's no waste in nature. Not the littlest atom is destroyed. It changes, that's all, as you see this pine wood go up in smoke an' feel somethin' that's heat come out of it. Where does that go? It's not lost. Nothin' is lost. So, the beautiful an' savin' thought is, maybe all rock an' wood, water an' blood an' flesh, are resolved back into the elements, to come to life somewhere again sometime."

"Oh, what you say is wonderful, but it's terrible!" exclaimed Helen. He had struck deep into her soul.

"Terrible? I reckon," he replied, sadly.

Then ensued a little interval of silence.

"Milt Dale, I lose the bet," declared Bo, with earnestness behind her frivolity.

"I'd forgotten that. Reckon I talked a lot," he said, apologetically. "You see, I don't get much chance to talk, except to myself or Tom. Years ago, when I found the habit of silence settlin' down on me, I took to thinkin' out loud an' talkin' to anythin'."

"I could listen to you all night," returned Bo, dreamily.

"Do you read - do you have books?" inquired Helen, suddenly.

"Yes, I read tolerable well; a good deal better than I talk or write," he replied. "I went to school till I was fifteen. Always hated study, but liked to read. Years ago an old friend of mine down here at Pine - Widow Cass - she gave me a lot of old books. An' I packed them up here. Winter's the time I read."

Conversation lagged after that, except for desultory remarks, and presently Dale bade the girls good night and left them. Helen watched his tall form vanish in the gloom under the pines, and after he had disappeared she still stared.

"Nell!" called Bo, shrilly. "I've called you three times. I want to go to bed."

"Oh! I - I was thinking," rejoined Helen, half embarrassed, half wondering at herself. "I didn't hear you."

"I should smile you didn't," retorted Bo. "Wish you could just have seen your eyes. Nell, do you want me to tell you something?

"Why - yes," said Helen, rather feebly. She did not at all, when Bo talked like that.

"You're going to fall in love with that wild hunter," declared Bo in a voice that rang like a bell.

Helen was not only amazed, but enraged. She caught her breath preparatory to giving this incorrigible sister a piece of her mind. Bo went calmly on.

"I can feel it in my bones."

"Bo, you're a little fool - a sentimental, romancing, gushy little fool!" retorted Helen. "All you seem to hold in your head is some rot about love. To hear you talk one would think there's nothing else in the world but love."

Bo's eyes were bright, shrewd, affectionate, and laughing as she bent their steady gaze upon Helen.

"Nell, that's just it. There is nothing else!"

CHAPTER X

The night of sleep was so short that it was difficult for Helen to believe that hours had passed. Bo appeared livelier this morning, with less complaint of aches.

"Nell, you've got color!" exclaimed Bo. "And your eyes are bright. Isn't the morning perfectly lovely? . . . Couldn't you get drunk on that air? I smell flowers. And oh! I'm hungry!"

"Bo, our host will soon have need of his hunting abilities if your appetite holds," said Helen, as she tried to keep her hair out of her eyes while she laced her boots.

"Look! there's a big dog - a hound."

Helen looked as Bo directed, and saw a hound of unusually large proportions, black and tan in color, with long, drooping ears. Curiously he trotted nearer to the door of their hut and then stopped to gaze at them. His head was noble, his eyes shone dark and sad. He seemed neither friendly nor unfriendly.

"Hello, doggie! Come right in - we won't hurt you," called Bo, but without enthusiasm.

This made Helen laugh. "Bo, you're simply delicious," she said. "You're afraid of that dog."

"Sure. Wonder if he's Dale's. Of course he must be."

Presently the hound trotted away out of sight. When the girls presented themselves at the camp-fire they espied their curious canine visitor lying down. His ears were so long that half of them lay on the ground.

"I sent Pedro over to wake you girls up," said Dale, after greeting them. "Did he scare you?"

"Pedro. So that's his name. No, he didn't exactly scare me. He did Nell, though. She's an awful tenderfoot," replied Bo.

"He's a splendid-looking dog," said Helen, ignoring her sister's sally. "I love dogs. Will he make friends?"

"He's shy an' wild. You see, when I leave camp he won't hang around. He an' Tom are jealous of each other. I had a pack of hounds an' lost all but Pedro on account of Tom. I think you can make friends with Pedro. Try it."

Whereupon Helen made overtures to Pedro, and not wholly in vain. The dog was matured, of almost stern aloofness, and manifestly not used to people. His deep, wine-dark eyes seemed to search Helen's soul. They were honest and wise, with a strange sadness.

"He looks intelligent," observed Helen, as she smoothed the long, dark ears.

"That hound is nigh human," responded Dale. "Come, an' while you eat I'll tell you about Pedro."

Dale had gotten the hound as a pup from a Mexican

sheep-herder who claimed he was part California bloodhound. He grew up, becoming attached to Dale. In his younger days he did not get along well with Dale's other pets and Dale gave him to a rancher down in the valley. Pedro was back in Dale's camp next day. From that day Dale began to care more for the hound, but he did not want to keep him, for various reasons, chief of which was the fact that Pedro was too fine a dog to be left alone half the time to shift for himself. That fall Dale had need to go to the farthest village, Snowdrop, where he left Pedro with a friend. Then Dale rode to Show Down and Pine, and the camp of the Beemans' and with them he trailed some wild horses for a hundred miles, over into New Mexico. The snow was flying when Dale got back to his camp in the mountains. And there was Pedro, gaunt and worn, overjoyed to welcome him home. Roy Beeman visited Dale that October and told that Dale's friend in Snowdrop had not been able to keep Pedro. He broke a chain and scaled a ten-foot fence to escape. He trailed Dale to Show Down, where one of Dale's friends, recognizing the hound, caught him, and meant to keep him until Dale's return. But Pedro refused to eat. It happened that a freighter was going out to the Beeman camp, and Dale's friend boxed Pedro up and put him on the wagon. Pedro broke out of the box, returned to Show Down, took up Dale's trail to Pine, and then on to the Beeman camp. That was as far as Roy could trace the movements of the hound. But he believed, and so did Dale, that Pedro had trailed them out on the wild-horse hunt. The following spring Dale learned more from the herder of a sheepman at whose camp he and the Beemans; had rested on the way into New Mexico. It appeared that after Dale had left this camp Pedro had arrived, and another Mexican herder had stolen the hound. But Pedro got away.

"An' he was here when I arrived," concluded Dale, smiling. "I never wanted to get rid of him after that. He's turned out to be the finest dog I ever knew. He knows what I say. He can almost talk. An' I swear he can cry. He does whenever I start off without him."

"How perfectly wonderful!" exclaimed Bo. "Aren't animals great? . . . But I love horses best."

It seemed to Helen that Pedro understood they were talking about him, for he looked ashamed, and swallowed hard, and dropped his gaze. She knew something of the truth about the love of dogs for their owners. This story of Dale's, however, was stranger than any she had ever heard.

Tom, the cougar, put in an appearance then, and there was scarcely love in the tawny eyes he bent upon Pedro. But the hound did not deign to notice him. Tom sidled up to Bo, who sat on the farther side of the tarpaulin table-cloth, and manifestly wanted part of her breakfast.

"Gee! I love the look of him," she said. "But when he's close he makes my flesh creep."

"Beasts are as queer as people," observed Dale. "They take likes an' dislikes. I believe Tom has taken a shine to you an' Pedro begins to be interested in your sister. I can tell."

"Where's Bud?" inquired Bo.

"He's asleep or around somewhere. Now, soon as I get the work done, what would you girls like to do?"

"Ride!" declared Bo, eagerly.

"Aren't you sore an' stiff?"

"I am that. But I don't care. Besides, when I used to go out to my uncle's farm near Saint Joe I always found riding to be a cure for aches."

"Sure is, if you can stand it. An' what will your sister like to do?" returned Dale, turning to Helen.

"Oh, I'll rest, and watch you folks - and dream," replied Helen.

"But after you've rested you must be active," said Dale, seriously. "You must do things. It doesn't matter what, just as long as you don't sit idle."

"Why?" queried Helen, in surprise. "Why not be idle here in this beautiful, wild place? just to dream away the hours - the days! I could do it."

"But you mustn't. It took me years to learn how bad that was for me. An' right now I would love nothin' more than to forget my work, my horses an' pets - everythin', an' just lay around, seein' an' feelin'."

"Seeing and feeling? Yes, that must be what I mean. But why - what is it? There are the beauty and color - the wild, shaggy slopes - the gray cliffs - the singing wind - the lulling water - the clouds - the sky. And the silence, loneliness, sweetness of it all."

"It's a driftin' back. What I love to do an' yet fear most. It's what makes a lone hunter of a man. An' it can grow so strong that it binds a man to the wilds."

"How strange!" murmured Helen. "But that could never bind me. Why, I must live and fulfil my mission, my work in the civilized
world."

It seemed to Helen that Dale almost imperceptibly shrank at her earnest words.

"The ways of Nature are strange," he said. "I look at it different. Nature's just as keen to wean you back to a savage state as you are to be civilized. An' if Nature won, you would carry out her design all the better."

This hunter's talk shocked Helen and yet stimulated her mind.

"Me - a savage? Oh no!" she exclaimed. "But, if that were possible, what would Nature's design be?"

"You spoke of your mission in life," he replied. "A woman's mission is to have children. The female of any species has only one mission - to reproduce its kind. An' Nature has only one mission - toward greater strength, virility, efficiency - absolute perfection, which is unattainable."

"What of mental and spiritual development of man and woman?" asked Helen.

"Both are direct obstacles to the design of Nature. Nature is physical. To create for limitless endurance for eternal life. That must be Nature's inscrutable design. An' why she must fail."

"But the soul!" whispered Helen.

"Ah! When you speak of the soul an' I speak of life we mean the same. You an' I will have some talks while you're here. I must brush up my thoughts."

"So must I, it seems," said Helen, with a slow smile. She had been rendered grave and thoughtful. "But I guess I'll risk dreaming under the pines."

Bo had been watching them with her keen blue eyes.

"Nell, it'd take a thousand years to make a savage of you," she said. "But a week will do for me."

"Bo, you were one before you left Saint Joe," replied Helen. "Don't you remember that school-teacher Barnes who said you were a wildcat and an Indian mixed? He spanked you with a ruler."

"Never! He missed me," retorted Bo, with red in her cheeks. "Nell, I wish you'd not tell things about me when I was a kid."

"That was only two years ago," expostulated Helen, in mild surprise.

"Suppose it was. I was a kid all right. I'll bet you -" Bo broke up abruptly, and, tossing her head, she gave Tom a pat and then ran away around the corner of cliff wall.

Helen followed leisurely.

"Say, Nell," said Bo, when Helen arrived at their little green ledge-pole hut, "do you know that hunter fellow will upset some of your theories?"

"Maybe. I'll admit he amazes me - and affronts me,

too, I'm afraid," replied Helen. "What surprises me is that in spite of his evident lack of schooling he's not raw or crude. He's elemental."

"Sister dear, wake up. The man's wonderful. You can learn more from him than you ever learned in your life. So can I. I always hated books, anyway."

When, a little later, Dale approached carrying some bridles, the hound Pedro trotted at his heels.

"I reckon you'd better ride the horse you had," he said to Bo.

"Whatever you say. But I hope you let me ride them all, by and by."

"Sure. I've a mustang out there you'll like. But he pitches a little," he rejoined, and turned away toward the park. The hound looked after him and then at Helen.

"Come, Pedro. Stay with me," called Helen.

Dale, hearing her, motioned the hound back. Obediently Pedro trotted to her, still shy and soberly watchful, as if not sure of her intentions, but with something of friendliness about him now. Helen found a soft, restful seat in the sun facing the park, and there composed herself for what she felt would be slow, sweet, idle hours. Pedro curled down beside her. The tall form of Dale stalked across the park, out toward the straggling horses. Again she saw a deer grazing among them. How erect and motionless it stood watching Dale! Presently it bounded away toward the edge of the forest. Some of the horses whistled and ran, kicking heels high in the air. The shrill whistles rang clear in the stillness.

"Gee! Look at them go!" exclaimed Bo, gleefully, coming up to where Helen sat. Bo threw herself down upon the fragrant pine-needles and stretched herself languorously, like a lazy kitten. There was something feline in her lithe, graceful outline. She lay flat and looked up through the pines.

"Wouldn't it be great, now," she murmured, dreamily, half to herself, "if that Las Vegas cowboy would happen somehow to come, and then an earthquake would shut us up here in this Paradise valley so we'd never get out?"

"Bo! What would mother say to such talk as that?" gasped Helen.

"But, Nell, wouldn't it be great?"

"It would be terrible."

"Oh, there never was any romance in you, Nell Rayner," replied Bo. "That very thing has actually happened out here in this wonderful country of wild places. You need not tell me! Sure it's happened. With the cliff-dwellers and the Indians and then white people. Every place I look makes me feel that. Nell, you'd have to see people in the moon through a telescope before you'd believe that."

"I'm practical and sensible, thank goodness!"

"But, for the sake of argument," protested Bo, with flashing eyes, "suppose it might happen. Just to please me, suppose we did get shut up here with Dale and that cowboy we saw from the train. Shut in without any hope of ever climbing out. . . . What would you do? Would you give up and pine away and die? Or would you fight for life and whatever joy it might mean?"

"Self-preservation is the first instinct," replied Helen, surprised at a strange, deep thrill in the depths of her. "I'd fight for life, of course."

"Yes. Well, really, when I think seriously I don't want anything like that to happen. But, just the same, if it did happen I would glory in it."

While they were talking Dale returned with the horses.

"Can you bridle an' saddle your own horse?" he asked.

"No. I'm ashamed to say I can't," replied Bo.

"Time to learn then. Come on. Watch me first when I saddle mine."

Bo was all eyes while Dale slipped off the bridle from his horse and then with slow, plain action readjusted it. Next he smoothed the back of the horse, shook out the blanket, and, folding it half over, he threw it in place, being careful to explain to Bo just the right position. He lifted his saddle in a certain way and put that in place, and then he tightened the cinches.

"Now you try," he said.

According to Helen's judgment Bo might have been a Western girl all her days. But Dale shook his head and made her do it over.

"That was better. Of course, the saddle is too heavy for you to sling it up. You can learn that with a light one. Now put the bridle on again. Don't be afraid of your hands. He won't bite. Slip the bit in sideways. . . . There. Now let's see you mount."

When Bo got into the saddle Dale continued: "You went up quick an' light, but the wrong way. Watch me."

Bo had to mount several times before Dale was satisfied. Then he told her to ride off a little distance. When Bo had gotten out of earshot Dale said to Helen: "She'll take to a horse like a duck takes to water." Then, mounting, he rode out after her.

Helen watched them trotting and galloping and running the horses round the grassy park, and rather regretted she had not gone with them. Eventually Bo rode back, to dismount and fling herself down, red-cheeked and radiant, with disheveled hair, and curls damp on her temples. How alive she seemed! Helen's senses thrilled with the grace and charm and vitality of this surprising sister, and she was aware of a sheer physical joy in her presence. Bo rested, but she did not rest long. She was soon off to play with Bud. Then she coaxed the tame doe to eat out of her hand. She dragged Helen off for wild flowers, curious and thoughtless by turns. And at length she fell asleep, quickly, in a way that reminded Helen of the childhood now gone forever.

Dale called them to dinner about four o'clock, as the sun was reddening the western rampart of the park. Helen wondered where the day had gone. The hours had flown swiftly, serenely, bringing her scarcely a thought of her uncle or dread of her forced detention there or possible discovery by those outlaws supposed to be hunting for her. After she realized the passing of those hours she had an intangible and indescribable feeling of what Dale had meant about dreaming the hours away. The nature of Paradise Park was inimical to the kind of thought that had habitually been hers, She found the new thought absorbing, yet when she tried to name it she found that, after all, she had only felt. At the meal hour she was more than usually quiet. She saw that Dale noticed it and was trying to interest her or distract her attention. He succeeded, but she did not choose to let him see that. She strolled away alone to her seat under the pine. Bo passed her once, and cried, tantalizingly:

"My, Nell, but you're growing romantic!"

Never before in Helen's life had the beauty of the evening star seemed so exquisite or the twilight so moving and shadowy or the darkness so charged with loneliness. It was their environment - the accompaniment of wild wolf-mourn, of the murmuring waterfall, of this strange man of the forest and the unfamiliar elements among which he made his home.

Next morning, her energy having returned, Helen shared Bo's lesson in bridling and saddling her horse, and in riding. Bo, however, rode so fast and so hard that for Helen to share her company was impossible. And Dale, interested and amused, yet anxious, spent most of his time with Bo. It was thus that Helen rode all over the park alone. She was astonished at its size, when from almost any point it looked so small. The atmosphere deceived her. How clearly she could see! And she began to judge distance by the size of familiar things. A horse, looked at across the longest length of the park, seemed very small indeed. Here and there she rode upon dark, swift, little brooks, exquisitely clear and amber-colored and almost hidden from sight by the long grass. These all ran one way, and united to form a deeper brook that apparently wound under the cliffs at the west end, and plunged to an outlet in narrow clefts. When Dale and Bo came to her once she made inquiry, and she was surprised to learn from Dale that this brook disappeared in a hole in the rocks and had an outlet on the other side of the mountain. Sometime he would take them to the lake it formed.

"Over the mountain?" asked Helen, again remembering that she must regard herself as a fugitive. "Will it be safe to leave our hiding-place? I forget so often why we are here."

"We would be better hidden over there than here," replied Dale. "The valley on that side is accessible only from that ridge. An' don't worry about bein' found. I told you Roy Beeman is watchin' Anson an' his gang. Roy will keep between them an' us."

Helen was reassured, yet there must always linger in the background of her mind a sense of dread. In spite of this, she determined to make the most of her opportunity. Bo was a stimulus. And so Helen spent the rest of that day riding and tagging after her sister.

The next day was less hard on Helen. Activity, rest, eating, and sleeping took on a wonderful new meaning to her. She had really never known them as strange joys. She rode, she walked, she climbed a little, she dozed under her pine-tree, she worked helping Dale at camp-fire tasks, and when night came she said she did not know herself. That fact haunted her in vague, deep dreams. Upon awakening she forgot her resolve to study herself. That day passed. And then several more went swiftly before she adapted herself to a situation she had reason to believe might last for weeks and even months.

It was afternoon that Helen loved best of all the time of the day. The sunrise was fresh, beautiful; the morning was windy, fragrant; the sunset was rosy, glorious; the twilight was sad, changing; and night seemed infinitely sweet with its stars and silence and sleep. But the afternoon, when nothing changed, when all was serene, when time seemed to halt, that was her choice, and her solace.

One afternoon she had camp all to herself. Bo was riding. Dale had climbed the mountain to see if he could find any trace of tracks or see any smoke from camp-fire. Bud was nowhere to be seen, nor any of the other pets. Tom had gone off to some sunny ledge where he could bask in the sun, after the habit of the wilder brothers of his species. Pedro had not been seen for a night and a day, a fact that Helen had noted with concern. However, she had forgotten him, and there-fore was the more surprised to see him coming limping into camp on three legs.

"Why, Pedro! You have been fighting. Come here," she called.

The hound did not look guilty. He limped to her and held up his right fore paw. The action was unmis-takable. Helen examined the injured member and presently found a piece of what looked like mussel-shell embedded deeply between the toes. The wound was swollen, bloody, and evidently very painful. Pedro whined. Helen had to exert all the strength of her fingers to pull it out. Then Pedro howled. But immediately he showed his gratitude by licking her hand. Helen bathed his paw and bound it up.

When Dale returned she related the incident and, showing the piece of shell, she asked: "Where did that come from ? Are there shells in the mountains?"

"Once this country was under the sea," replied Dale. "I've found things that 'd make you wonder."

"Under the sea!" ejaculated Helen. It was one thing to have read of such a strange fact, but a vastly different one to realize it here among these lofty peaks. Dale was always showing her something or telling her something that astounded her.

"Look here," he said one day. "What do you make of that little bunch of aspens?"

They were on the farther side of the park and were resting under a pine-tree. The forest here encroached upon the park with its straggling lines of spruce and groves of aspen. The little clump of aspens did not differ from hundreds Helen had seen.

"I don't make anything particularly of it," replied Helen, dubiously. "Just a tiny grove of aspens - some very small, some larger, but none very big. But it's pretty with its green and yellow leaves fluttering and quivering."

"It doesn't make you think of a fight?"

"Fight? No, it certainly does not," replied Helen.

"Well, it's as good an example of fight, of strife, of selfishness, as you will find in the forest," he said. "Now come over, you an' Bo, an' let me show you what I mean."

"Come on, Nell," cried Bo, with enthusiasm. "He'll open our eyes some more."

Nothing loath, Helen went with them to the little clump of aspens.

"About a hundred altogether," said Dale. "They're pretty well shaded by the spruces, but they get the sunlight from east an' south. These little trees all came from the same seedlings. They're all the same age. Four of them stand, say, ten feet or more high an' they're as large around as my wrist. Here's one that's largest. See how full-foliaged he is - how he stands over most of the others, but not so much over these four next to him. They all stand close together, very close, you see. Most of them are no larger than my thumb. Look how few branches they have, an' none low down. Look at how few leaves. Do you see how all the branches stand out toward the east an' south - how the leaves, of course, face the same way? See how one branch of one tree bends aside one from another tree. That's a fight for the sunlight. Here are one - two - three dead trees. Look, I can snap them off . An' now look down under them. Here are little trees five feet high - four feet high - down to these only a foot high. Look how pale, delicate, fragile, unhealthy! They get so little sunshine. They were born with the other trees, but did not get an equal start. Position gives the advantage, perhaps."

Dale led the girls around the little grove, illustrating

his words by action. He seemed deeply in earnest.

"You understand it's a fight for water an' sun. But mostly sun, because, if the leaves can absorb the sun, the tree an' roots will grow to grasp the needed moisture. Shade is death - slow death to the life of trees. These little aspens are fightin' for place in the sunlight. It is a merciless battle. They push an' bend one another's branches aside an' choke them. Only perhaps half of these aspens will survive, to make one of the larger clumps, such as that one of full-grown trees over there. One season will give advantage to this saplin' an' next year to that one. A few seasons' advantage to one assures its dominance over the others. But it is never sure of holdin' that dominance. An 'if wind or storm or a strong-growin' rival does not overthrow it, then sooner or later old age will. For there is absolute and continual fight. What is true of these aspens is true of all the trees in the forest an' of all plant life in the forest. What is most wonderful to me is the tenacity of life."

And next day Dale showed them an even more striking example of this mystery of nature.

He guided them on horseback up one of the thick, verdant-wooded slopes, calling their attention at various times to the different growths, until they emerged on the summit of the ridge where the timber grew scant and dwarfed. At the edge of timber-line he showed a gnarled and knotted spruce-tree, twisted out of all semblance to a beautiful spruce, bent and storm-blasted, with almost bare branches, all reaching one' way. The tree was a specter. It stood alone. It had little green upon it. There seemed something tragic about its contortions. But it was alive and strong. It had no rivals to take sun or moisture. Its enemies were the snow and wind and cold of the heights.

Helen felt, as the realization came to her, the knowledge Dale wished to impart, that it was as sad as wonderful, and as mysterious as it was inspiring. At that moment there were both the sting and sweetness of life - the pain and the joy - in Helen's heart. These strange facts were going to teach her - to transform her. And even if they hurt, she welcomed them.

CHAPTER XI

"I'll ride you if it breaks - my neck!" panted Bo, passionately, shaking her gloved fist at the gray pony.

Dale stood near with a broad smile on his face. Helen was within earshot, watching from the edge of the park, and she felt so fascinated and frightened that she could not call out for Bo to stop. The little gray mustang was a beauty, clean-limbed and racy, with long black mane and tail, and a fine, spirited head. There was a blanket strapped on his back, but no saddle. Bo held the short halter that had been fastened in a hackamore knot round his nose. She wore no coat; her blouse was covered with grass and seeds, and it was open at the neck; her hair hung loose and disheveled; one side of her face bore a stain of grass and dirt and a suspicion of blood; the other was red and white; her eyes blazed; beads of sweat stood out on her brow and wet places shone on her cheeks. As she began to strain on the halter, pulling herself closer to the fiery pony, the outline of her slender shape stood out lithe and strong.

Bo had been defeated in her cherished and determined ambition to ride Dale's mustang, and she was furious. The mustang did not appear to be vicious or mean. But he was spirited, tricky, mischievous, and he had thrown her six times. The scene of Bo's defeat was at the edge of the park, where thick moss and grass afforded soft places for her to fall. It also afforded poor foothold for the gray mustang, obviously placing him at a disadvantage. Dale did not bridle him, because he had not been broken to a bridle; and though it was harder for Bo to try to ride him bareback, there was less risk of her being hurt. Bo had begun in all eagerness and enthusiasm, loving and petting the mustang, which she named "Pony." She had evidently anticipated an adventure, but her smiling, resolute face had denoted confidence. Pony had stood fairly well to be mounted, and then had pitched and tossed until Bo had slid off or been upset or thrown. After each fall Bo bounced up with less of a smile, and more of spirit, until now the Western passion to master a horse had suddenly leaped to life within her. It was no longer fun, no more a daring circus trick to scare Helen and rouse Dale's admiration. The issue now lay between Bo and the mustang.

Pony reared, snorting, tossing his head, and pawing with front feet.

"Pull him down!" yelled Dale.

Bo did not have much weight, but she had strength, an she hauled with all her might, finally bringing him down.

"Now hold hard an' take up rope an' get in to him," called Dale. "Good! You're sure not afraid of him. He sees that. Now hold him, talk to him, tell him you're goin' to ride him. Pet him a little. An' when he quits shakin', grab his mane an' jump up an' slide a leg over him. Then hook your feet under him, hard as you can, an' stick on."

If Helen had not been so frightened for Bo she would have been able to enjoy her other sensations. Creeping, cold thrills chased over her as Bo, supple and quick, slid an arm and a leg over Pony and straightened up on him with a defiant cry. Pony jerked his head down, brought his feet together in one jump, and began to bounce. Bo got the swing of him this time and stayed on.

"You're ridin' him," yelled Dale. "Now squeeze hard with your knees. Crack him over the head with your rope. . . . That's the way. Hang on now an' you'll have him beat."

The mustang pitched all over the space adjacent to Dale and Helen, tearing up the moss and grass. Several times he tossed Bo high, but she slid back to grip him again with her legs, and he could not throw her. Suddenly he raised his head and bolted. Dale answered Bo's triumphant cry. But Pony had not run fifty feet before he tripped and fell, throwing Bo far over his head. As luck would have it - good luck, Dale afterward said - she landed in a boggy place and the force of her momentum was such that she slid several yards, face down, in wet moss and black ooze.

Helen uttered a scream and ran forward. Bo was getting to her knees when Dale reached her. He helped her up and half led, half carried her out of the boggy place. Bo was not recognizable. From head to foot she was dripping black ooze.

"Oh, Bo! Are you hurt?" cried Helen.

Evidently Bo's mouth was full of mud.

"Pp-su-tt! Ough! Whew!" she sputtered. "Hurt? No! Can't you see what I lit in? Dale, the sun-of-a-gun didn't throw me. He fell, and I went over his head."

"Right. You sure rode him. An' he tripped an' slung you a mile," replied Dale. "It's lucky you lit in that bog."

"Lucky! With eyes and nose stopped up? Oooo! I'm full of mud. And my nice - new riding-suit!"

Bo's tones indicated that she was ready to cry. Helen, realizing Bo had not been hurt, began to laugh. Her sister was the funniest-looking object that had ever come before her eyes.

"Nell Rayner - are you - laughing - at me?" demanded Bo, in most righteous amaze and anger.

"Me laugh-ing? N-never, Bo, "replied Helen. "Can't you see I'm just - just -"

"See? You idiot! my eyes are full of mud!" flashed Bo. "But I hear you. I'll - I'll get even."

Dale was laughing, too, but noiselessly, and Bo, being blind for the moment, could not be aware of that. By this time they had reached camp. Helen fell flat and laughed as she had never laughed before. When Helen forgot herself so far as to roll on the ground it was indeed a laughing matter. Dale's big frame shook as he possessed himself of a towel and, wetting it at the spring, began to wipe the mud off Bo's face. But that did not serve. Bo asked to be led to the water, where she knelt and, with splashing, washed out her eyes, and then her face, and then the bedraggled strands of hair.

"That mustang didn't break my neck, but he rooted my face in the mud. I'll fix him," she muttered, as she got up. "Please let me have the towel, now. . . . Well! Milt Dale, you're laughing!"

"Ex-cuse me, Bo. I - Haw! haw! haw!" Then Dale lurched off, holding his sides.

Bo gazed after him and then back at Helen.

"I suppose if I'd been kicked and smashed and killed you'd laugh," she said. And then she melted. "Oh, my pretty riding-suit! What a mess! I must be a sight. . . . Nell, I rode that wild pony - the sun-of-a-gun! I rode him! That's enough for me. You try it. Laugh all you want. It was funny. But if you want to square yourself with me, help me clean my clothes."

Late in the night Helen heard Dale sternly calling Pedro. She felt some little alarm. However, nothing happened, and she soon went to sleep again. At the morning meal Dale explained.

"Pedro an' Tom were uneasy last night. I think there are lions workin' over the ridge somewhere. I heard one scream."

"Scream?" inquired Bo, with interest.

"Yes, an' if you ever hear a lion scream you will think it a woman in mortal agony. The cougar cry, as Roy calls it, is the wildest to be heard in the woods. A wolf howls. He is sad. hungry, and wild. But a cougar seems human an' dyin' an' wild. We'll saddle up an' ride over there. Maybe Pedro will tree a lion. Bo, if he does will you shoot it?"

"Sure," replied Bo, with her mouth full of biscuit.

That was how they came to take a long, slow, steep ride under cover of dense spruce. Helen liked the ride after they got on the heights. But they did not get to any point where she could indulge in her pleasure of gazing afar over the ranges. Dale led up and down, and finally mostly down, until they came out within sight of sparser wooded ridges with parks lying below and streams shining in the sun.

More than once Pedro had to be harshly called by Dale. The hound scented game.

"Here's an old kill," said Dale, halting to point at some bleached bones scattered under a spruce. Tufts of grayish-white hair lay strewn around.

"What was it?" asked Bo.

"Deer, of course. Killed there an' eaten by a lion. Sometime last fall. See, even the skull is split. But I could not say that the lion did it."

Helen shuddered. She thought of the tame deer down at Dale's camp. How beautiful and graceful, and responsive to kindness!

They rode out of the woods into a grassy swale with rocks and clumps of some green bushes bordering it. Here Pedro barked, the first time Helen had heard him. The hair on his neck bristled, and it required stern calls from Dale to hold him in. Dale dismounted.

"Hyar, Pede, you get back," he ordered. "I'll let you go presently. . . . Girls, you're goin' to see somethin'. But stay on your horses."

Dale, with the hound tense and bristling beside him, strode here and there at the edge of the swale. Presently he halted on a slight elevation and beckoned for the girls to ride over.

"Here, see where the grass is pressed down all nice an' round," he said, pointing. "A lion made that. He sneaked there, watchin' for deer. That was done this mornin'. Come on, now. Let's see if we can trail him."

Dale stooped now, studying the grass, and holding Pedro. Suddenly he straightened up with a flash in his gray eyes.

"Here's where he jumped."

But Helen could not see any reason why Dale should say that. The man of the forest took a long stride then another.

"An' here's where that lion lit on the back of the deer. It was a big jump. See the sharp hoof tracks of the deer." Dale pressed aside tall grass to show dark, rough, fresh tracks of a deer, evidently made by violent action.

"Come on," called Dale, walking swiftly. "You're sure goin' to see somethin' now. . . . Here's where the deer bounded, carryin' the lion."

"What!" exclaimed Bo, incredulously.

"The deer was runnin' here with the lion on his back. I'll prove it to you. Come on, now. Pedro, you stay with me. Girls, it's a fresh trail." Dale walked along, leading his horse, and occasionally he pointed down into the grass. "There! See that! That's hair."

Helen did see some tufts of grayish hair scattered on the ground, and she believed she saw little, dark separations in the grass, where an animal had recently passed. All at once Dale halted. When Helen reached him Bo was already there and they were gazing down at a wide, flattened space in the grass. Even Helen's inexperienced eyes could make out evidences of a struggle. Tufts of gray-white hair lay upon the crushed grass. Helen did not need to see any more, but Dale silently pointed to a patch of blood. Then he spoke:

"The lion brought the deer down here an' killed him. Probably broke his neck. That deer ran a hundred yards with the lion. See, here's the trail left where the lion dragged the deer off."

A well-defined path showed across the swale.

"Girls, you'll see that deer pretty quick," declared Dale, starting forward. "This work has just been done. Only a few minutes ago."

"How can you tell?" queried Bo.

"Look! See that grass. It has been bent down by the deer bein' dragged over it. Now it's springin' up."

Dale's next stop was on the other side of the swale, under a spruce with low, spreading branches. The look of Pedro quickened Helen's pulse. He was wild to give chase. Fearfully Helen looked where Dale pointed, expecting to see the lion. But she saw instead a deer lying prostrate with tongue out and sightless eyes and bloody hair.

"Girls, that lion heard us an' left. He's not far," said Dale, as he stooped to lift the head of the deer. "Warm! Neck broken. See the lion's teeth an' claw marks. . . . It's a doe. Look here. Don't be squeamish, girls. This is only an hourly incident of everyday life in the forest. See where the lion has rolled the skin down as neat as I could do it, an' he'd just begun to bite in there when he heard us."

"What murderous work, The sight sickens me!" exclaimed Helen.

"It is nature," said Dale, simply.

"Let's kill the lion," added Bo.

For answer Dale took a quick turn at their saddle-girths, and then, mounting, he called to the hound. "Hunt him up, Pedro."

Like a shot the hound was off.

"Ride in my tracks an' keep close to me," called Dale, as he wheeled his horse.

"We're off!" squealed Bo, in wild delight, and she made her mount plunge.

Helen urged her horse after them and they broke across a comer of the swale to the woods. Pedro was running straight, with his nose high. He let out one short bark. He headed into the woods, with Dale not far behind. Helen was on one of Dale's best horses, but that fact scarcely manifested itself, because the others began to increase their lead. They entered the woods. It was open, and fairly good going. Bo's horse ran as fast in the woods as he did in the open. That frightened Helen and she yelled to Bo to hold him in. She yelled to deaf ears. That was Bo's great risk - she did not intend to be careful. Suddenly the forest rang with Dale's encouraging yell, meant to aid the girls in following him. Helen's horse caught the spirit of the chase. He gained somewhat on Bo, hurdling logs, sometimes two at once. Helen's blood leaped with a strange excitement, utterly unfamiliar and as utterly resistless. Yet her natural fear, and the intelligence that reckoned with the foolish risk of this ride, shared alike in her sum of sensations. She tried to remember Dale's caution about dodging branches and snags, and sliding her knees back to avoid knocks from trees. She barely missed some frightful reaching branches. She received a hard knock, then another, that unseated her, but frantically she held on and slid back, and at the end of a long run through comparatively open forest she got a stinging blow in the face from a far-spreading branch of pine. Bo missed, by what seemed only an inch, a solid snag that would have broken her in two. Both Pedro and Dale got out of Helen's sight. Then Helen, as she began to lose Bo, felt that she would rather run greater risks than be left behind to get lost in the forest, and she urged her horse. Dale's yell pealed back. Then it seemed even more thrilling to follow by sound than by sight. Wind and brush tore at her. The air was heavily pungent with odor of pine. Helen heard a wild, full bay of the hound, ringing back, full of savage eagerness, and she believed Pedro had roused out the lion from some covert. It lent more stir to her blood and it surely urged her horse on faster.

Then the swift pace slackened. A windfall of timber delayed Helen. She caught a glimpse of Dale far ahead, climbing a slope. The forest seemed full of his ringing yell. Helen strangely wished for level ground and the former swift motion. Next she saw Bo working down to the right, and Dale's yell now came from that direction. Helen followed, got out of the timber, and made better time on a gradual slope down to another park.

When she reached the open she saw Bo almost across this narrow open ground. Here Helen did not need to urge her mount. He snorted and plunged at the level and he got to going so fast that Helen would have screamed aloud in mingled fear and delight if she had not been breathless.

Her horse had the bad luck to cross soft ground. He went to his knees and Helen sailed out of the saddle over his head. Soft willows and wet grass broke her fall. She was surprised to find herself unhurt. Up she bounded and certainly did not know this new Helen Rayner. Her horse was coming, and he had patience with her, but he wanted to hurry. Helen made the quickest mount of her experience and somehow felt a pride in it. She would tell Bo that. But just then Bo flashed into the woods out of sight. Helen fairly charged into that green foliage, breaking brush and branches. She broke through into open forest. Bo was inside, riding down an aisle between pines and spruces. At that juncture Helen heard Dale's melodious yell near at hand. Coming into still more open forest, with rocks here and there, she saw Dale dismounted under a pine, and Pedro standing with fore paws upon the tree-trunk, and then high up on a branch a huge tawny colored lion, just like Tom.

Bo's horse slowed up and showed fear, but he kept on as far as Dale's horse. But Helen's refused to go any nearer. She had difficulty in halting him. Presently she dismounted and, throwing her bridle over a stump, she ran on, panting and fearful, yet tingling all over, up to her sister and Dale.

"Nell, you did pretty good for a tenderfoot," was Bo's greeting.

"It was a fine chase," said Dale. "You both rode well. I wish you could have seen the lion on the ground. He bounded - great long bounds with his tail up in the air - very funny. An' Pedro almost caught up with him. That scared me, because he would have killed the hound. Pedro was close to him when he treed. An' there he is - the yellow deer-killer. He's a male an' full grown."

With that Dale pulled his rifle from its saddle-sheath and looked expectantly at Bo. But she was gazing with great interest and admiration up at the lion.

"Isn't he just beautiful?" she burst out. "Oh, look at him spit! Just like a cat! Dale, he looks afraid he might fall off."

"He sure does. Lions are never sure of their balance in a tree. But I never saw one make a misstep. He knows he doesn't belong there."

To Helen the lion looked splendid perched up there. He was long and round and graceful and tawny. His tongue hung out and his plump sides heaved, showing what a quick, hard run he had been driven to. What struck Helen most forcibly about him was something in his face as he looked down at the hound. He was scared. He realized his peril. It was not possible for Helen to watch him killed, yet she could not bring herself to beg Bo not to shoot. Helen confessed she was a tenderfoot.

"Get down, Bo, an' let's see how good a shot you are, said Dale. Bo slowly withdrew her fascinated gaze from the lion and looked with a rueful smile at Dale.

"I've changed my mind. I said I would kill him, but now I can't. He looks so - so different from what I'd imagined."

Dale's answer was a rare smile of understanding and approval that warmed Helen's heart toward him. All the same, he was amused. Sheathing the gun, he mounted his horse.

"Come on, Pedro," he called. "Come, I tell you," he added, sharply, "Well, girls, we treed him, anyhow, an, it was fun. Now we'll ride back to the deer he killed an' pack a haunch to camp for our own use."

"Will the lion go back to his - his kill, I think you called it?" asked Bo.

"I've chased one away from his kill half a dozen times. Lions are not plentiful here an' they don't get overfed. I reckon the balance is pretty even."

This last remark made Helen inquisitive. And as they slowly rode on the back-trail Dale talked.

"You girls, bein' tender-hearted an' not knowin' the life of the forest, what's good an' what's bad, think it was a pity the poor deer was killed by a murderous lion. But you're wrong. As I told you, the lion is absolutely necessary to the health an' joy of wild life - or deer's wild life, so to speak. When deer were created or came into existence, then the lion must have come, too. They can't live without each other. Wolves, now, are not particularly deer-killers. They live off elk an' anythin' they can catch. So will lions, for that matter. But I mean lions follow the deer to an' fro from winter to summer feedin'-grounds. Where there's no deer you will find no lions. Well, now, if left alone deer would multiply very fast. In a few years there would be hundreds where now there's only one. An' in time, as the generations passed, they'd lose the fear, the alertness, the speed an' strength, the eternal vigilance that is love of life - they'd lose that an' begin to deteriorate, an' disease would carry them off. I saw one season of black-tongue among deer. It killed them off, an' I believe that is one of the diseases of over-production. The lions, now, are forever on the trail of the deer. They have learned. Wariness is an instinct born in the fawn. It makes him keen, quick, active, fearful, an' so he grows up strong an' healthy to become the smooth, sleek, beautiful, soft-eyed, an' wild-lookin' deer you girls love to watch. But if it wasn't for the lions, the deer would not thrive. Only the strongest an' swiftest survive. That is the meanin' of nature. There is always a perfect balance kept by nature. It may vary in different years, but on the whole, in the long years, it averages an even balance."

"How wonderfully you put it!" exclaimed Bo, with all her impulsiveness. "Oh, I'm glad I didn't kill the lion."

"What you say somehow hurts me," said Helen, wistfully, to the hunter. "I see - I feel how true - how inevitable it is. But it changes my - my feelings.

Almost I'd rather not acquire such knowledge as yours. This balance of nature - how tragic – how sad!"

"But why?" asked Dale. "You love birds, an' birds are the greatest killers in the forest."

"Don't tell me that - don't prove it," implored Helen. It is not so much the love of life in a deer or any creature, and the terrible clinging to life, that gives me distress. It is suffering. I can't bear to see pain. I can stand pain myself, but I can't bear to see or think of it."

"Well," replied. Dale, thoughtfully, "There you stump me again. I've lived long in the forest an' when a man's alone he does a heap of thinkin'. An' always I couldn't understand a reason or a meanin' for pain. Of all the bafflin' things of life, that is the hardest to understand an' to forgive - pain!"

That evening, as they sat in restful places round the camp-fire, with the still twilight fading into night, Dale seriously asked the girls what the day's chase had meant to them. His manner of asking was productive of thought. Both girls were silent for a moment.

"Glorious!" was Bo's brief and eloquent reply.

"Why?" asked. Dale, curiously. "You are a girl. You've been used to home, people, love, comfort, safety, quiet."

"Maybe that is just why it was glorious," said Bo, earnestly. "I can hardly explain. I loved the motion of the horse, the feel of wind in my face, the smell of the pine, the sight of slope and forest glade and windfall and rocks, and the black shade under the spruces. My blood beat and burned. My teeth clicked. My nerves all quivered. My heart sometimes, at dangerous moments, almost choked me, and all the time it pounded hard. Now my skin was hot and then it was cold. But I think the best of that chase for me was that I was on a fast horse, guiding him, controlling him. He was alive. Oh, how I felt his running!"

"Well, what you say is as natural to me as if I felt it," said Dale. "I wondered. You're certainly full of fire, An', Helen, what do you say?"

"Bo has answered you with her feelings," replied Helen, "I could not do that and be honest. The fact that Bo wouldn't shoot the lion after we treed him acquits her. Nevertheless, her answer is purely physical. You know, Mr. Dale, how you talk about the physical. I should say my sister was just a young, wild, highly sensitive, hot-blooded female of the species. She exulted in that chase as an Indian. Her sensations were inherited ones - certainly not acquired by education. Bo always hated study. The ride was a revelation to me. I had a good many of Bo's feelings - though not so strong. But over against them was the opposition of reason, of consciousness. A new-born side of my nature confronted me, strange, surprising, violent, irresistible. It was as if another side of my personality suddenly said: 'Here I am. Reckon with me now!' And there was no use for the moment to oppose that strange side. I - the thinking Helen Rayner, was powerless. Oh yes, I had such thoughts even when the branches were stinging my face and I was thrilling to the bay of the hound. Once my horse fell and threw me. . . . You needn't look alarmed. It was fine. I went into a soft place and was unhurt. But when I was sailing through the air a thought flashed: this is the end of me! It was like a dream when you are falling dreadfully. Much of what I felt and thought on that chase must have been because of what I have studied and read and taught. The reality of it, the action and flash, were splendid. But fear of danger, pity for the chased lion, consciousness of foolish risk, of a reckless disregard for the serious responsibility I have taken - all these worked in my mind and held back what might have been a sheer physical, primitive joy of the wild moment."

Dale listened intently, and after Helen had finished he studied the fire and thoughtfully poked the red embers with his stick. His face was still and serene, untroubled and unlined, but to Helen his eyes seemed sad, pensive, expressive of an unsatisfied yearning and wonder. She had carefully and earnestly spoken, because she was very curious to hear what he might say.

"I understand you," he replied, presently. "An' I'm sure surprised that I can. I've read my books - an' reread them, but no one ever talked like that to me. What I make of it is this. You've the same blood in you that's in Bo. An' blood is stronger than brain. Remember that blood is life. It would be good for you to have it run an' beat an' burn, as Bo's did. Your blood did that a thousand years or ten thousand before intellect was born in your ancestors. Instinct may not be greater than reason, but it's a million years older. Don't fight your instincts so hard. If they were not good the God of Creation would not have given them to you. To-day your mind was full of self-restraint that did not altogether restrain. You couldn't forget yourself. You couldn't feel only, as Bo did. You couldn't be true to your real nature."

"I don't agree with you," replied Helen, quickly. "I don't have to be an Indian to be true to myself."

"Why, yes you do," said Dale.

"But I couldn't be an Indian," declared Helen, spiritedly. "I couldn't feel only, as you say Bo did. I couldn't go back in the scale, as you hint. What would all my education amount to - though goodness knows it's little enough - if I had no control over primitive feelings that happened to be born in me?"

"You'll have little or no control over them when the right time comes," replied Dale. "Your sheltered life an' education have led you away from natural instincts. But they're in you an' you'll learn the proof of that out here."

"No. Not if I lived a hundred years in the West," asserted Helen.

"But, child, do you know what you're talkin' about?"

Here Bo let out a blissful peal of laughter.

"Mr. Dale!" exclaimed Helen, almost affronted. She was stirred. "I know myself, at least."

"But you do not. You've no idea of yourself. You've education, yes, but not in nature an' life. An' after all, they are the real things. Answer me, now - honestly, will you?"

"Certainly, if I can. Some of your questions are hard to answer."

"Have you ever been starved?" he asked.

"No," replied Helen.

"Have you ever been lost away from home ?"

"No."

"Have you ever faced death - real stark an' naked death, close an' terrible?"

"No, indeed."

"Have you ever wanted to kill any one with your bare hands?"

"Oh, Mr. Dale, you - you amaze me. No! . . . No!"

"I reckon I know your answer to my last question, but I'll ask it, anyhow. . . . Have you ever been so madly in love with a man that you could not live without him?"

Bo fell off her seat with a high, trilling laugh. "Oh, you two are great!"

"Thank Heaven, I haven't been," replied Helen, shortly.

"Then you don't know anythin' about life," declared Dale, with finality.

Helen was not to be put down by that, dubious and troubled as it made her.

"Have you experienced all those things?" she queried, stubbornly.

"All but the last one. Love never came my way. How could it? I live alone. I seldom go to the villages where there are girls. No girl would ever care for me. I have nothin'. . . . But, all the same, I understand love a little, just by comparison with strong feelin's I've lived."

Helen watched the hunter and marveled at his simplicity. His sad and penetrating gaze was on the fire, as if in its white heart to read the secret denied him. He had said that no girl would ever love him. She imagined he might know considerably less about the nature of girls than of the forest.

"To come back to myself," said Helen, wanting to continue the argument. "You declared I didn't know myself. That I would have no self-control. I will!"

"I meant the big things of life," he said, patiently.

"What things?"

"I told you. By askin' what had never happened to you I learned what will happen."

"Those experiences to come to me!" breathed Helen, incredulously. "Never!"

"Sister Nell, they sure will - particularly the last-named one - the mad love," chimed in Bo, mischievously, yet believingly.

Neither Dale nor Helen appeared to hear her interruption.

"Let me put it simpler," began Dale, evidently racking his brain for analogy. His perplexity appeared painful to him, because he had a great faith, a great conviction that he could not make clear. "Here I am, the natural physical man, livin' in the wilds. An' here you come, the complex, intellectual woman. Remember, for my argument's sake, that you're here. An' suppose circumstances forced you to stay here. You'd fight the elements with me an' work with me to sustain life. There must be a great change in either you or me, accordin' to the other's influence. An' can't you see that change must come in you, not because of anythin' superior in me - I'm really inferior to you - but because of our environment? You'd lose your complexity. An' in years to come you'd be a natural physical woman, because you'd live through an' by the physical."

"Oh dear, will not education be of help to the Western woman?" queried Helen, almost in despair.

"Sure it will," answered Dale, promptly. "What the West needs is women who can raise an' teach children. But you don't understand me. You don't get under your skin. I reckon I can't make you see my argument as I feel it. You take my word for this, though. Sooner or later you will wake up an' forget yourself. Remember."

"Nell, I'll bet you do, too," said Bo, seriously for her. "It may seem strange to you, but I understand Dale. I feel what he means. It's a sort of shock. Nell, we're not what we seem. We're not what we fondly imagine we are. We've lived too long with people - too far away from the earth. You know the Bible says something like this: 'Dust thou art and to dust thou shalt return.' Where do we come from?"

CHAPTER XII

Days passed.

Every morning Helen awoke with a wondering question as to what this day would bring forth, especially with regard to possible news from her uncle. It must come sometime and she was anxious for it. Something about this simple, wild camp life had begun to grip her. She found herself shirking daily attention to the clothes she had brought West. They needed it, but she had begun to see how superficial they really were. On the other hand, camp-fire tasks had come to be a pleasure. She had learned a great deal more about them than had Bo. Worry and dread were always impinging upon the fringe of her thoughts - always vaguely present, though seldom annoying. They were like shadows in dreams. She wanted to get to her uncle's ranch, to take up the duties of her new life. But she was not prepared to believe she would not regret this wild experience. She must get away from that in order to see it clearly, and she began to have doubts of herself.

Meanwhile the active and restful outdoor life went on. Bo leaned more and more toward utter reconciliation to it. Her eyes had a wonderful flash, like blue lightning; her cheeks were gold and brown; her hands tanned dark as an Indian's.

She could vault upon the gray mustang, or, for that matter, clear over his back. She learned to shoot a rifle accurately enough to win Dale's praise, and vowed she would like to draw a bead upon a grizzly bear or upon Snake Anson.

"Bo, if you met that grizzly Dale said has been prowling round camp lately you'd run right up a tree," declared Helen, one morning, when Bo seemed particularly boastful.

"Don't fool yourself," retorted Bo.

"But I've seen you run from a mouse!"

"Sister, couldn't I be afraid of a mouse and not a bear?"

"I don't see how."

"Well, bears, lions, outlaws, and other wild beasts are to be met with here in the West, and my mind's made up," said Bo, in slow-nodding deliberation.

They argued as they had always argued, Helen for reason and common sense and restraint, Bo on the principle that if she must fight it was better to get in the first blow.

The morning on which this argument took place Dale was a long time in catching the horses. When he did come in he shook his head seriously.

"Some varmint's been chasin' the horses," he said, as he reached for his saddle. "Did you hear them snortin' an' runnin' last night?"

Neither of the girls had been awakened.

"I missed one of the colts," went on Dale, "an' I'm goin' to ride across the park."

Dale's movements were quick and stern. It was significant that he chose his heavier rifle, and, mounting, with a sharp call to Pedro, he rode off without another word to the girls.

Bo watched him for a moment and then began to saddle the mustang.

"You won't follow him?" asked Helen, quickly.

"I sure will," replied Bo. "He didn't forbid it."

"But he certainly did not want us."

"He might not want you, but I'll bet he wouldn't object to me, whatever's up," said Bo, shortly.

"Oh! So you think -" exclaimed Helen, keenly hurt. She bit her tongue to keep back a hot reply. And it was certain that a bursting gush of anger flooded over her. Was she, then, such a coward? Did Dale think this slip of a sister, so wild and wilful, was a stronger woman than she? A moment's silent strife convinced her that no doubt he thought so and no doubt he was right. Then the anger centered upon herself, and Helen neither understood nor trusted herself.

The outcome proved an uncontrollable impulse. Helen began to saddle her horse. She had the task half accomplished when Bo's call made her look up.

"Listen!"

Helen heard a ringing, wild bay of the hound.

"That's Pedro," she said, with a thrill.

"Sure. He's running. We never heard him bay like that before."

"Where's Dale?"

"He rode out of sight across there," replied Bo, pointing. "And Pedro's running toward us along that slope. He must be a mile - two miles from Dale."

"But Dale will follow."

"Sure. But he'd need wings to get near that hound now. Pedro couldn't have gone across there with him. . . . just listen."

The wild note of the hound manifestly stirred Bo to irrepressible action. Snatching up Dale's lighter rifle, she shoved it into her saddle-sheath, and, leaping on the mustang, she ran him over brush and brook, straight down the park toward the place Pedro was climbing. For an instant Helen stood amazed beyond speech. When Bo sailed over a big log, like a steeple-chaser, then Helen answered to further unconsidered impulse by frantically getting her saddle fastened. Without coat or hat she mounted. The nervous horse bolted almost before she got into the saddle. A strange, trenchant trembling coursed through all her veins. She wanted to scream for Bo to wait. Bo was out of sight, but the deep, muddy tracks in wet places and the path through the long grass afforded Helen an easy trail to follow. In fact, her horse needed no guiding. He ran in and out of the straggling spruces along the edge of the park, and suddenly wheeled around a corner of trees to come upon the gray mustang standing still. Bo was looking up and listening.

"There he is!" cried Bo, as the hound bayed ringingly, closer to them this time, and she spurred away.

Helen's horse followed without urging. He was excited. His ears were up. Something was in the wind. Helen had never ridden along this broken end of the park, and Bo was not easy to keep up with. She led across bogs, brooks, swales, rocky little ridges, through stretches of timber and groves of aspen so thick Helen could scarcely squeeze through. Then Bo came out into a large open offshoot of the park, right under the mountain slope, and here she sat, her horse watching and listening. Helen rode up to her, imagining once that she had heard the hound.

"Look! Look!" Bo's scream made her mustang stand almost straight up.

Helen gazed up to see a big brown bear with a frosted coat go lumbering across an opening on the slope.

"It's a grizzly! He'll kill Pedro! Oh, where is Dale!" cried Bo, with intense excitement.

"Bo! That bear is running down! We - we must get - out of his road," panted Helen, in breathless alarm.

"Dale hasn't had time to be close. . . . Oh, I wish he'd come! I don't know what to do."

"Ride back. At least wait for him."

Just then Pedro spoke differently, in savage barks, and following that came a loud growl and crashings in the brush. These sounds appeared to be not far up the slope.

"Nell! Do you hear? Pedro's fighting the bear," burst out Bo. Her face paled, her eyes flashed like blue steel. "The bear 'll kill him!"

"Oh, that would be dreadful!" replied Helen, in distress. "But what on earth can we do?"

"Hel-lo, Dale!" called Bo, at the highest pitch of her piercing voice.

No answer came. A heavy crash of brush, a rolling of stones, another growl from the slope told Helen that the hound had brought the bear to bay.

"Nell, I'm going up," said Bo, deliberately.

"No-no! Are you mad?" returned Helen.

"The bear will kill Pedro."

"He might kill you."

"You ride that way and yell for Dale," rejoined Bo.

"What will - you do?" gasped Helen.

"I'll shoot at the bear - scare him off. If he chases me he can't catch me coming downhill. Dale said that."

"You're crazy!" cried Helen, as Bo looked up the slope, searching for open ground. Then she pulled the rifle from its sheath.

But Bo did not hear or did not care. She spurred the mustang, and he, wild to run, flung grass and dirt from his heels. What Helen would have done then she never knew, but the fact was that her horse bolted after the mustang. In an instant, seemingly, Bo had disappeared in the gold and green of the forest slope. Helen's mount climbed on a run, snorting and heaving, through aspens, brush, and timber, to come out into a narrow, long opening extending lengthwise up the slope.

A sudden prolonged crash ahead alarmed Helen and halted her horse. She saw a shaking of aspens. Then a huge brown beast leaped as a cat out of the woods. It was a bear of enormous size. Helen's heart stopped - her tongue clove to the roof of her mouth. The bear turned. His mouth was open, red and dripping. He looked shaggy, gray. He let out a terrible bawl. Helen's every muscle froze stiff. Her horse plunged high and sidewise, wheeling almost in the air, neighing his terror. Like a stone she dropped from the saddle. She did not see the horse break into the woods, but she heard him. Her gaze never left the bear even while she was falling, and it seemed she alighted in an upright position with her back against a bush. It upheld her. The bear wagged his huge head from side to side. Then, as the hound barked close at hand, he turned to run heavily uphill and out of the opening.

The instant of his disappearance was one of collapse for Helen. Frozen with horror, she had been unable to move or feel or think. All at once she was a quivering mass of cold, helpless flesh, wet with perspiration, sick with a shuddering, retching, internal convulsion, her mind liberated from paralyzing shock. The moment was as horrible as that in which the bear had bawled his frightful rage. A stark, icy, black emotion seemed in possession of her. She could not lift a hand, yet all of her body appeared shaking. There was a fluttering, a strangling in her throat. The crushing weight that surrounded her heart eased before she recovered use of her limbs. Then, the naked and terrible thing was gone, like a nightmare giving way to consciousness. What blessed relief! Helen wildly gazed about her. The bear and hound were out of sight, and so was her horse. She stood up very dizzy and weak. Thought of Bo then seemed to revive her, to shock different life and feeling throughout all her cold extremities. She listened.

She heard a thudding of hoofs down the slope, then Dale's clear, strong call. She answered. It appeared long before he burst out of the woods, riding hard and leading her horse. In that time she recovered fully, and when he reached her, to put a sudden halt upon the fiery Ranger, she caught the bridle he threw and swiftly mounted her horse. The feel of the saddle seemed different. Dale's piercing gray glance thrilled her strangely.

"You're white. Are you hurt?" he said.

"No. I was scared."

"But he threw you?"

"Yes, he certainly threw me."

"What happened?"

"We heard the hound and we rode along the timber. Then we saw the bear - a monster - white - coated -"

"I know. It's a grizzly. He killed the colt - your pet. Hurry now. What about Bo?"

"Pedro was fighting the bear. Bo said he'd be killed. She rode right up here. My horse followed. I couldn't have stopped him. But we lost Bo. Right there the bear came out. He roared. My horse threw me and ran off. Pedro's barking saved me - my life, I think. Oh! that was awful! Then the bear went up - there. . . . And you came."

"Bo's followin' the hound!" ejaculated Dale. And, lifting his hands to his mouth, he sent out a stentorian yell that rolled up the slope, rang against the cliffs, pealed and broke and died away. Then he waited, listening. From far up the slope came a faint, wild cry, high-pitched and sweet, to create strange echoes, floating away to die in the ravines.

"She's after him!" declared Dale, grimly.

"Bo's got your rifle," said Helen. "Oh, we must hurry."

"You go back," ordered Dale, wheeling his horse.

"No!" Helen felt that word leave her lips with the force of a bullet.

Dale spurred Ranger and took to the open slope. Helen kept at his heels until timber was reached. Here a steep trail led up. Dale dismounted.

"Horse tracks - bear tracks - dog tracks," he said,

bending over. "We'll have to walk up here. It'll save our horses an' maybe time, too."

"Is Bo riding up there?" asked Helen, eying the steep ascent.

"She sure is." With that Dale started up, leading his horse. Helen followed. It was rough and hard work. She was lightly clad, yet soon she was hot, laboring, and her heart began to hurt. When Dale halted to rest Helen was just ready to drop. The baying of the hound, though infrequent, inspirited her. But presently that sound was lost. Dale said bear and hound had gone over the ridge and as soon as the top was gained he would hear them again.

"Look there," he said, presently, pointing to fresh tracks, larger than those made by Bo's mustang. "Elk tracks. We've scared a big bull an' he's right ahead of us. Look sharp an' you'll see him."

Helen never climbed so hard and fast before, and when they reached the ridge-top she was all tuckered out. It was all she could do to get on her horse. Dale led along the crest of this wooded ridge toward the western end, which was considerably higher. In places open rocky ground split the green timber. Dale pointed toward a promontory.

Helen saw a splendid elk silhouetted against the sky. He was a light gray over all his hindquarters, with shoulders and head black. His ponderous, wide-spread antlers towered over him, adding to the wildness of his magnificent poise as he stood there, looking down into the valley, no doubt listening for the bay of the hound. When he heard Dale's horse he gave one bound, gracefully and wonderfully carrying his antlers, to disappear in the green.

Again on a bare patch of ground Dale pointed down. Helen saw big round tracks, toeing in a little, that gave her a chill. She knew these were grizzly tracks.

Hard riding was not possible on this ridge crest, a fact that gave Helen time to catch her breath. At length, coming out upon the very summit of the mountain, Dale heard the hound. Helen's eyes feasted afar upon a wild scene of rugged grandeur, before she looked down on this western slope at her feet to see bare, gradual descent, leading down to sparsely wooded bench and on to deep-green cañon.

"Ride hard now!" yelled Dale. "I see Bo, an' I'll have to ride to catch her."

Dale spurred down the slope. Helen rode in his tracks and, though she plunged so fast that she felt her hair stand up with fright, she saw him draw away from her. Sometimes her horse slid on his haunches for a few yards, and at these hazardous moments she got her feet out of the stirrups so as to fall free from him if he went down. She let him choose the way, while she gazed ahead at Dale, and then farther on, in the hope of seeing Bo. At last she was rewarded. Far Down the wooded bench she saw a gray flash of the little mustang and a bright glint of Bo's hair. Her heart swelled. Dale would soon overhaul Bo and come between her and peril. And on the instant, though Helen was unconscious of it then, a remarkable change came over her spirit. Fear left her. And a hot, exalting, incomprehensible something took possession of her.

She let the horse run, and when he had plunged to the foot of that slope of soft ground he broke out across the open bench at a pace that made the wind bite Helen's cheeks and roar in her ears. She lost sight of Dale. It gave her a strange, grim exultance. She bent her eager gaze to find the tracks of his horse, and she found them. Also she made out the tracks of Bo's mustang and the bear and the hound. Her horse, scenting game, perhaps, and afraid to be left alone, settled into a fleet and powerful stride, sailing over logs and brush. That open bench had looked short, but it was long, and Helen rode down the gradual descent at breakneck speed. She would not be left behind. She had awakened to a heedlessness of risk. Something burned steadily within her. A grim, hard anger of joy! When she saw, far down another open, gradual descent, that Dale had passed Bo and that Bo was riding the little mustang as never before, then Helen flamed with a madness to catch her, to beat her in that wonderful chase, to show her and Dale what there really was in the depths of Helen Rayner.

Her ambition was to be short-lived, she divined from the lay of the land ahead, but the ride she lived then for a flying mile was something that would always blanch her cheeks and prick her skin in remembrance.

The open ground was only too short. That thundering pace soon brought Helen's horse to the timber. Here it took all her strength to check his headlong flight over deadfalls and between small jack-pines. Helen lost sight of Bo, and she realized it would take all her wits to keep from getting lost. She had to follow the trail, and in some places it was hard to see from horseback.

Besides, her horse was mettlesome, thoroughly

aroused, and he wanted a free rein and his own way. Helen tried that, only to lose the trail and to get sundry knocks from trees and branches. She could not hear the hound, nor Dale. The pines were small, close together, and tough. They were hard to bend. Helen hurt her hands, scratched her face, barked her knees. The horse formed a habit suddenly of deciding to go the way he liked instead of the way Helen guided him, and when he plunged between saplings too close to permit easy passage it was exceedingly hard on her. That did not make any difference to Helen. Once worked into a frenzy, her blood stayed at high pressure. She did not argue with herself about a need of desperate hurry. Even a blow on the head that nearly blinded her did not in the least retard her. The horse could hardly be held, and not at all in the few open places.

At last Helen reached another slope. Coming out upon cañon rim, she heard Dale's clear call, far down, and Bo's answering peal, high and piercing, with its note of exultant wildness. Helen also heard the bear and the hound fighting at the bottom of this cañon.

Here Helen again missed the tracks made by Dale and Bo. The descent looked impassable. She rode back along the rim, then forward. Finally she found where the ground had been plowed deep by hoofs, down over little banks. Helen's horse balked at these jumps. When she goaded him over them she went forward on his neck. It seemed like riding straight downhill. The mad spirit of that chase grew more stingingly keen to Helen as the obstacles grew. Then, once more the bay of the hound and the bawl of the bear made a demon of her horse. He snorted a shrill defiance. He plunged with fore hoofs in the air. He slid and broke a way down the steep, soft banks, through the thick brush and thick clusters of saplings, sending loose rocks and earth into avalanches ahead of him. He fell over one bank, but a thicket of aspens upheld him so that he rebounded and gained his feet. The sounds of fight ceased, but Dale's thrilling call floated up on the pine-scented air.

Before Helen realized it she was at the foot of the slope, in a narrow cañon-bed, full of rocks and trees, with a soft roar of running water filling her ears. Tracks were everywhere, and when she came to the first open place she saw where the grizzly had plunged off a sandy bar into the water. Here he had fought Pedro. Signs of that battle were easy to read. Helen saw where his huge tracks, still wet, led up the opposite sandy bank.

Then down-stream Helen did some more reckless and splendid riding. On level ground the horse was great. Once he leaped clear across the brook. Every plunge, every turn Helen expected to come upon Dale and Bo facing the bear. The cañon narrowed, the stream-bed deepened. She had to slow down to get through the trees and rocks. Quite unexpectedly she rode pell-mell upon Dale and Bo and the panting Pedro. Her horse plunged to a halt, answering the shrill neighs of the other horses.

Dale gazed in admiring amazement at Helen.

"Say, did you meet the bear again?" he queried, blankly.

"No. Didn't - you - kill him?" panted Helen, slowly sagging in her saddle.

"He got away in the rocks. Rough country down here.

Helen slid off her horse and fell with a little panting cry of relief. She saw that she was bloody, dirty, disheveled, and wringing wet with perspiration. Her riding habit was torn into tatters. Every muscle seemed to burn and sting, and all her bones seemed broken. But it was worth all this to meet Dale's penetrating glance, to see Bo's utter, incredulous astonishment.

"Nell - Rayner!" gasped Bo.

"If - my horse 'd been - any good - in the woods," panted Helen, "I'd not lost - so much time - riding down this mountain. And I'd caught you - beat you."

"Girl, did you ride down this last slope?" queried Dale.

"I sure did," replied Helen, smiling.

"We walked every step of the way, and was lucky to get down at that," responded Dale, gravely. "No horse should have been ridden down there. Why, he must have slid down."

"We slid - yes. But I stayed on him."

Bo's incredulity changed to wondering, speechless admiration. And Dale's rare smile changed his gravity.

"I'm sorry. It was rash of me. I thought you'd go back. . . . But all's well that ends well. . . . Helen, did you wake up to-day?"

She dropped her eyes, not caring to meet the questioning gaze upon her.

"Maybe - a little," she replied, and she covered her face

with her hands. Remembrance of his questions - of his assurance that she did not know the real meaning of life - of her stubborn antagonism - made her somehow ashamed. But it was not for long.

"The chase was great," she said. "I did not know myself. You were right."

"In how many ways did you find me right?" he asked.

"I think all - but one," she replied, with a laugh and a shudder. "I'm near starved now - I was so furious at Bo that I could have choked her. I faced that horrible brute. . . . Oh, I know what it is to fear death! . . . I was lost twice on the ride - absolutely lost. That's all."

Bo found her tongue. "The last thing was for you to fall wildly in love, wasn't it?"

"According to Dale, I must add that to my new experiences of to-day - before I can know real life," replied Helen, demurely.

The hunter turned away. "Let us go," he said, soberly.

CHAPTER XIII

After more days of riding the grassy level of that wonderfully gold and purple park, and dreamily listening by day to the ever-low and ever-changing murmur of the waterfall, and by night to the wild, lonely mourn of a hunting wolf, and climbing to the dizzy heights where the wind stung sweetly, Helen Rayner lost track of time and forgot her peril.

Roy Beeman did not return. If occasionally Dale mentioned Roy and his quest, the girls had little to say beyond a recurrent anxiety for the old uncle, and then they forgot again. Paradise Park, lived in a little while at that season of the year, would have claimed any one, and ever afterward haunted sleeping or waking dreams.

Bo gave up to the wild life, to the horses and rides, to the many pets, and especially to the cougar, Tom. The big cat followed her everywhere, played with her, rolling and pawing, kitten-like, and he would lay his massive head in her lap to purr his content. Bo had little fear of anything, and here in the wilds she soon lost that.

Another of Dale's pets was a half-grown black bear named Muss. He was abnormally jealous of little Bud and he had a well-developed hatred of Tom, otherwise he was a very good-tempered bear, and enjoyed Dale's impartial regard. Tom, however, chased Muss out of camp whenever Dale's back was turned, and sometimes Muss stayed away, shifting for himself. With the advent of Bo, who spent a good deal of time on the animals, Muss manifestly found the camp more attractive. Whereupon, Dale predicted trouble between Tom and Muss.

Bo liked nothing better than a rough-and-tumble frolic with the black bear. Muss was not very big nor very heavy, and in a wrestling bout with the strong and wiry girl he sometimes came out second best. It spoke well of him that he seemed to be careful not to hurt Bo. He never bit or scratched, though he sometimes gave her sounding slaps with his paws. Whereupon, Bo would clench her gauntleted fists and sail into him in earnest.

One afternoon before the early supper they always had, Dale and Helen were watching Bo teasing the bear. She was in her most vixenish mood, full of life and fight. Tom lay his long length on the grass, watching with narrow, gleaming eyes.

When Bo and Muss locked in an embrace and went down to roll over and over, Dale called Helen's attention to the cougar.

"Tom's jealous. It's strange how animals are like people. Pretty soon I'll have to corral Muss, or there'll be a fight."

Helen could not see anything wrong with Tom except that he did not look playful.

During supper-time both bear and cougar disappeared, though this was not remarked until afterward. Dale whistled and called, but the rival pets did not return.

Next morning Tom was there, curled up snugly at the foot of Bo's bed, and when she arose he followed her around as usual. But Muss did not return.

The circumstance made Dale anxious. He left camp, taking Tom with him, and upon returning stated that he had followed Muss's track as far as possible, and then had tried to put Tom on the trail, but the cougar would not or could not follow it. Dale said Tom never liked a bear trail, anyway, cougars and bears being common enemies. So, whether by accident or design, Bo lost one of her playmates.

The hunter searched some of the slopes next day and even went up on one of the mountains. He did not discover any sign of Muss, but he said he had found something else.

"Bo you girls want some more real excitement?" he asked.

Helen smiled her acquiescence and Bo replied with one of her forceful speeches.

"Don't mind bein' good an' scared?" he went on.

"You can't scare me," bantered Bo. But Helen looked doubtful.

"Up in one of the parks I ran across one of my horses - a lame bay you haven't seen. Well, he had been killed by that old silvertip. The one we chased. Hadn't been dead over an hour. Blood was still runnin' an' only a little meat eaten. That bear heard me or saw me an' made off into the woods. But he'll come back to-night. I'm goin' up there, lay for him, an' kill him this time.

Reckon you'd better go, because I don't want to leave you here alone at night."

"Are you going to take Tom?" asked Bo.

"No. The bear might get his scent. An', besides, Tom ain't reliable on bears. I'll leave Pedro home, too."

When they had hurried supper, and Dale had gotten in the horses, the sun had set and the valley was shadowing low down, while the ramparts were still golden. The long zigzag trail Dale followed up the slope took nearly an hour to climb, so that when that was surmounted and he led out of the woods twilight had fallen. A rolling park extended as far as Helen could see, bordered by forest that in places sent out straggling stretches of trees. Here and there, like islands, were isolated patches of timber.

At ten thousand feet elevation the twilight of this clear and cold night was a rich and rare atmospheric effect. It looked as if it was seen through perfectly clear smoked glass. Objects were singularly visible, even at long range, and seemed magnified. In the west, where the afterglow of sunset lingered over the dark, ragged, spruce-speared horizon-line, there was such a transparent golden line melting into vivid star-fired blue that Helen could only gaze and gaze in wondering admiration.

Dale spurred his horse into a lope and the spirited mounts of the girls kept up with him. The ground was rough, with tufts of grass growing close together, yet the horses did not stumble. Their action and snorting betrayed excitement. Dale led around several clumps of timber, up a long grassy swale, and then straight westward across an open flat toward where the dark-fringed forest-line raised itself wild and clear against the cold sky. The horses went swiftly, and the wind cut like a blade of ice. Helen could barely get her breath and she panted as if she had just climbed a laborsome hill. The stars began to blink out of the blue, and the gold paled somewhat, and yet twilight lingered. It seemed long across that flat, but really was short. Coming to a thin line of trees that led down over a slope to a deeper but still isolated patch of woods, Dale dismounted and tied his horse. When the girls got off he haltered their horses also.

"Stick close to me an' put your feet down easy," he whispered. How tall and dark he loomed in the fading light! Helen thrilled, as she had often of late, at the strange, potential force of the man. Stepping softly, without the least sound, Dale entered this straggly bit of woods, which appeared to have narrow byways and nooks. Then presently he came to the top of a well-wooded slope, dark as pitch, apparently. But as Helen followed she perceived the trees, and they were thin dwarf spruce, partly dead. The slope was soft and springy, easy to step upon without noise. Dale went so cautiously that Helen could not hear him, and some-times in the gloom she could not see him. Then the chill thrills ran over her. Bo kept holding on to Helen, which fact hampered Helen as well as worked somewhat to disprove Bo's boast. At last level ground was reached. Helen made out a light-gray background crossed by black bars. Another glance showed this to be the dark tree-trunks against the open park.

Dale halted, and with a touch brought Helen to a straining pause. He was listening. It seemed wonderful to watch him bend his head and stand as silent and motionless as one of the dark trees.

"He's not there yet," Dale whispered, and he stepped forward very slowly. Helen and Bo began to come up against thin dead branches that were invisible and then cracked. Then Dale knelt down, seemed to melt into the ground.

"You'll have to crawl," he whispered.

How strange and thrilling that was for Helen, and hard work! The ground bore twigs and dead branches, which had to be carefully crawled over; and lying flat, as was necessary, it took prodigious effort to drag her body inch by inch. Like a huge snake, Dale wormed his way along.

Gradually the wood lightened. They were nearing the edge of the park. Helen now saw a strip of open with a high, black wall of spruce beyond. The afterglow flashed or changed, like a dimming northern light, and then failed. Dale crawled on farther to halt at length between two tree-trunks at the edge of the wood.

"Come up beside me," he whispered.

Helen crawled on, and presently Bo was beside her panting, with pale face and great, staring eyes, plain to be seen in the wan light.

"Moon's comin' up. We're just in time. The old grizzly's not there yet, but I see coyotes. Look."

Dale pointed across the open neck of park to a dim blurred patch standing apart some little distance from the black wall.

"That's the dead horse," whispered Dale. "An' if you watch close you can see the coyotes. They're gray an' they move. . . .Can't you hear them?"

Helen's excited ears, so full of throbs and imaginings, presently registered low snaps and snarls. Bo gave her arm a squeeze.

"I hear them. They're fighting. Oh, gee!" she panted, and drew a long, full breath of unutterable excitement.

"Keep quiet now an' watch an' listen," said the hunter.

Slowly the black, ragged forest-line seemed to grow blacker and lift; slowly the gray neck of park lightened under some invisible influence; slowly the stars paled and the sky filled over. Somewhere the moon was rising. And slowly that vague blurred patch grew a little clearer.

Through the tips of the spruce, now seen to be rather close at hand, shone a slender, silver crescent moon, darkening, hiding, shining again, climbing until its exquisite sickle-point topped the trees, and then, magically, it cleared them, radiant and cold. While the eastern black wall shaded still blacker, the park blanched and the border-line opposite began to stand out as trees.

"Look! Look!" cried Bo, very low and fearfully, as she pointed.

"Not so loud," whispered Dale.

"But I see something!"

"Keep quiet," he admonished.

Helen, in the direction Bo pointed, could not see anything but moon-blanched bare ground, rising close at hand to a little ridge.

"Lie still," whispered Dale. "I'm goin' to crawl around to get a look from another angle. I'll be right back."

He moved noiselessly backward and disappeared. With him gone, Helen felt a palpitating of her heart and a prickling of her skin.

"Oh, my! Nell! Look!" whispered Bo, in fright. "I know I saw something."

On top of the little ridge a round object moved slowly, getting farther out into the light. Helen watched with suspended breath. It moved out to be silhouetted against the sky - apparently a huge, round, bristling animal, frosty in color. One instant it seemed huge - the next small - then close at hand - and far away. It swerved to come directly toward them. Suddenly Helen realized that the beast was not a dozen yards distant. She was just beginning a new experience - a real and horrifying terror in which her blood curdled, her heart gave a tremendous leap and then stood still, and she wanted to fly, but was rooted to the spot - when Dale returned to her side.

"That's a pesky porcupine," he whispered. "Almost crawled over you. He sure would have stuck you full of quills."

Whereupon he threw a stick at the animal. It bounced straight up to turn round with startling quickness, and it gave forth a rattling sound; then it crawled out of sight.

"Por - cu - pine!" whispered Bo, pantingly. "It might - as well - have been - an elephant!"

Helen uttered a long, eloquent sigh. She would not have cared to describe her emotions at sight of a harmless hedgehog.

"Listen!" warned Dale, very low. His big hand closed over Helen's gauntleted one. "There you have - the real cry of the wild."

Sharp and cold on the night air split the cry of a wolf, distant, yet wonderfully distinct. How wild and mournful and hungry! How marvelously pure! Helen shuddered through all her frame with the thrill of its music, the wild and unutterable and deep emotions it aroused. Again a sound of this forest had pierced beyond her life, back into the dim remote past from which she had come.

The cry was not repeated. The coyotes were still. And silence fell, absolutely unbroken.

Dale nudged Helen, and then reached over to give Bo a tap. He was peering keenly ahead and his strained intensity could be felt. Helen looked with all her might and she saw the shadowy gray forms of the coyotes skulk away, out of the moonlight into the gloom of the woods, where they disappeared. Not only Dale's intensity, but the very silence, the wildness of the moment and place, seemed fraught with wonderful potency. Bo must have felt it, too, for she was trembling all over, and holding tightly to Helen, and breathing quick and fast.

"A-huh!" muttered Dale, under his breath.

Helen caught the relief and certainty in his exclamation, and she divined, then, something of what the moment must have been to a hunter.

Then her roving, alert glance was arrested by a looming gray shadow coming out of the forest. It moved, but surely that huge thing could not be a bear. It passed out of gloom into silver moonlight. Helen's heart bounded. For it was a great frosty-coated bear lumbering along toward the dead horse. Instinctively Helen's hand sought the arm of the hunter. It felt like iron under a rippling surface. The touch eased away the oppression over her lungs, the tightness of her throat. What must have been fear left her, and only a powerful excitement remained. A sharp expulsion of breath from Bo and a violent jerk of her frame were signs that she had sighted the grizzly.

In the moonlight he looked of immense size, and that wild park with the gloomy blackness of forest furnished a fit setting for him. Helen's quick mind, so taken up with emotion, still had a thought for the wonder and the meaning of that scene. She wanted the bear killed, yet that seemed a pity.

He had a wagging, rolling, slow walk which took several moments to reach his quarry. When at length he reached it he walked around with sniffs plainly heard and then a cross growl. Evidently he had discovered that his meal had been messed over. As a whole the big bear could be seen distinctly, but only in outline and color. The distance was perhaps two hundred yards. Then it looked as if he had begun to tug at the carcass. Indeed, he was dragging it, very slowly, but surely.

"Look at that!" whispered Dale. "If he ain't strong! . . . Reckon I'll have to stop him."

The grizzly, however, stopped of his own accord, just outside of the shadow-line of the forest. Then he hunched in a big frosty heap over his prey and began to tear and rend.

"Jess was a mighty good horse," muttered Dale, grimly; "too good to make a meal for a hog silvertip."

Then the hunter silently rose to a kneeling position, swinging the rifle in front of him. He glanced up into the low branches of the tree overhead.

"Girls, there's no tellin' what a grizzly will do. If I yell, you climb up in this tree, an' do it quick."

With that he leveled the rifle, resting his left elbow on his knee. The front end of the rifle, reaching out of the shade, shone silver in the moonlight. Man and weapon became still as stone. Helen held her breath. But Dale relaxed, lowering the barrel.

"Can't see the sights very well," he whispered, shaking his head. "Remember, now - if I yell you climb!"

Again he aimed and slowly grew rigid. Helen could not take her fascinated eyes off him. He knelt, bareheaded, and in the shadow she could make out the gleam of his clear-cut profile, stern and cold.

A streak of fire and a heavy report startled her. Then she heard the bullet hit. Shifting her glance, she saw the bear lurch with convulsive action, rearing on his hind legs. Loud clicking snaps must have been a clashing of his jaws in rage. But there was no other sound. Then again Dale's heavy gun boomed. Helen heard again that singular spatting thud of striking lead. The bear went down with a flop as if he had been dealt a terrific blow. But just as quickly he was up on all-fours and began to whirl with hoarse, savage bawls of agony and fury. His action quickly carried him out of the moonlight into the shadow, where he disappeared. There the bawls gave place to gnashing snarls, and crashings in the brush, and snapping of branches, as he made his way into the forest.

"Sure he's mad," said Dale, rising to his feet. "An' I reckon hard hit. But I won't follow him to-night."

Both the girls got up, and Helen found she was shaky on her feet and very cold.

"Oh-h, wasn't - it - won-wonder-ful!" cried Bo.

"Are you scared? Your teeth are chatterin'," queried Dale.

"I'm - cold."

"Well, it sure is cold, all right," he responded. "Now the fun's over, you'll feel it. . . . Nell, you're froze, too?"

Helen nodded. She was, indeed, as cold as she had ever been before. But that did not prevent a strange warmness along her veins and a quickened pulse, the cause of which she did not conjecture.

"Let's rustle," said Dale, and led the way out of the wood and skirted its edge around to the slope. There they climbed to the flat, and went through the straggling line of trees to where the horses were tethered.

Up here the wind began to blow, not hard through the forest, but still strong and steady out in the open, and bitterly cold. Dale helped Bo to mount, and then Helen.

"I'm - numb," she said. "I'll fall off - sure."

"No. You'll be warm in a jiffy," he replied, "because we'll ride some goin' back. Let Ranger pick the way an' you hang on."

With Ranger's first jump Helen's blood began to run. Out he shot, his lean, dark head beside Dale's horse. The wild park lay clear and bright in the moonlight, with strange, silvery radiance on the grass. The patches of timber, like spired black islands in a moon-blanched lake, seemed to harbor shadows, and places for bears to hide, ready to spring out. As Helen neared each little grove her pulses shook and her heart beat. Half a mile of rapid riding burned out the cold. And all seemed glorious - the sailing moon, white in a dark-blue sky, the white, passionless stars, so solemn, so far away, the beckoning fringe of forest-land at once mysterious and friendly, and the fleet horses, running with soft, rhythmic thuds over the grass, leaping the ditches and the hollows, making the bitter wind sting and cut. Coming up that park the ride had been long; going back was as short as it was thrilling. In Helen, experiences gathered realization slowly, and it was this swift ride, the horses neck and neck, and all the wildness and beauty, that completed the slow, insidious work of years. The tears of excitement froze on her cheeks and her heart heaved full. All that pertained to this night got into her blood. It was only to feel, to live now, but it could be understood and remembered forever afterward.

Dale's horse, a little in advance, sailed over a ditch. Ranger made a splendid leap, but he alighted among some grassy tufts and fell. Helen shot over his head. She struck lengthwise, her arms stretched, and slid hard to a shocking impact that stunned her.

Bo's scream rang in her ears; she felt the wet grass under her face and then the strong hands that lifted her. Dale loomed over her, bending down to look into her face; Bo was clutching her with frantic hands. And Helen could only gasp. Her breast seemed caved in. The need to breathe was torture.

"Nell! - you're not hurt. You fell light, like a feather. All grass here. . . . You can't be hurt!" said Dale, sharply.

His anxious voice penetrated beyond her hearing, and his strong hands went swiftly over her arms and shoulders, feeling for broken bones.

"Just had the wind knocked out of you," went on Dale. It feels awful, but it's nothin'."

Helen got a little air, that was like hot pin-points in her lungs, and then a deeper breath, and then full, gasping respiration.

"I guess - I'm not hurt - not a bit," she choked out.

"You sure had a header. Never saw a prettier spill. Ranger doesn't do that often. I reckon we were travelin' too fast. But it was fun, don't you think?"

It was Bo who answered. "Oh, glorious! . . . But, gee! I was scared."

Dale still held Helen's hands. She released them while looking up at him. The moment was realization for her of what for days had been a vague, sweet uncertainty, becoming near and strange, disturbing and present. This accident had been a sudden, violent end to the wonderful ride. But its effect, the knowledge of what had got into her blood, would never change. And inseparable from it was this man of the forest.

CHAPTER XIV

On the next morning Helen was awakened by what she imagined had been a dream of some one shouting. With a start she sat up. The sunshine showed pink and gold on the ragged spruce line of the mountain rims. Bo was on her knees, braiding her hair with shaking hands, and at the same time trying to peep out.

And the echoes of a ringing cry were cracking back from the cliffs. That had been Dale's voice.

"Nell! Nell! Wake up!" called Bo, wildly. "Oh, some one's come! Horses and men!"

Helen got to her knees and peered out over Bo's shoulder. Dale, standing tall and striking beside the campfire, was waving his sombrero. Away down the open edge of the park came a string of pack-burros with mounted men behind. In the foremost rider Helen recognized Roy Beeman.

"That first one's Roy!" she exclaimed. "I'd never forget him on a horse. . . . Bo, it must mean Uncle Al's come!"

"Sure! We're born lucky. Here we are safe and sound - and all this grand camp trip. . . . Look at the cowboys. . . . Look! Oh, maybe this isn't great!" babbled Bo.

Dale wheeled to see the girls peeping out.

"It's time you're up!" he called. "Your uncle Al is here."

For an instant after Helen sank back out of Dale's sight she sat there perfectly motionless, so struck was she by the singular tone of Dale's voice. She imagined that he regretted what this visiting cavalcade of horsemen meant - they had come to take her to her ranch in Pine. Helen's heart suddenly began to beat fast, but thickly, as if muffled within her breast.

"Hurry now, girls," called Dale.

Bo was already out, kneeling on the flat stone at the little brook, splashing water in a great hurry. Helen's hands trembled so that she could scarcely lace her boots or brush her hair, and she was long behind Bo in making herself presentable. When Helen stepped out, a short, powerfully built man in coarse garb and heavy boots stood holding Bo's hands.

"Wal, wal! You favor the Rayners," he was saying I remember your dad, an' a fine feller he was."

Beside them stood Dale and Roy, and beyond was a group of horses and riders.

"Uncle, here comes Nell," said Bo, softly.

"Aw!" The old cattle-man breathed hard as he turned.

Helen hurried. She had not expected to remember this uncle, but one look into the brown, beaming face, with the blue eyes flashing, yet sad, and she recognized him, at the same instant recalling her mother.

He held out his arms to receive her.

"Nell Auchincloss all over again!" he exclaimed, in deep voice, as he kissed her. "I'd have knowed you anywhere!"

"Uncle Al!" murmured Helen. "I remember you - though I was only four."

"Wal, wal, - that's fine," he replied. "I remember you straddled my knee once, an' your hair was brighter - an' curly. It ain't neither now. . . . Sixteen years! An' you're twenty now? What a fine, broad-shouldered girl you are! An', Nell, you're the handsomest Auchincloss I ever seen!"

Helen found herself blushing, and withdrew her hands from his as Roy stepped forward to pay his respects. He stood bareheaded, lean and tall, with neither his clear eyes nor his still face, nor the proffered hand expressing anything of the proven quality of fidelity, of achievement, that Helen sensed in him.

"Howdy, Miss Helen? Howdy, Bo?" he said. "You all both look fine an' brown. . . . I reckon I was shore slow rustlin' your uncle Al up here. But I was figgerin' you'd like Milt's camp for a while."

"We sure did," replied Bo, archly.

"Aw!" breathed Auchincloss, heavily. "Lemme set down."

He drew the girls to the rustic seat Dale had built for

them under the big pine.

"Oh, you must be tired! How - how are you?" asked Helen, anxiously.

"Tired! Wal, if I am it's jest this here minit. When Joe Beeman rode in on me with thet news of you - wal, I jest fergot I was a worn-out old hoss. Haven't felt so good in years. Mebbe two such young an' pretty nieces will make a new man of me."

"Uncle Al, you look strong and well to me," said Bo. "And young, too, and -"

"Haw! Haw! Thet 'll do," interrupted Al. "I see through you. What you'll do to Uncle Al will be aplenty. . . . Yes, girls, I'm feelin' fine. But strange - strange! Mebbe thet's my joy at seein' you safe - safe when I feared so thet damned greaser Beasley -"

In Helen's grave gaze his face changed swiftly - and all the serried years of toil and battle and privation showed, with something that was not age, nor resignation, yet as tragic as both.

"Wal, never mind him - now," he added, slowly, and the warmer light returned to his face. "Dale - come here."

The hunter stepped closer.

"I reckon I owe you more 'n I can ever pay," said Auchincloss, with an arm around each niece.

"No, Al, you don't owe me anythin'," returned Dale, thoughtfully, as he looked away.

"A-huh!" grunted Al. "You hear him, girls. . . . Now listen, you wild hunter. An' you girls listen. . . . Milt, I never thought you much good, 'cept for the wilds. But I reckon I'll have to swallow thet. I do. Comin' to me as you did - an' after bein' druv off - keepin' your council an' savin' my girls from thet hold-up, wal, it's the biggest deal any man ever did for me. . . . An' I'm ashamed of my hard feelin's, an' here's my hand."

"Thanks, Al," replied Dale, with his fleeting smile, and he met the proffered hand. "Now, will you be makin' camp here?"

"Wal, no. I'll rest a little, an' you can pack the girls' outfit - then we'll go. Sure you're goin' with us?"

"I'll call the girls to breakfast," replied Dale, and he moved away without answering Auchincloss's query.

Helen divined that Dale did not mean to go down to Pine with them, and the knowledge gave her a blank feeling of surprise. Had she expected him to go?

"Come here, Jeff," called Al, to one of his men.

A short, bow-legged horseman with dusty garb and sun-bleached face hobbled forth from the group. He was not young, but he had a boyish grin and bright little eyes. Awkwardly he doffed his slouch sombrero.

"Jeff, shake hands with my nieces," said Al. "This 's Helen, an' your boss from now on. An' this 's Bo, fer short. Her name was Nancy, but when she lay a baby in her cradle I called her Bo-Peep, an' the name's stuck. . . . Girls, this here's my foreman, Jeff Mulvey, who's been with me twenty years."

The introduction caused embarrassment to all three principals, particularly to Jeff.

"Jeff, throw the packs an' saddles fer a rest," was Al's order to his foreman.

"Nell, reckon you'll have fun bossin' thet outfit," chuckled Al. "None of 'em's got a wife. Lot of scalawags they are; no women would have them!"

"Uncle, I hope I'll never have to be their boss," replied Helen.

"Wal, you're goin' to be, right off," declared Al. "They ain't a bad lot, after all. An' I got a likely new man."

With that he turned to Bo, and, after studying her pretty face, he asked, in apparently severe tone, "Did you send a cowboy named Carmichael to ask me for a job?"

Bo looked quite startled.

"Carmichael! Why, Uncle, I never heard that name before," replied Bo, bewilderedly.

"A-huh! Reckoned the young rascal was lyin'," said Auchincloss. "But I liked the fellar's looks an' so let him stay."

Then the rancher turned to the group of lounging riders.

"Las Vegas, come here," he ordered, in a loud voice.

Helen thrilled at sight of a tall, superbly built cowboy

reluctantly detaching himself from the group. He had a red-bronze face, young like a boy's. Helen recognized it, and the flowing red scarf, and the swinging gun, and the slow, spur-clinking gait. No other than Bo's Las Vegas cowboy admircr!

Then Helen flashed a look at Bo, which look gave her a delicious, almost irresistible desire to laugh. That young lady also recognized the reluctant individual approaching with flushed and downcast face. Helen recorded her first experience of Bo's utter discomfiture. Bo turned white then red as a rose.

"Say, my niece said she never heard of the name Carmichael," declared Al, severely, as the cowboy halted before him. Helen knew her uncle had the repute of dealing hard with his men, but here she was reassured and pleased at the twinkle in his eye.

"Shore, boss, I can't help thet," drawled the cowboy. "It's good old Texas stock."

He did not appear shamefaced now, but just as cool, easy, clear-eyed, and lazy as the day Helen had liked his warm young face and intent gaze.

"Texas! You fellars from the Pan Handle are always hollerin' Texas. I never seen thet Texans had any one else beat - say from Missouri," returned Al, testily.

Carmichael maintained a discreet silence, and carefully avoided looking at the girls.

"Wal, reckon we'll all call you Las Vegas, anyway," continued the rancher. "Didn't you say my niece sent you to me for a job?"

Whereupon Carmichael's easy manner vanished.

"Now, boss, shore my memory's pore," he said. "I only says -"

"Don't tell me thet. My memory's not p-o-r-e," replied Al, mimicking the drawl. "What you said was thet my niece would speak a good word for you."

Here Carmichael stole a timid glance at Bo, the result of which was to render him utterly crestfallen. Not improbably he had taken Bo's expression to mean something it did not, for Helen read it as a mingling of consternation and fright. Her eyes were big and blazing; a red spot was growing in each cheek as she gathered strength from his confusion.

"Well, didn't you?" demanded Al.

From the glance the old rancher shot from the cowboy to the others of his employ it seemed to Helen that they were having fun at Carmichael's expense.

"Yes, sir, I did," suddenly replied the cowboy.

"A-huh! All right, here's my niece. Now see thet she speaks the good word."

Carmichael looked at Bo and Bo looked at him. Their glances were strange, wondering, and they grew shy. Bo dropped hers. The cowboy apparently forgot what had been demanded of him.

Helen put a hand on the old rancher's arm.

"Uncle, what happened was my fault," she said. "The

train stopped at Las Vegas. This young man saw us at the open window. He must have guessed we were lonely, homesick girls, getting lost in the West. For he spoke to us - nice and friendly. He knew of you. And he asked, in what I took for fun, if we thought you would give him a job. And I replied, just to tease Bo, that she would surely speak a good word for him."

"Haw! Haw! So thet's it," replied Al, and he turned to Bo with merry eyes. "Wal, I kept this here Las Vegas Carmichael on his say-so. Come on with your good word, unless you want to see him lose his job."

Bo did not grasp her uncle's bantering, because she was seriously gazing at the cowboy. But she had grasped something.

"He - he was the first person - out West - to speak kindly to us," she said, facing her uncle.

"Wal, thet's a pretty good word, but it ain't enough," responded Al.

Subdued laughter came from the listening group. Carmichael shifted from side to side.

"He - he looks as if he might ride a horse well," ventured Bo.

"Best hossman I ever seen," agreed Al, heartily.

"And - and shoot?" added Bo, hopefully.

"Bo, he packs thet gun low, like Jim Wilson an' all them Texas gun-fighters. Reckon thet ain't no good word."

"Then - I'll vouch for him," said Bo, with finality.

"Thet settles it." Auchincloss turned to the cowboy. "Las Vegas, you're a stranger to us. But you're welcome to a place in the outfit an' I hope you won't never disappoint us."

Auchincloss's tone, passing from jest to earnest, betrayed to Helen the old rancher's need of new and true men, and hinted of trying days to come.

Carmichael stood before Bo, sombrero in hand, rolling it round and round, manifestly bursting with words he could not speak. And the girl looked very young and sweet with her flushed face and shining eyes. Helen saw in the moment more than that little by-play of confusion.

"Miss - Miss Rayner - I shore - am obliged," he stammered, presently.

"You're very welcome," she replied, softly. "I - I got on the next train," he added.

When he said that Bo was looking straight at him, but she seemed not to have heard.

"What's your name?" suddenly she asked.

"Carmichael."

"I heard that. But didn't uncle call you Las Vegas?"

"Shore. But it wasn't my fault. Thet cow-punchin' outfit saddled it on me, right off . They Don't know no better. Shore I jest won't answer to thet handle. . . .

Now - Miss Bo - my real name is Tom."

"I simply could not call you - any name but Las Vegas," replied Bo, very sweetly.

"But - beggin' your pardon - I - I don't like thet," blustered Carmichael.

"People often get called names - they don't like," she said, with deep intent.

The cowboy blushed scarlet. Helen as well as he got Bo's inference to that last audacious epithet he had boldly called out as the train was leaving Las Vegas. She also sensed something of the disaster in store for Mr. Carmichael. Just then the embarrassed young man was saved by Dale's call to the girls to come to breakfast.

That meal, the last for Helen in Paradise Park, gave rise to a strange and inexplicable restraint. She had little to say. Bo was in the highest spirits, teasing the pets, joking with her uncle and Roy, and even poking fun at Dale. The hunter seemed somewhat somber. Roy was his usual dry, genial self. And Auchincloss, who sat near by, was an interested spectator. When Tom put in an appearance, lounging with his feline grace into the camp, as if he knew he was a privileged pet, the rancher could scarcely contain himself.

"Dale, it's thet damn cougar!" he ejaculated.

"Sure, that's Tom."

"He ought to be corralled or chained. I've no use for cougars," protested Al.

"Tom is as tame an' safe as a kitten."

"A-huh! Wal, you tell thet to the girls if you like. But not me! I'm an old hoss, I am."

"Uncle Al, Tom sleeps curled up at the foot of my bed," said Bo.

"Aw - what?"

"Honest Injun," she responded. "Well, isn't it so?"

Helen smilingly nodded her corroboration. Then Bo called Tom to her and made him lie with his head on his stretched paws, right beside her, and beg for bits to eat.

"Wal! I'd never have believed thet!" exclaimed Al, shaking his big head. "Dale, it's one on me. I've had them big cats foller me on the trails, through the woods, moonlight an' dark. An' I've heard 'em let out thet awful cry. They ain't any wild sound on earth thet can beat a cougar's. Does this Tom ever let out one of them wails?"

"Sometimes at night," replied Dale.

"Wal, excuse me. Hope you don't fetch the yaller rascal down to Pine."

"I won't."

"What'll you do with this menagerie?"

Dale regarded the rancher attentively. "Reckon, Al, I'll take care of them."

"But you're goin' down to my ranch."

"What for?"

Al scratched his head and gazed perplexedly at the hunter. "Wal, ain't it customary to visit friends?"

"Thanks, Al. Next time I ride down Pine way - in the spring, perhaps - I'll run over an' see how you are."

"Spring!" ejaculated Auchincloss. Then he shook his head sadly and a far-away look filmed his eyes. "Reckon you'd call some late."

"Al, you'll get well now. These, girls - now - they'll cure you. Reckon I never saw you look so good."

Auchincloss did not press his point farther at that time, but after the meal, when the other men came to see Dale's camp and pets, Helen's quick ears caught the renewal of the subject.

"I'm askin' you - will you come?" Auchincloss said, low and eagerly.

"No. I wouldn't fit in down there," replied Dale.

"Milt, talk sense. You can't go on forever huntin' bear an' tamin' cats," protested the old rancher.

"Why not?" asked the hunter, thoughtfully.

Auchincloss stood up and, shaking himself as if to ward off his testy temper, he put a hand on Dale's arm.

"One reason is you're needed in Pine."

"How? Who needs me?"

"I do. I'm playin' out fast. An' Beasley's my enemy. The ranch an' all I got will go to Nell. Thet ranch will have to be run by a man an' held by a man. Do you savvy? It's a big job. An' I'm offerin' to make you my foreman right now."

"Al, you sort of take my breath," replied Dale. "An' I'm sure grateful. But the fact is, even if I could handle the job, I - I don't believe I'd want to."

"Make yourself want to, then. Thet 'd soon come. You'd get interested. This country will develop. I seen thet years ago. The government is goin' to chase the Apaches out of here. Soon homesteaders will be flockin' in. Big future, Dale. You want to get in now. An' -"

Here Auchincloss hesitated, then spoke lower:

"An' take your chance with the girl! . . . I'll be on your side."

A slight vibrating start ran over Dale's stalwart form.

"Al - you're plumb dotty!" he exclaimed.

"Dotty! Me? Dotty!" ejaculated Auchincloss. Then he swore. "In a minit I'll tell you what you are."

"But, Al, that talk's so - so - like an old fool's."

"Huh! An' why so?"

"Because that - wonderful girl would never look at

me," Dale replied, simply.

"I seen her lookin' already," declared Al, bluntly.

Dale shook his head as if arguing with the old rancher was hopeless.

"Never mind thet," went on Al. "Mebbe I am a dotty old fool - 'specially for takin' a shine to you. But I say again - will you come down to Pine and be my foreman?"

"No," replied Dale.

"Milt, I've no son - an' I'm - afraid of Beasley." This was uttered in an agitated whisper.

"Al, you make me ashamed," said Dale, hoarsely. "I can't come. I've no nerve."

"You've no what?"

"Al, I don't know what's wrong with me. But I'm afraid I'd find out if I came down there."

"A-huh! It's the girl!"

"I don't know, but I'm afraid so. An' I won't come."

"Aw yes, you will -"

Helen rose with beating heart and tingling ears, and moved away out of hearing. She had listened too long to what had not been intended for her ears, yet she could not be sorry. She walked a few rods along the brook, out from under the pines, and, standing in the open edge of the park, she felt the beautiful scene still her agitation. The following moments, then, were the happiest she had spent in Paradise Park, and the profoundest of her whole life.

Presently her uncle called her.

"Nell, this here hunter wants to give you thet black hoss. An' I say you take him."

"Ranger deserves better care than I can give him," said Dale. "He runs free in the woods most of the time. I'd be obliged if she'd have him. An' the hound, Pedro, too."

Bo swept a saucy glance from Dale to her sister.

"Sure she'll have Ranger. Just offer him to me!"

Dale stood there expectantly, holding a blanket in his hand, ready to saddle the horse. Carmichael walked around Ranger with that appraising eye so keen in cowboys.

"Las Vegas, do you know anything about horses?" asked Bo.

"Me! Wal, if you ever buy or trade a hoss you shore have me there," replied Carmichael.

"What do you think of Ranger?" went on Bo.

"Shore I'd buy him sudden, if I could."

"Mr. Las Vegas, you're too late," asserted Helen, as she advanced to lay a hand on the horse.

"Ranger is mine."

Dale smoothed out the blanket and, folding it, he threw it over the horse; and then with one powerful swing he set the saddle in place.

"Thank you very much for him," said Helen, softly.

"You're welcome, an' I'm sure glad," responded Dale, and then, after a few deft, strong pulls at the straps, he continued. "There, he's ready for you."

With that he laid an arm over the saddle, and faced Helen as she stood patting and smoothing Ranger. Helen, strong and calm now, in feminine possession of her secret and his, as well as her composure, looked frankly and steadily at Dale. He seemed composed, too, yet the bronze of his fine face was a trifle pale.

"But I can't thank you - I'll never be able to repay you - for your service to me and my sister," said Helen.

"I reckon you needn't try," Dale returned. "An' my service, as you call it, has been good for me."

"Are you going down to Pine with us?"

"No."

"But you will come soon?"

"Not very soon, I reckon," he replied, and averted his gaze.

"When?"

"Hardly before spring."

"Spring? . . . That is a long time. Won't you come to see me sooner than that?"

"If I can get down to Pine."

"You're the first friend I've made in the West," said Helen, earnestly.

"You'll make many more - an' I reckon soon forget him you called the man of the forest."

"I never forget any of my friends. And you've been the - the biggest friend I ever had."

"I'll be proud to remember."

"But will you remember - will you promise to come to Pine?"

"I reckon."

"Thank you. All's well, then. . . . My friend, goodby."

"Good-by," he said, clasping her hand. His glance was clear, warm, beautiful, yet it was sad.

Auchincloss's hearty voice broke the spell. Then Helen saw that the others were mounted. Bo had ridden up close; her face was earnest and happy and grieved all at once, as she bade good-by to Dale. The pack-burros were hobbling along toward the green slope. Helen was the last to mount, but Roy was the last to leave the hunter. Pedro came reluctantly.

It was a merry, singing train which climbed that brown odorous trail, under the dark spruces. Helen assuredly was happy, yet a pang abided in her breast.

She remembered that half-way up the slope there was a turn in the trail where it came out upon an open bluff. The time seemed long, but at last she got there. And she checked Ranger so as to have a moment's gaze down into the park.

It yawned there, a dark-green and bright-gold gulf, asleep under a westering sun, exquisite, wild, lonesome. Then she saw Dale standing in the open space between the pines and the spruces. He waved to her. And she returned the salute.

Roy caught up with her then and halted his horse. He waved his sombrero to Dale and let out a piercing yell that awoke the sleeping echoes, splitting strangely from cliff to cliff .

"Shore Milt never knowed what it was to be lonesome," said Roy, as if thinking aloud. "But he'll know now."

Ranger stepped out of his own accord and, turning off the ledge, entered the spruce forest. Helen lost sight of Paradise Park. For hours then she rode along a shady, fragrant trail, seeing the beauty of color and wildness, hearing the murmur and rush and roar of water, but all the while her mind revolved the sweet and momentous realization which had thrilled her - that the hunter, this strange man of the forest, so deeply versed in nature and so unfamiliar with emotion, aloof and simple and strong like the elements which had developed him, had fallen in love with her and did not know it.

CHAPTER XV

Dale stood with face and arm upraised, and he watched Helen ride off the ledge to disappear in the forest. That vast spruce slope seemed to have swallowed her. She was gone! Slowly Dale lowered his arm with gesture expressive of a strange finality, an eloquent despair, of which he was unconscious.

He turned to the park, to his camp, and the many duties of a hunter. The park did not seem the same, nor his home, nor his work.

"I reckon this feelin's natural," he soliloquized, resignedly, "but it's sure queer for me. That's what comes of makin' friends. Nell an' Bo, now, they made a difference, an' a difference I never knew before."

He calculated that this difference had been simply one of responsibility, and then the charm and liveliness of the companionship of girls, and finally friendship. These would pass now that the causes were removed.

Before he had worked an hour around camp he realized a change had come, but it was not the one anticipated. Always before he had put his mind on his tasks, whatever they might be; now he worked while his thoughts were strangely involved.

The little bear cub whined at his heels; the tame deer

seemed to regard him with deep, questioning eyes, the big cougar padded softly here and there as if searching for something.

"You all miss them - now - I reckon," said Dale. "Well, they're gone an' you'll have to get along with me."

Some vague approach to irritation with his pets surprised him. Presently he grew both irritated and surprised with himself - a state of mind totally unfamiliar. Several times, as old habit brought momentary abstraction, he found himself suddenly looking around for Helen and Bo. And each time the shock grew stronger. They were gone, but their presence lingered. After his camp chores were completed he went over to pull down the lean-to which the girls had utilized as a tent. The spruce boughs had dried out brown and sear; the wind had blown the roof awry; the sides were leaning in. As there was now no further use for this little habitation, he might better pull it down. Dale did not acknowledge that his gaze had involuntarily wandered toward it many times. There-fore he strode over with the intention of destroying it.

For the first time since Roy and he had built the lean-to he stepped inside. Nothing was more certain than the fact that he experienced a strange sensation, perfectly incomprehensible to him. The blankets lay there on the spruce boughs, disarranged and thrown back by hurried hands, yet still holding something of round folds where the slender forms had nestled. A black scarf often worn by Bo lay covering the pillow of pine-needles; a red ribbon that Helen had worn on her hair hung from a twig. These articles were all that had been forgotten. Dale gazed at them attentively, then at the blankets, and all around the fragrant little shelter; and he stepped outside with an uncomfortable knowledge that he could not destroy the place where Helen and Bo had spent so many hours.

Whereupon, in studious mood, Dale took up his rifle and strode out to hunt. His winter supply of venison had not yet been laid in. Action suited his mood; he climbed far and passed by many a watching buck to slay which seemed murder; at last he jumped one that was wild and bounded away. This he shot, and set himself a Herculean task in packing the whole carcass back to camp. Burdened thus, be staggered under the trees, sweating freely, many times laboring for breath, aching with toil, until at last he had reached camp. There he slid the deer carcass off his shoulders, and, standing over it, he gazed down while his breast labored. It was one of the finest young bucks he had ever seen. But neither in stalking it, nor making a wonderful shot, nor in packing home a weight that would have burdened two men, nor in gazing down at his beautiful quarry, did Dale experience any of the old joy of the hunter.

"I'm a little off my feed," he mused, as he wiped sweat from his heated face. "Maybe a little dotty, as I called Al. But that'll pass."

Whatever his state, it did not pass. As of old, after a long day's hunt, he reclined beside the camp-fire and watched the golden sunset glows change on the ramparts; as of old he laid a hand on the soft, furry head of the pet cougar; as of old he watched the gold change to red and then to dark, and twilight fall like a blanket; as of old he listened to the dreamy, lulling murmur of the water fall. The old familiar beauty, wildness, silence, and loneliness were there, but the old content seemed strangely gone.

Soberly he confessed then that he missed the happy company of the girls. He did not distinguish Helen from Bo in his slow introspection. When he sought his bed he did not at once fall to sleep. Always, after a few moments of wakefulness, while the silence settled down or the wind moaned through the pines, he had fallen asleep. This night he found different. Though he was tired, sleep would not soon come. The wilderness, the mountains, the park, the camp - all seemed to have lost something. Even the darkness seemed empty. And when at length Dale fell asleep it was to be troubled by restless dreams.

Up with the keen-edged, steely-bright dawn, he went at the his tasks with the springy stride of the deer-stalker.

At the end of that strenuous day, which was singularly full of the old excitement and action and danger, and of new observations, he was bound to confess that no longer did the chase suffice for him.

Many times on the heights that day, with the wind keen in his face, and the vast green billows of spruce below him, he had found that be was gazing without seeing, halting without object, dreaming as he had never dreamed before.

Once, when a magnificent elk came out upon a rocky ridge and, whistling a challenge to invisible rivals, stood there a target to stir any hunter's pulse, Dale did not even raise his rifle. Into his ear just then rang Helen's voice: "Milt Dale, you are no Indian. Giving yourself to a hunter's wildlife is selfish. It is wrong. You love this lonely life, but it is not work. Work that does not help others is not a real man's work."

From that moment conscience tormented him. It was not what he loved, but what he ought to do, that counted in the sum of good achieved in the world. Old Al Auchincloss had been right. Dale was wasting strength and intelligence that should go to do his share in the development of the West. Now that he had reached maturity, if through his knowledge of nature's law he had come to see the meaning of the strife of men for existence, for place, for possession, and to hold them in contempt, that was no reason why he should keep himself aloof from them, from some work that was needed in an incomprehensible world.

Dale did not hate work, but he loved freedom. To be alone, to live with nature, to feel the elements, to labor and dream and idle and climb and sleep unhampered by duty, by worry, by restriction, by the petty interests of men - this had always been his ideal of living. Cowboys, riders, sheep-herders, farmers - these toiled on from one place and one job to another for the little money doled out to them. Nothing beautiful, nothing significant had ever existed in that for him. He had worked as a boy at every kind of range-work, and of all that humdrum waste of effort he had liked sawing wood best. Once he had quit a job of branding cattle because the smell of burning hide, the bawl of the terrified calf, had sickened him. If men were honest there would be no need to scar cattle. He had never in the least desired to own land and droves of stock, and make deals with ranchmen, deals advantageous to himself. Why should a man want to make a deal or trade a horse or do a piece of work to another man's disadvantage? Self-preservation was the first law of life. But as the plants and trees and birds and beasts interpreted that law, merciless and inevitable as they were, they had neither greed nor dishonesty. They lived by the grand rule of what was best for the greatest number.

But Dale's philosophy, cold and clear and inevitable, like nature itself, began to be pierced by the human appeal in Helen Rayner's words. What did she mean? Not that he should lose his love of the wilderness, but that he realize himself! Many chance words of that girl had depth. He was young, strong, intelligent, free from taint of disease or the fever of drink. He could do something for others. Who? If that mattered, there, for instance, was poor old Mrs. Cass, aged and lame now; there was Al Auchincloss, dying in his boots, afraid of enemies, and wistful for his blood and his property to receive the fruit of his labors; there were the two girls, Helen and Bo, new and strange to the West, about to be confronted by a big problem of ranch life and rival interests. Dale thought of still more people in the little village of Pine - of others who had failed, whose lives were hard, who could have been made happier by kindness and assistance.

What, then, was the duty of Milt Dale to himself? Because men preyed on one another and on the weak, should he turn his back upon a so-called civilization or should he grow like them? Clear as a bell came the answer that his duty was to do neither. And then he saw how the little village of Pine, as well as the whole world, needed men like him. He had gone to nature, to the forest, to the wilderness for his development; and all the judgments and efforts of his future would be a result of that education.

Thus Dale, lying in the darkness and silence of his

lonely park, arrived at a conclusion that he divined was but the beginning of a struggle.

It took long introspection to determine the exact nature of that struggle, but at length it evolved into the paradox that Helen Rayner had opened his eyes to his duty as a man, that he accepted it, yet found a strange obstacle in the perplexing, tumultuous, sweet fear of ever going near her again.

Suddenly, then, all his thought revolved around the girl, and, thrown off his balance, he weltered in a wilderness of unfamiliar strange ideas.

When he awoke next day the fight was on in earnest. In his sleep his mind had been active. The idea that greeted him, beautiful as the sunrise, flashed in memory of Auchincloss's significant words, "Take your chance with the girl!"

The old rancher was in his dotage. He hinted of things beyond the range of possibility. That idea of a chance for Dale remained before his consciousness only an instant. Stars were unattainable; life could not be fathomed; the secret of nature did not abide alone on the earth - these theories were not any more impossible of proving than that Helen Rayner might be for him.

Nevertheless, her strange coming into his life had played havoc, the extent of which he had only begun to realize.

For a month he tramped through the forest. It was October, a still golden, fulfilling season of the year; and everywhere in the vast dark green a glorious blaze of oak and aspen made beautiful contrast. He carried his rifle, but he never used it. He would climb miles and go this way and that with no object in view. Yet his eye and ear had never been keener. Hours he would spend on a promontory, watching. the distance, where the golden patches of aspen shone bright out of dark-green mountain slopes. He loved to fling himself down in an aspen-grove at the edge of a senaca, and there lie in that radiance like a veil of gold and purple and red, with the white tree-trunks striping the shade. Always, whether there were breeze or not, the aspen-leaves quivered, ceaselessly, wonderfully, like his pulses, beyond his control. Often he reclined against a mossy rock beside a mountain stream to listen, to watch, to feel all that was there, while his mind held a haunting, dark-eyed vision of a girl. On the lonely heights, like an eagle, he sat gazing down into Paradise Park, that was more and more beautiful, but would never again be the same, never fill him with content, never be all and all to him.

Late in October the first snow fell. It melted at once on the south side of the park, but the north slopes and the rims and domes above stayed white.

Dale had worked quick and hard at curing and storing his winter supply of food, and now he spent days chopping and splitting wood to burn during the months he would be snowed-in. He watched for the dark-gray, fast-scudding storm-clouds, and welcomed them when they came. Once there lay ten feet of snow on the trails he would be snowed-in until spring. It would be impossible to go down to Pine. And perhaps during the long winter he would be cured of this strange, nameless disorder of his feelings.

November brought storms up on the peaks. Flurries of

snow fell in the park every day, but the sunny south side, where Dale's camp lay, retained its autumnal color and warmth. Not till late in winter did the snow creep over this secluded nook.

The morning came at last, piercingly keen and bright, when Dale saw that the heights were impassable; the realization brought him a poignant regret. He had not guessed how he had wanted to see Helen Rayner again until it was too late. That opened his eyes. A raging frenzy of action followed, in which he only tired himself physically without helping himself spiritually.

It was sunset when he faced the west, looking up at the pink snow-domes and the dark-golden fringe of spruce, and in that moment he found the truth.

"I love that girl! I love that girl!" he spoke aloud, to the distant white peaks, to the winds, to the loneliness and silence of his prison, to the great pines and to the murmuring stream, and to his faithful pets. It was his tragic confession of weakness, of amazing truth, of hopeless position, of pitiful excuse for the transformation wrought in him.

Dale's struggle ended there when he faced his soul. To understand himself was to be released from strain, worry, ceaseless importuning doubt and wonder and fear. But the fever of unrest, of uncertainty, had been nothing compared to a sudden upflashing torment of love.

With somber deliberation he set about the tasks needful, and others that he might make - his camp-fires and meals, the care of his pets and horses, the mending of saddles and pack-harness, the curing of buckskin for moccasins and hunting-suits. So his days were not idle. But all this work was habit for him and needed no application of mind.

And Dale, like some men of lonely wilderness lives who did not retrograde toward the savage, was a thinker. Love made him a sufferer.

The surprise and shame of his unconscious surrender, the certain hopelessness of it, the long years of comm-union with all that was wild, lonely, and beautiful, the wonderfully developed insight into nature's secrets, and the sudden-dawning revelation that he was no omniscient being exempt from the ruthless ordinary destiny of man - all these showed him the strength of his manhood and of his passion, and that the life he had chosen was of all lives the one calculated to make love sad and terrible.

Helen Rayner haunted him. In the sunlight there was not a place around camp which did not picture her lithe, vigorous body, her dark, thoughtful eyes, her eloquent, resolute lips, and the smile that was so sweet and strong. At night she was there like a slender specter, pacing beside him under the moaning pines. Every camp-fire held in its heart the glowing white radiance of her spirit.

Nature had taught Dale to love solitude and silence, but love itself taught him their meaning. Solitude had been created for the eagle on his crag, for the blasted mountain fir, lonely and gnarled on its peak, for the elk and the wolf. But it had not been intended for man. And to live always in the silence of wild places was to become obsessed with self - to think and dream - to be happy, which state, however pursued by man, was not good for him. Man must be given imperious longings for the unattainable.

It needed, then, only the memory of an unattainable woman to render solitude passionately desired by a man, yet almost unendurable. Dale was alone with his secret; and every pine, everything in that park saw him shaken and undone.

In the dark, pitchy deadness of night, when there was no wind and the cold on the peaks had frozen the waterfall, then the silence seemed insupportable. Many hours that should have been given to slumber were paced out under the cold, white, pitiless stars, under the lonely pines.

Dale's memory betrayed him, mocked his restraint, cheated him of any peace; and his imagination, sharpened by love, created pictures, fancies, feelings, that drove him frantic.

He thought of Helen Rayner's strong, shapely brown hand. In a thousand different actions it haunted him. How quick and deft in camp-fire tasks! how graceful and swift as she plaited her dark hair! how tender and skilful in its ministration when one of his pets had been injured! how eloquent when pressed tight against her breast in a moment of fear on the dangerous heights! How expressive of unutterable things when laid on his arm!

Dale saw that beautiful hand slowly creep up his arm, across his shoulder, and slide round his neck to clasp there. He was powerless to inhibit the picture. And what he felt then was boundless, unutterable. No woman had ever yet so much as clasped his hand, and heretofore no such imaginings had ever crossed his mind, yet deep in him, somewhere hidden, had been this waiting, sweet, and imperious need. In the bright day he appeared to ward off such fancies, but at night he was helpless. And every fancy lcft him weaker, wilder.

When, at the culmination of this phase of his passion, Dale, who had never known the touch of a woman's lips, suddenly yielded to the illusion of Helen Rayner's kisses, he found himself quite mad, filled with rapture and despair, loving her as he hated himself. It seemed as if he had experienced all these terrible feelings in some former life and had forgotten them in this life. He had no right to think of her, but he could not resist it. Imagining the sweet surrender of her lips was a sacrilege, yet here, in spite of will and honor and shame, he was lost.

Dale, at length, was vanquished, and he ceased to rail at himself, or restrain his fancies. He became a dreamy, sad-eyed, camp-fire gazer, like many another lonely man, separated, by chance or error, from what the heart hungered most for. But this great experience, when all its significance had clarified in his mind, immeasurably broadened his understanding of the principles of nature applied to life.

Love had been in him stronger than in most men, because of his keen, vigorous, lonely years in the forest, where health of mind and body were intensified and preserved. How simple, how natural, how inevitable! He might have loved any fine-spirited, healthy-bodied girl. Like a tree shooting its branches and leaves, its whole entity, toward the sunlight, so had he grown toward a woman's love. Why? Because the thing he revered in nature, the spirit, the universal, the life that was God, had created at his birth or before his birth the three tremendous instincts of nature - to fight for life, to feed himself, to reproduce his kind. That was all there was to it. But oh! the mystery, the beauty, the torment, and the terror of this third instinct - this hunger for the sweetness and the glory of a woman's love!

CHAPTER XVI

Helen Rayner dropped her knitting into her lap and sat pensively gazing out of the window over the bare yellow ranges of her uncle's ranch.

The winter day was bright, but steely, and the wind that whipped down from the white-capped mountains had a keen, frosty edge. A scant snow lay in protected places; cattle stood bunched in the lee of ridges; low sheets of dust scurried across the flats.

The big living-room of the ranch-house was warm and comfortable with its red adobe walls, its huge stone fireplace where cedar logs blazed, and its many-colored blankets. Bo Rayner sat before the fire, curled up in an armchair, absorbed in a book. On the floor lay the hound Pedro, his racy, fine head stretched toward the warmth.

"Did uncle call?" asked Helen, with a start out of her reverie.

"I didn't hear him," replied Bo.

Helen rose to tiptoe across the floor, and, softly parting some curtains, she looked into the room where her uncle lay. He was asleep. Sometimes he called out in his slumbers. For weeks now he had been confined to his bed, slowly growing weaker. With a sigh Helen returned to her window-seat and took up her work.

"Bo, the sun is bright," she said. "The days are growing longer. I'm so glad."

"Nell, you're always wishing time away. For me it passes quickly enough," replied the sister.

"But I love spring and summer and fall - and I guess I hate winter," returned Helen, thoughtfully.

The yellow ranges rolled away up to the black ridges and they in turn swept up to the cold, white mountains. Helen's gaze seemed to go beyond that snowy barrier. And Bo's keen eyes studied her sister's earnest, sad face.

"Nell, do you ever think of Dale?" she queried, suddenly.

The question startled Helen. A slow blush suffused neck and cheek.

"Of course," she replied, as if surprised that Bo should ask such a thing.

"I - I shouldn't have asked that," said Bo, softly, and then bent again over her book.

Helen gazed tenderly at that bright, bowed head. In this swift-flying, eventful, busy winter, during which the management of the ranch had devolved wholly upon Helen, the little sister had grown away from her. Bo had insisted upon her own free will and she had followed it, to the amusement of her uncle, to the concern of Helen, to the dismay and bewilderment of the faithful Mexican housekeeper, and to the undoing of all the young men on the ranch.

Helen had always been hoping and waiting for a favorable hour in which she might find this wilful sister once more susceptible to wise and loving influence. But while she hesitated to speak, slow footsteps and a jingle of spurs sounded without, and then came a timid knock. Bo looked up brightly and ran to open the door.

"Oh! It's only - you!" she uttered, in withering scorn, to the one who knocked.

Helen thought she could guess who that was.

"How are you-all?" asked a drawling voice.

"Well, Mister Carmichael, if that interests you - I'm quite ill," replied Bo, freezingly.

"Ill! Aw no, now?"

"It's a fact. If I don't die right off I'll have to be taken back to Missouri," said Bo, casually.

"Are you goin' to ask me in?" queried Carmichael, bluntly. "It's cold - an' I've got somethin' to say to -"

"To me? Well, you're not backward, I declare," retorted Bo.

"Miss Rayner, I reckon it 'll be strange to you - findin' out I didn't come to see you."

"Indeed! No. But what was strange was the deluded

idea I had - that you meant to apologize to me - like a gentleman. . ..Come in, Mr. Carmichael. My sister is here."

The door closed as Helen turned round. Carmichael stood just inside with his sombrero in hand, and as he gazed at Bo his lean face seemed hard. In the few months since autumn he had changed - aged, it seemed, and the once young, frank, alert, and careless cowboy traits had merged into the making of a man. Helen knew just how much of a man he really was. He had been her mainstay during all the complex working of the ranch that had fallen upon her shoulders.

"Wal, I reckon you was deluded, all right - if you thought I'd crawl like them other lovers of yours," he said, with cool deliberation.

Bo turned pale, and her eyes fairly blazed, yet even in what must have been her fury Helen saw amaze and pain.

"Other lovers? I think the biggest delusion here is the way you flatter yourself," replied Bo, stingingly.

"Me flatter myself? Nope. You don't savvy me. I'm shore hatin' myself these days."

"Small wonder. I certainly hate you - with all my heart!"

At this retort the cowboy dropped his head and did not see Bo flaunt herself out of the room. But he heard the door close, and then slowly came toward Helen.

"Cheer up, Las Vegas," said Helen, smiling. "Bo's hot-tempered."

"Miss Nell, I'm just like a dog. The meaner she treats me the more I love her," he replied, dejectedly.

To Helen's first instinct of liking for this cowboy there had been added admiration, respect, and a growing appreciation of strong, faithful, developing character. Carmichael's face and hands were red and chapped from winter winds; the leather of wrist-bands, belt, and boots was all worn shiny and thin; little streaks of dust fell from him as he breathed heavily. He no longer looked the dashing cowboy, ready for a dance or lark or fight.

"How in the world did you offend her so?" asked Helen. "Bo is furious. I never saw her so angry as that."

"Miss Nell, it was jest this way," began Carmichael. "Shore Bo's knowed I was in love with her. I asked her to marry me an' she wouldn't say yes or no. . . . An', mean as it sounds - she never run away from it, thet's shore. We've had some quarrels - two of them bad, an' this last's the worst."

"Bo told me about one quarrel," said Helen. "It was - because you drank - that time."

"Shore it was. She took one of her cold spells an' I jest got drunk."

"But that was wrong," protested Helen.

"I ain't so shore. You see, I used to get drunk often -

before I come here. An' I've been drunk only once. Back at Las Vegas the outfit would never believe thet. Wal, I promised Bo I wouldn't do it again, an' I've kept my word."

"That is fine of you. But tell me, why is she angry now?"

"Bo makes up to all the fellars," confessed Carmichael, hanging his head. "I took her to the dance last week - over in the town-hall. Thet's the first time she'd gone anywhere with me. I shore was proud. . . . But thet dance was hell. Bo carried on somethin' turrible, an' I -"

"Tell me. What did she do?" demanded Helen, anxiously. "I'm responsible for her. I've got to see that she behaves."

"Aw, I ain't sayin' she didn't behave like a lady," replied Carmichael. "It was - she - wal, all them fellars are fools over her - an' Bo wasn't true to me."

"My dear boy, is Bo engaged to you?"

"Lord - if she only was!" he sighed.

"Then how can you say she wasn't true to you? Be reasonable."

"I reckon now, Miss Nell, thet no one can be in love an' act reasonable," rejoined the cowboy. "I don't know how to explain, but the fact is I feel thet Bo has played the - the devil with me an' all the other fellars."

"You mean she has flirted?"

"I reckon."

"Las Vegas, I'm afraid you're right," said Helen, with growing apprehension. "Go on. Tell me what's happened."

"Wal, thet Turner boy, who rides for Beasley, he was hot after Bo," returned Carmichael, and he spoke as if memory hurt him. "Reckon I've no use for Turner. He's a fine-lookin', strappin', big cow-puncher, an' calculated to win the girls. He brags thet he can, an' I reckon he's right. Wal, he was always hangin' round Bo. An' he stole one of my dances with Bo. I only had three, an' he comes up to say this one was his; Bo, very innocent - oh, she's a cute one! - she says, 'Why, Mister Turner - is it really yours?' An' she looked so full of joy thet when he says to me, 'Excoose us, friend Carmichael,' I sat there like a locoed jackass an' let them go. But I wasn't mad at thet. He was a better dancer than me an' I wanted her to have a good time. What started the hell was I seen him put his arm round her when it wasn't just time, accordin' to the dance, an' Bo - she didn't break any records gettin' away from him. She pushed him away - after a little - after I near died. Wal, on the way home I had to tell her. I shore did. An' she said what I'd love to forget. Then - then, Miss Nell, I grabbed her - it was outside here by the porch an' all bright moonlight - I grabbed her an' hugged an' kissed her good. When I let her go I says, sorta brave, but I was plumb scared - I says, "Wal, are you goin' to marry me now?"'

He concluded with a gulp, and looked at Helen with woe in his eyes.

"Oh! What did Bo do?" breathlessly queried Helen.

"She slapped me," he replied. "An' then she says, I did like you best, but now I hate you!' An' she slammed the door in my face."

"I think you made a great mistake," said Helen, gravely.

"Wal, if I thought so I'd beg her forgiveness. But I reckon I don't. What's more, I feel better than before. I'm only a cowboy an' never was much good till I met her. Then I braced. I got to havin' hopes, studyin' books, an' you know how I've been lookin' into this ranchin' game. I stopped drinkin' an' saved my money. Wal, she knows all thet. Once she said she was proud of me. But it didn't seem to count big with her. An' if it can't count big I don't want it to count at all. I reckon the madder Bo is at me the more chance I've got. She knows I love her - thet I'd die for her - thet I'm a changed man. An' she knows I never before thought of darin' to touch her hand. An' she knows she flirted with Turner."

"She's only a child," replied Helen. "And all this change - the West - the wildness - and you boys making much of her - why, it's turned her head. But Bo will come out of it true blue. She is good, loving. Her heart is gold."

"I reckon I know, an' my faith can't be shook," rejoined Carmichael, simply. "But she ought to believe thet she'll make bad blood out here. The West is the West. Any kind of girls are scarce. An' one like Bo - Lord! we cowboys never seen none to compare with her. She'll make bad blood an' some of it will be spilled."

"Uncle Al encourages her," said Helen, apprehensively. "It tickles him to hear how the boys are after her. Oh, she doesn't tell him. But he hears. And I, who must stand in mother's place to her, what can I do?"

"Miss Nell, are you on my side?" asked the cowboy, wistfully. He was strong and elemental, caught in the toils of some power beyond him.

Yesterday Helen might have hesitated at that question. But to-day Carmichael brought some proven quality of loyalty, some strange depth of rugged sincerity, as if she had learned his future worth.

"Yes, I am," Helen replied, earnestly. And she offered her hand.

"Wal, then it 'll shore turn out happy," he said, squeezing her hand. His smile was grateful, but there was nothing in it of the victory he hinted at. Some of his ruddy color had gone. "An' now I want to tell you why I come."

He had lowered his voice. "Is Al asleep?" he whispered.

"Yes," replied Helen. "He was a little while ago."

"Reckon I'd better shut his door."

Helen watched the cowboy glide across the room and carefully close the door, then return to her with intent eyes. She sensed events in his look, and she divined suddenly that he must feel as if he were her brother.

"Shore I'm the one thet fetches all the bad news to

you," he said, regretfully.

Helen caught her breath. There had indeed been many little calamities to mar her management of the ranch - loss of cattle, horses, sheep - the desertion of herders to Beasley - failure of freighters to arrive when most needed - fights among the cowboys - and disagreements over long-arranged deals.

"Your uncle Al makes a heap of this here Jeff Mulvey," asserted Carmichael.

"Yes, indeed. Uncle absolutely relies on Jeff," replied Helen.

"Wal, I hate to tell you, Miss Nell," said the cowboy, bitterly, "thet Mulvey ain't the man he seems."

"Oh, what do you mean?"

"When your uncle dies Mulvey is goin' over to Beasley an' he's goin' to take all the fellars who'll stick to him."

"Could Jeff be so faithless - after so many years my uncle's foreman? Oh, how do you know?"

"Reckon I guessed long ago. But wasn't shore. Miss Nell, there's a lot in the wind lately, as poor old Al grows weaker. Mulvey has been particular friendly to me an' I've nursed him along, 'cept I wouldn't drink. An' his pards have been particular friends with me, too, more an' more as I loosened up. You see, they was shy of me when I first got here. To-day the whole deal showed clear to me like a hoof track in soft ground. Bud Lewis, who's bunked with me, come out an' tried to win me over to Beasley - soon as Auchincloss dies. I palavered with Bud an' I wanted to know. But Bud would only say he was goin' along with Jeff an' others of the outfit. I told him I'd reckon over it an' let him know. He thinks I'll come round."

"Why - why will these men leave me when - when - Oh, poor uncle! They bargain on his death. But why - tell me why?"

"Beasley has worked on them - won them over," replied Carmichael, grimly. "After Al dies the ranch will go to you. Beasley means to have it. He an' Al was pards once, an' now Beasley has most folks here believin' he got the short end of thet deal. He'll have papers - shore - an' he'll have most of the men. So he'll just put you off an' take possession. Thet's all, Miss Nell, an' you can rely on its bein' true."

"I - I believe you - but I can't believe such - such robbery possible," gasped Helen.

"It's simple as two an' two. Possession is law out here. Once Beasley gets on the ground it's settled. What could you do with no men to fight for your property?"

"But, surely, some of the men will stay with me?"

"I reckon. But not enough."

"Then I can hire more. The Beeman boys. And Dale would come to help me."

"Dale would come. An' he'd help a heap. I wish he was here," replied Carmichael, soberly. "But there's no way to get him. He's snowed-up till May."

"I dare not confide in uncle," said Helen, with agitation. "The shock might kill him. Then to tell him of the unfaithfulness of his old men - that would be cruel. . . . Oh, it can't be so bad as you think."

"I reckon it couldn't be no worse. An' - Miss Nell, there's only one way to get out of it - an' thet's the way of the West."

"How?" queried Helen, eagerly.

Carmichael lunged himself erect and stood gazing down at her. He seemed completely detached now from that frank, amiable cowboy of her first impressions. The redness was totally gone from his face. Something strange and cold and sure looked out of his eyes.

"I seen Beasley go in the saloon as I rode past. Suppose I go down there, pick a quarrel with him - an' kill him?"

Helen sat bolt-upright with a cold shock.

"Carmichael! you're not serious?" she exclaimed.

"Serious? I shore am. Thet's the only way, Miss Nell. An' I reckon it's what Al would want. An' between you an' me - it would be easier than ropin' a calf. These fellars round Pine don't savvy guns. Now, I come from where guns mean somethin'. An' when I tell you I can throw a gun slick an' fast, why I shore ain't braggin'. You needn't worry none about me, Miss Nell."

Helen grasped that he had taken the signs of her shocked sensibility to mean she feared for his life. But what had sickened her was the mere idea of bloodshed in her behalf.

"You'd - kill Beasley - just because there are rumors of his - treachery?" gasped Helen.

"Shore. It'll have to be done, anyhow," replied the cowboy.

"No! No! It's too dreadful to think of. Why, that would be murder. I - I can't understand how you speak of it - so - so calmly."

"Reckon I ain't doin' it calmly. I'm as mad as hell," said Carmichael, with a reckless smile.

"Oh, if you are serious then, I say no - no - no! I forbid you. I don't believe I'll be robbed of my property."

"Wal, supposin' Beasley does put you off - an' takes possession. What 're you goin' to say then?" demanded the cowboy, in slow, cool deliberation.

"I'd say the same then as now," she replied.

He bent his head thoughtfully while his red hands smoothed his sombrero.

"Shore you girls haven't been West very long," be muttered, as if apologizing for them. "An' I reckon it takes time to learn the ways of a country."

"West or no West, I won't have fights deliberately picked, and men shot, even if they do threaten me," declared Helen, positively.

"All right, Miss Nell, shore I respect your wishes," he returned. "But I'll tell you this. If Beasley turns you an' Bo out of your home - wal, I'll look him up on my own account."

Helen could only gaze at him as he backed to the door, and she thrilled and shuddered at what seemed his loyalty to her, his love for Bo, and that which was inevitable in himself.

"Reckon you might save us all some trouble - now if you'd - just get mad - an' let me go after thet greaser."

"Greaser! Do you mean Beasley?"

"Shore. He's a half-breed. He was born in Magdalena, where I heard folks say nary one of his parents was no good."

"That doesn't matter. I'm thinking of humanity of law and order. Of what is right."

"Wal, Miss Nell, I'll wait till you get real mad - or till Beasley -"

"But, my friend, I'll not get mad," interrupted Helen. "I'll keep my temper."

"I'll bet you don't," he retorted. "Mebbe you think you've none of Bo in you. But I'll bet you could get so mad - once you started - thet you'd be turrible. What 've you got them eyes for, Miss Nell, if you ain't an Auchincloss ?"

He was smiling, yet he meant every word. Helen felt the truth as something she feared.

"Las Vegas, I won't bet. But you - you will always come to me - first - if there's trouble."

"I promise," he replied, soberly, and then went out.

Helen found that she was trembling, and that there was a commotion in her breast. Carmichael had frightened her. No longer did she hold doubt of the gravity of the situation. She had seen Beasley often, several times close at hand, and once she had been forced to meet him. That time had convinced her that he had evinced personal interest in her. And on this account, coupled with the fact that Riggs appeared to have nothing else to do but shadow her, she had been slow in developing her intention of organizing and teaching a school for the children of Pine. Riggs had become rather a doubtful celebrity in the settlements. Yet his bold, apparent badness had made its impression. From all reports he spent his time gambling, drinking, and bragging. It was no longer news in Pine what his intentions were toward Helen Rayner. Twice he had ridden up to the ranch-house, upon one occasion securing an interview with Helen. In spite of her contempt and indifference, he was actually influencing her life there in Pine. And it began to appear that the other man, Beasley, might soon direct stronger significance upon the liberty of her actions.

The responsibility of the ranch had turned out to be a heavy burden. It could not be managed, at least by her, in the way Auchincloss wanted it done. He was old, irritable, irrational, and hard. Almost all the neighbors were set against him, and naturally did not take kindly to Helen.

She had not found the slightest evidence of unfair

dealing on the part of her uncle, but he had been a hard driver. Then his shrewd, far-seeing judgment had made all his deals fortunate for him, which fact had not brought a profit of friendship.

Of late, since Auchincloss had grown weaker and less dominating, Helen had taken many decisions upon herself, with gratifying and hopeful results. But the wonderful happiness that she had expected to find in the West still held aloof. The memory of Paradise Park seemed only a dream, sweeter and more intangible as time passed, and fuller of vague regrets. Bo was a comfort, but also a very considerable source of anxiety. She might have been a help to Helen if she had not assimilated Western ways so swiftly. Helen wished to decide things in her own way, which was as yet quite far from Western. So Helen had been thrown more and more upon her own resources, with the cowboy Carmichael the only one who had come forward voluntarily to her aid.

For an hour Helen sat alone in the room, looking out of the window, and facing stern reality with a colder, graver, keener sense of intimacy than ever before. To hold her property and to live her life in this community according to her ideas of honesty, justice, and law might well be beyond her powers. To-day she had been convinced that she could not do so without fighting for them, and to fight she must have friends. That conviction warmed her toward Carmichael, and a thoughtful consideration of all he had done for her proved that she had not fully appreciated him. She would make up for her oversight.

There were no Mormons in her employ, for the good reason that Auchincloss would not hire them. But in one of his kindlier hours, growing rare now, he had admitted that the Mormons were the best and the most sober, faithful workers on the ranges, and that his sole objection to them was just this fact of their superiority. Helen decided to hire the four Beemans and any of their relatives or friends who would come; and to do this, if possible, without letting her uncle know. His temper now, as well as his judgment, was a hindrance to efficiency. This decision regarding the Beemans; brought Helen back to Carmichael's fervent wish for Dale, and then to her own.

Soon spring would be at hand, with its multiplicity of range tasks. Dale had promised to come to Pine then, and Helen knew that promise would be kept. Her heart beat a little faster, in spite of her business-centered thoughts. Dale was there, over the black-sloped, snowy-tipped mountain, shut away from the world. Helen almost envied him. No wonder he loved loneliness, solitude, the sweet, wild silence and beauty of Paradise Park! But he was selfish, and Helen meant to show him that. She needed his help. When she recalled his physical prowess with animals, and imagined what it must be in relation to men, she actually smiled at the thought of Beasley forcing her off her property, if Dale were there. Beasley would only force disaster upon himself. Then Helen experienced a quick shock. Would Dale answer to this situation as Carmichael had answered? It afforded her relief to assure herself to the contrary. The cowboy was one of a blood-letting breed; the hunter was a man of thought, gentleness, humanity. This situation was one of the kind that had made him despise the littleness of men. Helen assured herself that he was different from her uncle and from the cowboy, in all the relations of life which she had observed while with him. But a doubt lingered in her mind. She remembered his calm reference to Snake Anson, and that caused a recurrence of the little shiver Carmichael had given her. When the doubt augmented to a possibility that she might not be able to control Dale, then she tried not to think of it any more. It confused and perplexed her that into her mind should flash a thought that, though it would be dreadful for Carmichael to kill Beasley, for Dale to do it would be a calamity - a terrible thing. Helen did not analyze that strange thought. She was as afraid of it as she was of the stir in her blood when she visualized Dale.

Her meditation was interrupted by Bo, who entered the room, rebellious-eyed and very lofty. Her manner changed, which apparently owed its cause to the, fact that Helen was alone.

"Is that - cowboy gone?" she asked.

"Yes. He left quite some time ago," replied Helen.

"I wondered if he made your eyes shine - your color burn so. Nell, you're just beautiful."

"Is my face burning?" asked Helen, with a little laugh. "So it is. Well, Bo, you've no cause for jealousy. Las Vegas can't be blamed for my blushes."

"Jealous! Me? Of that wild-eyed, soft-voiced, two-faced cow-puncher? I guess not, Nell Rayner. What 'd he say about me?"

"Bo, he said a lot," replied Helen, reflectively. "I'll tell you presently. First I want to ask you - has Carmichael ever told you how he's helped me?"

"No! When I see him - which hasn't been often lately - he - I - Well, we fight. Nell, has he helped you?"

Helen smiled in faint amusement. She was going to be sincere, but she meant to keep her word to the cowboy. The fact was that reflection had acquainted her with her indebtedness to Carmichael.

"Bo, you've been so wild to ride half-broken mustangs - and carry on with cowboys - and read - and sew - and keep your secrets that you've had no time for your sister or her troubles."

"Nell!" burst out Bo, in amaze and pain. She flew to Helen and seized her hands. "What 're you saying?"

"It's all true," replied Helen, thrilling and softening. This sweet sister, once aroused, would be hard to resist. Helen imagined she should hold to her tone of reproach and severity.

"Sure it's true," cried Bo, fiercely. "But what's my fooling got to do with the - the rest you said? Nell, are you keeping things from me?"

"My dear, I never get any encouragement to tell you my troubles."

"But I've - I've nursed uncle - sat up with him - just the same as you," said Bo, with quivering lips.

"Yes, you've been good to him."

"We've no other troubles, have we, Nell?"

"You haven't, but I have," responded Helen, reproachfully.

"Why - why didn't you tell me?" cried Bo, passio-passionately. "What are they? Tell me now. You must think me a -- a selfish, hateful cat."

"Bo, I've had much to worry me - and the worst is yet to come," replied Helen. Then she told Bo how complicated and bewildering was the management of a big ranch - when the owner was ill, testy, defective in memory, and hard as steel - when he had hoards of gold and notes, but could not or would not remember his obligations - when the neighbor ranchers had just claims - when cowboys and sheep-herders were discontented, and wrangled among themselves - when great herds of cattle and flocks of sheep had to be fed in winter - when supplies had to be continually freighted across a muddy desert and lastly, when an enemy rancher was slowly winning away the best hands with the end in view of deliberately taking over the property when the owner died. Then Helen told how she had only that day realized the extent of Carmichael's advice and help and labor - how, indeed, he had been a brother to her - how -

But at this juncture Bo buried her face in Helen's breast and began to cry wildly.

"I - I - don't want - to hear - any more," she sobbed.

"Well, you've got to hear it," replied Helen, inexorably "I want you to know how he's stood by me."

"But I hate him."

"Bo, I suspect that's not true."

"I do - I do."

"Well, you act and talk very strangely then."

"Nell Rayner - are - you - you sticking up for that - that devil?"

"I am, yes, so far as it concerns my conscience," rejoined Helen, earnestly. "I never appreciated him as he deserved - not until now. He's a man, Bo, every inch of him. I've seen him grow up to that in three months. I'd never have gotten along without him. I think he's fine, manly, big. I -"

"I'll bet - he's made love - to you, too," replied Bo, woefully.

"Talk sense," said Helen, sharply. "He has been a brother to me. But, Bo Rayner, if he had made love to me I - I might have appreciated it more than you."

Bo raised her face, flushed in part and also pale, with tear-wet cheeks and the telltale blaze in the blue eyes.

"I've been wild about that fellow. But I hate him, too," she said, with flashing spirit. "And I want to go on hating him. So don't tell me any more."

Whereupon Helen briefly and graphically related how Carmichael had offered to kill Beasley, as the only way to save her property, and how, when she refused, that he threatened he would do it anyhow.

Bo fell over with a gasp and clung to Helen.

"Oh - Nell! Oh, now I love him more than - ever," she cried, in mingled rage and despair.

Helen clasped her closely and tried to comfort her as in the old days, not so very far back, when troubles were not so serious as now.

"Of course you love him," she concluded. "I guessed that long ago. And I'm glad. But you've been wilful - foolish. You wouldn't surrender to it. You wanted your fling with the other boys. You're - Oh, Bo, I fear you have been a sad little flirt."

"I - I wasn't very bad till - till he got bossy. Why, Nell, he acted - right off - just as if he owned me. But he didn't. . . . And to show him - I - I really did flirt with that Turner fellow. Then he - he insulted me. . . . Oh, I hate him!"

"Nonsense, Bo. You can't hate any one while you love him," protested Helen.

"Much you know about that," flashed Bo. "You just can! Look here. Did you ever see a cowboy rope and throw and tie up a mean horse?"

"Yes, I have."

"Do you have any idea how strong a cowboy is - how his hands and arms are like iron?"

"Yes, I'm sure I know that, too."

"And how savage he is?"

"Yes."

"And how he goes at anything he wants to do?"

"I must admit cowboys are abrupt," responded Helen, with a smile.

"Well, Miss Rayner, did you ever - when you were standing quiet like a lady - did you ever have a cowboy dive at you with a terrible lunge - grab you and hold you so you couldn't move or breathe or scream - hug you till all your bones cracked - and kiss you so fierce and so hard that you wanted to kill him and die?

Helen had gradually drawn back from this blazing-eyed, eloquent sister, and when the end of that remarkable question came it was impossible to reply.

"There! I see you never had that done to you," resumed Bo, with satisfaction. "So don't ever talk to me."

"I've heard his side of the story," said Helen, constrainedly.

With a start Bo sat up straighter, as if better to defend herself.

"Oh! So you have? And I suppose you'll take his part - even about that - that bearish trick."

"No. I think that rude and bold. But, Bo, I don't believe he meant to be either rude or bold. From what he confessed to me I gather that he believed he'd lose you outright or win you outright by that violence. It seems girls can't play at love out here in this wild West. He said there would be blood shed over you. I begin to realize what he meant. He's not sorry for what he did. Think how strange that is. For he has the instincts of a gentleman. He's kind, gentle, chivalrous. Evidently he had tried every way to win your favor except any familiar advance. He did that as a last resort. In my opinion his motives were to force you to accept or refuse him, and in case you refused him he'd always have those forbidden stolen kisses to assuage his self-respect - when he thought of Turner or any one else daring to be familiar with you. Bo, I see through Carmichael, even if I don't make him clear to you. You've got to be honest with yourself. Did that act of his win or lose you? In other words, do you love him or not?"

Bo hid her face.

"Oh, Nell! it made me see how I loved him - and that made me so - so sick I hated him. . . . But now - the hate is all gone."

CHAPTER XVII

When spring came at last and the willows drooped green and fresh over the brook and the range rang with bray of burro and whistle of stallion, old Al Auchincloss had been a month in his grave.

To Helen it seemed longer. The month had been crowded with work, events, and growing, more hopeful duties, so that it contained a world of living. The uncle had not been forgotten, but the innumerable restrictions to development and progress were no longer manifest. Beasley had not presented himself or any claim upon Helen; and she, gathering confidence day by day, began to believe all that purport of trouble had been exaggerated.

In this time she had come to love her work and all that pertained to it. The estate was large. She had no accurate knowledge of how many acres she owned, but it was more than two thousand. The fine, old, rambling ranch-house, set like a fort on the last of the foot-hills, corrals and fields and barns and meadows, and the rolling green range beyond, and innumerable sheep, horses, cattle - all these belonged to Helen, to her ever-wondering realization and ever-growing joy. Still, she was afraid to let herself go and be perfectly happy. Always there was the fear that had been too deep and strong to forget so soon.

This bright, fresh morning, in March, Helen came out upon the porch to revel a little in the warmth of sunshine and the crisp, pine-scented wind that swept down from the mountains. There was never a morning that she did not gaze mountainward, trying to see, with a folly she realized, if the snow had melted more perceptibly away on the bold white ridge. For all she could see it had not melted an inch, and she would not confess why she sighed. The desert had become green and fresh, stretching away there far below her range, growing dark and purple in the distance with vague buttes rising. The air was full of sound - notes of blackbirds and the baas of sheep, and blasts from the corrals, and the clatter of light hoofs on the court below.

Bo was riding in from the stables. Helen loved to watch her on one of those fiery little mustangs, but the sight was likewise given to rousing apprehensions. This morning Bo appeared particularly bent on frightening Helen. Down the lane Carmichael appeared, waving his arms, and Helen at once connected him with Bo's manifest desire to fly away from that particular place. Since that day, a month back, when Bo had confessed her love for Carmichael, she and Helen had not spoken of it or of the cowboy. The boy and girl were still at odds. But this did not worry Helen. Bo had changed much for the better, especially in that she devoted herself to Helen and to her work. Helen knew that all would turn out well in the end, and so she had been careful of her rather precarious position between these two young fire-brands.

Bo reined in the mustang at the porch steps. She wore a buckskin riding-suit which she had made herself, and its soft gray with the touches of red beads was mightily becoming to her. Then she had grown considerably during the winter and now looked too flashing and pretty to resemble a boy, yet singularly healthy and strong and lithe. Red spots shone in her cheeks and her eyes held that ever-dangerous blaze.

"Nell, did you give me away to that cowboy?" she demanded.

"Give you away!" exclaimed Helen, blankly.

"Yes. You know I told you - awhile back - that I was wildly in love with him. Did you give me away - tell on me? "

She might have been furious, but she certainly was not confused.

"Why, Bo! How could you? No. I did not," replied Helen.

"Never gave him a hint?"

"Not even a hint. You have my word for that. Why? What's happened?"

"He makes me sick."

Bo would not say any more, owing to the near approach of the cowboy.

"Mawnin', Miss Nell," he drawled. "I was just tellin' this here Miss Bo-Peep Rayner -"

"Don't call me that!" broke in Bo, with fire in her voice.

"Wal, I was just tellin' her thet she wasn't goin' off on any more of them long rides. Honest now, Miss Nell, it ain't safe, an' -"

"You're not my boss," retorted Bo.

"Indeed, sister, I agree with him. You won't obey me."

"Reckon some one's got to be your boss," drawled Carmichael. "Shore I ain't hankerin' for the job. You could ride to Kingdom Come or off among the Apaches - or over here a ways" - at this he grinned knowingly - "or anywheres, for all I cared. But I'm workin' for Miss Nell, an' she's boss. An' if she says you're not to take them rides - you won't. Savvy that, miss?"

It was a treat for Helen to see Bo look at the cowboy.

"Mis-ter Carmichael, may I ask how you are going to prevent me from riding where I like?"

"Wal, if you're goin' worse locoed this way I'll keep you off'n a hoss if I have to rope you an' tie you up. By golly, I will!"

His dry humor was gone and manifestly he meant what he said.

"Wal," she drawled it very softly and sweetly, but venomously, "if - you - ever - touch - me again!"

At this he flushed, then made a quick, passionate

gesture with his hand, expressive of heat and shame.

"You an' me will never get along," he said, with a dignity full of pathos. "I seen thet a month back when you changed sudden-like to me. But nothin' I say to you has any reckonin' of mine. I'm talkin' for your sister. It's for her sake. An' your own.. . . I never told her an' I never told you thet I've seen Riggs sneakin' after you twice on them desert rides. Wal, I tell you now."

The intelligence apparently had not the slightest effect on Bo. But Helen was astonished and alarmed.

"Riggs! Oh, Bo, I've seen him myself - riding around. He does not mean well. You must be careful."

"If I ketch him again," went on Carmichael, with his mouth lining hard, "I'm goin' after him."

He gave her a cool, intent, piercing look, then he dropped his head and turned away, to stride back toward the corrals.

Helen could make little of the manner in which her sister watched the cowboy pass out of sight.

"A month back - when I changed sudden-like," mused Bo. "I wonder what he meant by that. . . . Nell, did I change - right after the talk you had with me - about him?"

"Indeed you did, Bo," replied Helen. "But it was for the better. Only he can't see it. How proud and sensitive he is! You wouldn't guess it at first. Bo, your reserve has wounded him more than your flirting. He thinks it's indifference."

"Maybe that 'll be good for him," declared Bo. "Does he expect me to fall on his neck? He's that thick-headed! Why, he's the locoed one, not me."

"I'd like to ask you, Bo, if you've seen how he has changed?" queried Helen, earnestly. "He's older. He's worried. Either his heart is breaking for you or else he fears trouble for us. I fear it's both. How he watches you! Bo, he knows all you do - where you go. That about Riggs sickens me."

"If Riggs follows me and tries any of his four-flush desperado games he'll have his hands full," said Bo, grimly. "And that without my cowboy protector! But I just wish Riggs would do something. Then we'll see what Las Vegas Tom Carmichael cares. Then we'll see!"

Bo bit out the last words passionately and jealously, then she lifted her bridle to the spirited mustang,

"Nell, don't you fear for me," she said. "I can take care of myself."

Helen watched her ride away, all but willing to confess that there might be truth in what Bo said. Then Helen went about her work, which consisted of routine duties as well as an earnest study to familiarize herself with continually new and complex conditions of ranch life. Every day brought new problems. She made notes of all that she observed, and all that was told her, which habit she had found, after a few weeks of trial, was going to be exceedingly valuable to her. She did not intend always to be dependent upon the knowledge of hired men, however faithful some of them might be.

This morning on her rounds she had expected developments; of some kind, owing to the presence of Roy Beeman and two of his brothers, who had arrived yesterday. And she was to discover that Jeff Mulvey, accompanied by six of his co-workers and associates, had deserted her without a word or even sending for their pay. Carmichael had predicted this. Helen had half doubted. It was a relief now to be confronted with facts, however disturbing. She had fortified herself to withstand a great deal more trouble than had happened. At the gateway of the main corral, a huge inclosure fenced high with peeled logs, she met Roy Beeman, lasso in hand, the same tall, lean, limping figure she remembered so well. Sight of him gave her an inexplicable thrill - a flashing memory of an unforgettable night ride. Roy was to have charge of the horses on the ranch, of which there were several hundred, not counting many lost on range and mountain, or the unbranded colts.

Roy took off his sombrero and greeted her. This Mormon had a courtesy for women that spoke well for him. Helen wished she had more employees like him.

"It's jest as Las Vegas told us it 'd be," he said, regretfully. "Mulvey an' his pards lit out this mornin'. I'm sorry, Miss Helen. Reckon thet's all because I come over."

"I heard the news," replied Helen. "You needn't be sorry, Roy, for I'm not. I'm glad. I want to know whom I can trust."

"Las Vegas says we're shore in for it now."

"Roy, what do you think?"

"I reckon so. Still, Las Vegas is powerful cross these days an' always lookin' on the dark side. With us boys, now, it's sufficient unto the day is the evil thereof. But, Miss Helen, if Beasley forces the deal there will be serious trouble. I've seen thet happen. Four or five years ago Beasley rode some greasers off their farms an' no one ever knowed if he had a just claim."

"Beasley has no claim on my property. My uncle solemnly swore that on his death-bed. And I find nothing in his books or papers of those years when he employed Beasley. In fact, Beasley was never uncle's partner. The truth is that my uncle took Beasley up when he was a poor, homeless boy."

"So my old dad says," replied Roy. "But what's right don't always prevail in these parts."

"Roy, you're the keenest man I've met since I came West. Tell me what you think will happen."

Beeman appeared flattered, but be hesitated to reply. Helen had long been aware of the reticence of these outdoor men.

"I reckon you mean cause an' effect, as Milt Dale would say," responded Roy, thoughtfully.

"Yes. If Beasley attempts to force me off my ranch what will happen?"

Roy looked up and met her gaze. Helen remembered

that singular stillness, intentness of his face.

"Wal, if Dale an' John get here in time I reckon we can bluff thet Beasley outfit."

"You mean my friends - my men would confront Beasley - refuse his demands - and if necessary fight him off?"

"I shore do," replied Roy.

"But suppose you're not all here? Beasley would be smart enough to choose an opportune time. Suppose he did put me off and take possession? What then?"

"Then it 'd only be a matter of how soon Dale or Carmichael - or I - got to Beasley."

"Roy! I feared just that. It haunts me. Carmichael asked me to let him go pick a fight with Beasley. Asked me, just as he would ask me about his work! I was shocked. And now you say Dale - and you -"

Helen choked in her agitation.

"Miss Helen, what else could you look for? Las Vegas is in love with Miss Bo. Shore he told me so. An' Dale's in love with you! . . . Why, you couldn't stop them any more 'n you could stop the wind from blowin' down a pine, when it got ready. . . .Now, it's some different with me. I'm a Mormon an' I'm married. But I'm Dale's pard, these many years. An' I care a powerful sight for you an' Miss Bo. So I reckon I'd draw on Beasley the first chance I got."

Helen strove for utterance, but it was denied her. Roy's

simple statement of Dale's love had magnified her emotion by completely changing its direction. She forgot what she had felt wretched about. She could not look at Roy.

"Miss Helen, don't feel bad," he said, kindly. "Shore you're not to blame. Your comin' West hasn't made any difference in Beasley's fate, except mebbe to hurry it a little. My dad is old, an' when he talks it's like history. He looks back on happenin's. Wal, it's the nature of happenin's that Beasley passes away before his prime. Them of his breed don't live old in the West. . . .So I reckon you needn't feel bad or worry. you've got friends."

Helen incoherently thanked him, and, forgetting her usual round of corrals and stables, she hurried back toward the house, deeply stirred, throbbing and dim-eyed, with a feeling she could not control. Roy Beeman had made a statement that had upset her equilibrium. It seemed simple and natural, yet momentous and staggering. To hear that Dale loved her - to hear it spoken frankly, earnestly, by Dale's best friend, was strange, sweet, terrifying. But was it true? Her own consciousness had admitted it. Yet that was vastly different from a man's open statement. No longer was it a dear dream, a secret that seemed hers alone. How she had lived on that secret hidden deep in her breast!

Something burned the dimness from her eyes as she looked toward the mountains and her sight became clear, telescopic with its intensity. Magnificently the mountains loomed. Black inroads and patches on the slopes showed where a few days back all bad been white. The snow was melting fast. Dale would soon be free to ride down to Pine. And that was an event Helen prayed for, yet feared as she had never feared anything.

The noonday dinner-bell startled Helen from a reverie that was a pleasant aftermath of her unrestraint. How the hours had flown! This morning at least must be credited to indolence.

Bo was not in the dining-room, nor in her own room, nor was she in sight from window or door. This absence had occurred before, but not particularly to disturb Helen. In this instance, however, she grew worried. Her nerves presaged strain. There was an overcharge of sensibility in her feelings or a strange pressure in the very atmosphere. She ate dinner alone, looking her apprehension, which was not mitigated by the expressive fears of old Maria, the Mexican woman who served her.

After dinner she sent word to Roy and Carmichael that they had better ride out to look for Bo. Then Helen applied herself resolutely to her books until a rapid clatter of hoofs out in the court caused her to jump up and hurry to the porch. Roy was riding in.

"Did you find her?" queried Helen, hurriedly.

"Wasn't no track or sign of her up the north range," replied Roy, as he dismounted and threw his bridle. "An' I was ridin' back to take up her tracks from the corral an' trail her. But I seen Las Vegas comin' an' he waved his sombrero. He was comin' up from the south. There he is now."

Carmichael appeared swinging into the lane. He was mounted on Helen's big black Ranger, and he made the dust fly.

"Wal, he's seen her, thet's shore," vouchsafed Roy, with relief, as Carmichael rode up.

"Miss Neil, she's comin'," said the cowboy, as he reined in and slid down with his graceful single motion. Then in a violent action, characteristic of him, he slammed his sombrero down on the porch and threw up both arms. "I've a hunch it's come off!"

"Oh, what?" exclaimed Helen.

"Now, Las Vegas, talk sense," expostulated Roy. "Miss Helen is shore nervous to-day. Has anythin' happened?"

"I reckon, but I don't know what," replied Carmichael, drawing a, long breath. "Folks, I must be gettin' old. For I shore felt orful queer till I seen Bo. She was ridin' down the ridge across the valley. Ridin' some fast, too, an' she'll be here right off, if she doesn't stop in the village."

"Wal, I hear her comin' now," said Roy. "An' - if you asked me I'd say she was ridin' some fast."

Helen heard the light, swift, rhythmic beat of hoofs, and then out on the curve of the road that led down to Pine she saw Bo's mustang, white with lather, coming on a dead run.

"Las Vegas, do you see any Apaches?" asked Roy, quizzingly.

The cowboy made no reply, but he strode out from the porch, directly in front of the mustang. Bo was pulling hard on the bridle, and had him slowing down, but not controlled. When he reached the house it could easily be seen that Bo had pulled him to the limit of her strength, which was not enough to halt him. Carmichael lunged for the bridle and, seizing it, hauled him to a standstill.

At close sight of Bo Helen uttered a startled cry. Bo was white; her sombrero was gone and her hair undone; there were blood and dirt on her face, and her riding-suit was torn and muddy. She had evidently sustained a fall. Roy gazed at her in admiring consternation, but Carmichael never looked at her at all. Apparently he was examining the horse. "Well, help me off - somebody," cried Bo, peremptorily. Her voice was weak, but not her spirit.

Roy sprang to help her off, and when she was down it developed that she was lame.

"Oh, Bo! You've had a tumble," exclaimed Helen, anxiously, and she ran to assist Roy. They led her up the porch and to the door. There she turned to look at Carmichael, who was still examining the spent mustang.

"Tell him - to come in," she whispered.

"Hey, there, Las Vegas!" called Roy. "Rustle hyar, will you?"

When Bo had been led into the sitting-room and seated in a chair Carmichael entered. His face was a study, as slowly he walked up to Bo.

"Girl, you - ain't hurt?" he asked, huskily.

"It's no fault of yours that I'm not crippled - or dead or worse," retorted Bo. "You said the south range was the only safe ride for me. And there - I - it happened."

She panted a little and her bosom heaved. One of her gauntlets was gone, and the bare band, that was bruised and bloody, trembled as she held it out.

"Dear, tell us - are you badly hurt?" queried Helen, with hurried gentleness.

"Not much. I've had a spill," replied Bo. "But oh! I'm mad - I'm boiling!"

She looked as if she might have exaggerated her doubt of injuries, but certainly she had not overestimated her state of mind. Any blaze Helen had heretofore seen in those quick eyes was tame compared to this one. It actually leaped. Bo was more than pretty then. Manifestly Roy was admiring her looks, but Carmichael saw beyond her charm. And slowly he was growing pale.

"I rode out the south range - as I was told," began Bo, breathing hard and trying to control her feelings. "That's the ride you usually take, Nell, and you bet - if you'd taken it to-day - you'd not be here now. . . . About three miles out I climbed off the range up that cedar slope. I always keep to high ground. When I got up I saw two horsemen ride out of some broken rocks off to the east. They rode as if to come between me and home. I didn't like that. I circled south. About a mile farther on I spied another horseman and he showed up directly in front of me and came along slow. That I liked still less. It might have been accident, but it looked to me as if those riders had some intent. All I could do was head off to the southeast and ride. You bet I did ride. But I got into rough ground where I'd never been before. It was slow going. At last I made the cedars and here I cut loose, believing I could circle ahead of those strange riders and come round through Pine. I had it wrong."

Here she hesitated, perhaps for breath, for she had spoken rapidly, or perhaps to get better hold on her subject. Not improbably the effect she was creating on her listeners began to be significant. Roy sat absorbed, perfectly motionless, eyes keen as steel, his mouth open. Carmichael was gazing over Bo's head, out of the window, and it seemed that he must know the rest of her narrative. Helen knew that her own wide-eyed attention alone would have been all-compelling inspiration to Bo Rayner.

"Sure I had it wrong," resumed Bo. "Pretty soon heard a horse behind. I looked back. I saw a big bay riding down on me. Oh, but he was running! He just tore through the cedars. . . . I was scared half out of my senses. But I spurred and beat my mustang. Then began a race! Rough going - thick cedars - washes and gullies I had to make him run - to keep my saddle - to pick my way. Oh-h-h! but it was glorious! To race for fun - that's one thing; to race for your life is another! My heart was in my mouth - choking me. I couldn't have yelled. I was as cold as ice - dizzy sometimes - blind others - then my stomach turned - and I couldn't get my breath. Yet the wild thrills I had! . . . But I stuck on and held my own for several miles - to the edge of the cedars. There the big horse gained on me. He came pounding closer - perhaps as close as a hundred yards - I could hear him plain enough. Then I had my spill. Oh, my mustang tripped - threw me 'way over his head. I hit light, but slid far - and that's what scraped me so. I know my knee is raw. . . . When I got to my feet the big horse dashed up, throwing gravel all over me - and his rider jumped off. . . . Now who do you think he was?"

Helen knew, but she did not voice her conviction. Carmichael knew positively, yet he kept silent. Roy was smiling, as if the narrative told did not seem so alarming to him.

"Wal, the fact of you bein' here, safe an' sound, sorta makes no difference who thet son-of-a-gun was," he said.

"Riggs! Harve Riggs!" blazed Bo. "The instant I recognized him I got over my scare. And so mad I burned all through like fire. I don't know what I said, but it was wild - and it was a whole lot, you bet.

"You sure can ride,' he said.

"I demanded why he had dared to chase me, and he said he had an important message for Nell. This was it: 'Tell your sister that Beasley means to put her off an' take the ranch. If she'll marry me I'll block his deal. If she won't marry me, I'll go in with Beasley.' Then he told me to hurry home and not to breathe a word to any one except Nell. Well, here I am - and I seem to have been breathing rather fast."

She looked from Helen to Roy and from Roy to Las Vegas. Her smile was for the latter, and to any one not overexcited by her story that smile would have told volumes.

"Wal, I'll be doggoned!" ejaculated Roy, feelingly.

Helen laughed.

"Indeed, the working of that man's mind is beyond me. . . . Marry him to save my ranch? I wouldn't marry him to save my life!

Carmichael suddenly broke his silence.

"Bo, did you see the other men?"

"Yes. I was coming to that," she replied. "I caught a glimpse of them back in the cedars. The three were together, or, at least, three horsemen were there. They had halted behind some trees. Then on the way home I began to think. Even in my fury I had received impressions. Riggs was surprised when I got up. I'll bet he had not expected me to be who I was. He thought I was Nell! . . . I look bigger in this buckskin outfit. My hair was up till I lost my hat, and that was when I had the tumble. He took me for Nell. Another thing, I remember - he made some sign - some motion while I was calling him names, and I believe that was to keep those other men back. . . . I believe Riggs had a plan with those other men to waylay Nell and make off with her. I absolutely know it."

"Bo, you're so - so - you jump at wild ideas so," protested Helen, trying to believe in her own assurance. But inwardly she was trembling.

"Miss Helen, that ain't a wild idee," said Roy, seriously. "I reckon your sister is pretty close on the trail. Las Vegas, don't you savvy it thet way?"

Carmichael's answer was to stalk out of the room.

"Call him back!" cried Helen, apprehensively.

"Hold on, boy!" called Roy, sharply.

Helen reached the door simultaneously with Roy. The cowboy picked up his sombrero, jammed it on his head, gave his belt a vicious hitch that made the gun-sheath jump, and then in one giant step he was astride Ranger.

"Carmichael! Stay!" cried Helen.

The cowboy spurred the black, and the stones rang under iron-shod hoofs.

"Bo! Call him back! Please call him back!" importuned Helen, in distress.

"I won't," declared Bo Rayner. Her face shone whiter now and her eyes were like fiery flint. That was her answer to a loving, gentle-hearted sister; that was her answer to the call of the West.

"No use," said Roy, quietly. "An' I reckon I'd better trail him up."

He, too, strode out and, mounting his horse, galloped swiftly away.

It turned out that Bo, was more bruised and scraped and shaken than she had imagined. One knee was rather badly cut, which injury alone would have kept her from riding again very soon. Helen, who was somewhat skilled at bandaging wounds, worried a great deal over these sundry blotches on Bo's fair skin, and it took considerable time to wash and dress them. Long after this was done, and during the early supper, and afterward, Bo's excitement remained unabated. The whiteness stayed on her face and the blaze in her eyes. Helen ordered and begged her to go to bed, for the fact was Bo could not stand up and her hands shook.

"Go to bed? Not much," she said. "I want to know what he does to Riggs."

It was that possibility which had Helen in dreadful suspense. If Carmichael killed Riggs, it seemed to Helen that the bottom would drop out of this structure of Western life she had begun to build so earnestly and fearfully. She did not believe that he would do so. But the uncertainty was torturing.

"Dear Bo," appealed Helen, "you don't want - Oh! you do want Carmichael to - to kill Riggs?"

"No, I don't, but I wouldn't care if he did," replied Bo, bluntly.

"Do you think - he will?"

"Nell, if that cowboy really loves me he read my mind right here before he left," declared Bo. "And he knew what I thought he'd do."

"And what's - that?" faltered Helen.

"I want him to round Riggs up down in the village - somewhere in a crowd. I want Riggs shown up as the coward, braggart, four-flush that he is. And insulted, slapped, kicked - driven out of Pine!"

Her passionate speech still rang throughout the room when there came footsteps on the porch. Helen hurried to raise the bar from the door and open it just as a tap sounded on the door-post. Roy's face stood white out of the darkness. His eyes were bright. And his smile made Helen's fearful query needless.

"How are you-all this evenin'?" he drawled, as he came in.

A fire blazed on the hearth and a lamp burned on the table. By their light Bo looked white and eager-eyed as she reclined in the big arm-chair.

"What 'd he do?" she asked, with all her amazing force.

"Wal, now, ain't you goin' to tell me how you are?"

"Roy, I'm all bunged up. I ought to be in bed, but I just couldn't sleep till I hear what Las Vegas did. I'd forgive anything except him getting drunk."

"Wal, I shore can ease your mind on thet," replied Roy. "He never drank a drop."

Roy was distractingly slow about beginning the tale any child could have guessed he was eager to tell. For once the hard, intent quietness, the soul of labor, pain, and endurance so plain in his face was softened by pleasurable emotion. He poked at the burning logs with the toe of his boot. Helen observed that he had changed his boots and now wore no spurs. Then he had gone to his quarters after whatever had happened down in Pine.

"Where is he?" asked Bo.

"Who? Riggs? Wal, I don't know. But I reckon he's somewhere out in the woods nursin' himself."

"Not Riggs. First tell me where he is."

"Shore, then, you must mean Las Vegas. I just left him down at the cabin. He was gettin' ready for bed, early as it is. All tired out he was an' thet white you wouldn't have knowed him. But he looked happy at thet, an' the last words he said, more to himself than to me, I reckon, was, 'I'm some locoed gent, but if she doesn't call me Tom now she's no good!'"

Bo actually clapped her hands, notwithstanding that one of them was bandaged.

"Call him Tom? I should smile I will," she declared, in delight. "Hurry now - what 'd -"

"It's shore powerful strange how he hates thet handle Las Vegas," went on Roy, imperturbably.

"Roy, tell me what he did - what Tom did - or I'll scream," cried Bo.

"Miss Helen, did you ever see the likes of thet girl?" asked Roy, appealing to Helen.

"No, Roy, I never did," agreed Helen. "But please - please tell us what has happened."

Roy grinned and rubbed his hands together in a dark delight, almost fiendish in its sudden revelation of a gulf of strange emotion deep within him. Whatever had happened to Riggs had not been too much for Roy Beeman. Helen remembered hearing her uncle say that a real Westerner hated nothing so hard as the swaggering desperado, the make-believe gunman who pretended to sail under the true, wild, and reckoning colors of the West.

Roy leaned his lithe, tall form against the stone mantelpiece and faced the girls.

"When I rode out after Las Vegas I seen him 'way down the road," began Roy, rapidly. "An' I seen another man ridin' down into Pine from the other side. Thet was Riggs, only I didn't know it then. Las Vegas rode up to the store, where some fellars was hangin' round, an' he spoke to them. When I come up they was all headin' for Turner's saloon. I seen a dozen hosses hitched to the rails. Las Vegas rode on. But I got off at Turner's an' went in with the bunch. Whatever it was Las Vegas said to them fellars, shore they didn't give him away. Pretty soon more men strolled into Turner's an' there got to be 'most twenty altogether, I reckon. Jeff Mulvey was there with his pards. They had been drinkin' sorta free. An' I didn't like the way Mulvey watched me. So I went out an' into the store, but kept a-lookin' for Las Vegas. He wasn't in sight. But I seen Riggs ridin' up. Now, Turner's is where Riggs hangs out an' does his braggin'. He looked powerful deep an' thoughtful, dismounted slow without seein' the unusual number of hosses there, an' then he slouches into Turner's. No more 'n a minute after Las Vegas rode down there like a streak. An' just as quick he was off an' through thet door."

Roy paused as if to gain force or to choose his words. His tale now appeared all directed to Bo, who gazed at him, spellbound, a fascinated listener.

"Before I got to Turner's door - an' thet was only a little ways - I heard Las Vegas yell. Did you ever hear him? Wal, he's got the wildest yell of any cow-puncher I ever beard. Quicklike I opened the door an' slipped in. There was Riggs an' Las Vegas alone in the center of the big saloon, with the crowd edgin' to the walls an' slidin' back of the bar. Riggs was whiter 'n a dead man. I didn't hear an' I don't know what Las Vegas yelled at him. But Riggs knew an' so did the gang. All of a sudden every man there shore seen in Las Vegas what Riggs had always bragged he was. Thet time comes to every man like Riggs.

"'What 'd you call me?' he asked, his jaw shakin'.

"'I 'ain't called you yet,' answered Las Vegas. 'I just whooped.'

"'What d'ye want?'

"'You scared my girl.'

"'The hell ye say! Who's she?' blustered Riggs, an' he began to take quick looks 'round. But he never moved a hand. There was somethin' tight about the way he stood. Las Vegas had both arms half out, stretched as if he meant to leap. But he wasn't. I never seen Las Vegas do thet, but when I seen him then I understood it.

"'You know. An' you threatened her an' her sister. Go for your gun,' called Las Vegas, low an' sharp.

"Thet put the crowd right an' nobody moved. Riggs

turned green then. I almost felt sorry for him. He began to shake so he'd dropped a gun if he had pulled one.

"'Hyar, you're off - some mistake - I 'ain't seen no gurls - I -'

"'Shut up an' draw!' yelled Las Vegas. His voice just pierced holes in the roof, an' it might have been a bullet from the way Riggs collapsed. Every man seen in a second more thet Riggs wouldn't an' couldn't draw. He was afraid for his life. He was not what he had claimed to be. I don't know if he had any friends there. But in the West good men an' bad men, all alike, have no use for Riggs's kind. An' thet stony quiet broke with haw - haw. It shore was as pitiful to see Riggs as it was fine to see Las Vegas.

"When he dropped his arms then I knowed there would be no gun-play. An' then Las Vegas got red in the face. He slapped Riggs with one hand, then with the other. An' he began to cuss him. I shore never knowed thet nice-spoken Las Vegas Carmichael could use such language. It was a stream of the baddest names known out here, an' lots I never heard of. Now an' then I caught somethin' like low-down an' sneak an' four-flush an' long-haired skunk, but for the most part they was just the cussedest kind of names. An' Las Vegas spouted them till he was black in the face, an' foamin' at the mouth, an' hoarser 'n a bawlin' cow.

"When he got out of breath from cussin' he punched Riggs all about the saloon, threw him outdoors, knocked him down an' kicked him till he got kickin' him down the road with the whole haw-hawed gang behind. An' he drove him out of town!"

CHAPTER XVIII

For two days Bo was confined to her bed, suffering considerable pain, and subject to fever, during which she talked irrationally. Some of this talk afforded Helen as vast an amusement as she was certain it would have lifted Tom Carmichael to a seventh heaven.

The third day, however, Bo was better, and, refusing to remain in bed, she hobbled to the sitting-room, where she divided her time between staring out of the window toward the corrals and pestering Helen with questions she tried to make appear casual. But Helen saw through her case and was in a state of glee. What she hoped most for was that Carmichael would suddenly develop a little less inclination for Bo. It was that kind of treatment the young lady needed. And now was the great opportunity. Helen almost felt tempted to give the cowboy a hint.

Neither this day, nor the next, however, did he put in an appearance at the house, though Helen saw him twice on her rounds. He was busy, as usual, and greeted her as if nothing particular had happened.

Roy called twice, once in the afternoon, and again during the evening. He grew more likable upon longer acquaintance. This last visit he rendered Bo speechless by teasing her about another girl Carmichael was going to take to a dance. Bo's face showed that her vanity could not believe this statement, but that her intelligence of young men credited it with being possible. Roy evidently was as penetrating as he was kind. He made a dry, casual little remark about the snow never melting on the mountains during the latter part of March; and the look with which be accompanied this remark brought a blush to Helen's cheek.

After Roy had departed Bo said to Helen: "Confound that fellow! He sees right through me."

"My dear, you're rather transparent these days," murmured Helen.

"You needn't talk. He gave you a dig," retorted Bo. "He just knows you're dying to see the snow melt."

"Gracious! I hope I'm not so bad as that. Of course I want the snow melted and spring to come, and flowers -"

"Hal Ha! Ha!" taunted Bo. "Nell Rayner, do you see any green in my eyes? Spring to come! Yes, the poet said in the spring a young man's fancy lightly turns to thoughts of love. But that poet meant a young woman."

Helen gazed out of the window at the white stars.

"Nell, have you seen him - since I was hurt?" continued Bo, with an effort.

"Him? Who?"

"Oh, whom do you suppose? I mean Tom!" she responded, and the last word came with a burst.

"Tom? Who's he? Ah, you mean Las Vegas. Yes, I've seen him."

"Well, did he ask a-about me?"

"I believe he did ask how you were - something like that."

"Humph! Nell, I don't always trust you." After that she relapsed into silence, read awhile, and dreamed awhile, looking into the fire, and then she limped over to kiss Helen good night and left the room.

Next day she was rather quiet, seeming upon the verge of one of the dispirited spells she got infrequently. Early in the evening, just after the lights had been lit and she had joined Helen in the sitting-room, a familiar step sounded on the loose boards of the porch.

Helen went to the door to admit Carmichael. He was clean-shaven, dressed in his dark suit, which presented such marked contrast from his riding-garb, and he wore a flower in his buttonhole. Nevertheless, despite all this style, he seemed more than usually the cool, easy, careless cowboy.

"Evenin', Miss Helen," he said, as he stalked in. "Evenin', Miss Bo. How are you-all?"

Helen returned his greeting with a welcoming smile.

"Good evening - Tom," said Bo, demurely.

That assuredly was the first time she had ever called him Tom. As she spoke she looked distractingly pretty and tantalizing. But if she had calculated to floor Carmichael with the initial, half-promising, wholly mocking use of his name she had reckoned without cause. The cowboy received that greeting as if he had heard her use it a thousand times or had not heard it at all. Helen decided if he was acting a part he was certainly a clever actor. He puzzled her somewhat, but she liked his look, and his easy manner, and the something about him that must have been his unconscious sense of pride. He had gone far enough, perhaps too far, in his overtures to Bo.

"How are you feelin'?" be asked.

"I'm better to-day," she replied, with downcast eyes. "But I'm lame yet."

"Reckon that bronc piled you up. Miss Helen said there shore wasn't any joke about the cut on your knee. Now, a fellar's knee is a bad place to hurt, if he has to keep on ridin'."

"Oh, I'll be well soon. How's Sam? I hope he wasn't crippled."

"Thet Sam - why, he's so tough he never knowed he had a fall."

"Tom - I - I want to thank you for giving Riggs what he deserved."

She spoke it earnestly, eloquently, and for once she had no sly little intonation or pert allurement, such as was her wont to use on this infatuated young man.

"Aw, you heard about that," replied Carmichael, with a wave of his hand to make light of it. "Nothin' much. It had to be done. An' shore I was afraid of Roy. He'd been bad. An' so would any of the other boys. I'm sorta lookin' out for all of them, you know, actin' as Miss Helen's foreman now."

Helen was unutterably tickled. The effect of his speech upon Bo was stupendous. He had disarmed her. He had, with the finesse and tact and suavity of a diplomat, removed himself from obligation, and the detachment of self, the casual thing be apparently made out of his magnificent championship, was bewildering and humiliating to Bo. She sat silent for a moment or two while Helen tried to fit easily into the conversation. It was not likely that Bo would long be at a loss for words, and also it was immensely probable that with a flash of her wonderful spirit she would turn the tables on her perverse lover in a twinkling. Anyway, plain it was that a lesson had sunk deep. She looked startled, hurt, wistful, and finally sweetly defiant.

"But - you told Riggs I was your girl!" Thus Bo unmasked her battery. And Helen could not imagine how Carmichael would ever resist that and the soft, arch glance which accompanied it.

Helen did not yet know the cowboy, any more than did Bo.

"Shore. I had to say thet. I had to make it strong before thet gang. I reckon it was presumin' of me, an' I shore apologize."

Bo stared at him, and then, giving a little gasp, she drooped.

"Wal, I just run in to say howdy an' to inquire after you-all," said Carmichael. "I'm goin' to the dance, an' as Flo lives out of town a ways I'd shore better rustle . . . . Good night, Miss Bo; I hope you'll be ridin' Sam soon. An' good night, Miss Helen."

Bo roused to a very friendly and laconic little speech, much overdone. Carmichael strode out, and Helen, bidding him good-by, closed the door after him.

The instant he had departed Bo's transformation was tragic.

"Flo! He meant Flo Stubbs - that ugly, cross-eyed, bold, little frump!"

"Bo!" expostulated Helen. "The young lady is not beautiful, I grant, but she's very nice and pleasant. I liked her."

"Nell Rayner, men are no good! And cowboys are the worst!" declared Bo, terribly.

"Why didn't you appreciate Tom when you had him?" asked Helen.

Bo had been growing furious, but now the allusion, in past tense, to the conquest she had suddenly and amazingly found dear quite broke her spirit. It was a very pale, unsteady, and miserable girl who avoided Helen's gaze and left the room.

Next day Bo was not approachable from any direction.

Helen found her a victim to a multiplicity of moods, ranging from woe to dire, dark broodings, from them to' wistfulness, and at last to a pride that sustained her.

Late in the afternoon, at Helen's lcisure hour, when she and Bo were in the sitting-room, horses tramped into the court and footsteps mounted the porch. Opening to a loud knock, Helen was surprised to see Beasley. And out in the court were several mounted horsemen. Helen's heart sank. This visit, indeed, had been fore-shadowed.

"Afternoon, Miss Rayner," said Beasley, doffing his sombrero. "I've called on a little business deal. Will you see me?"

Helen acknowledged his greeting while she thought rapidly. She might just as well see him and have that inevitable interview done with.

"Come in," she said, and when he had entered she closed the door. "My sister, Mr. Beasley."

"How d' you do, Miss?" said the rancher, in bluff, loud voice.

Bo acknowledged the introduction with a frigid little bow.

At close range Beasley seemed a forceful personality as well as a rather handsome man of perhaps thirty-five, heavy of build, swarthy of skin, and sloe-black of eye, like that of the Mexicans whose blood was reported to be in him. He looked crafty, confident, and self-centered. If Helen had never heard of him before that visit she would have distrusted him.

"I'd called sooner, but I was waitin' for old José, the Mexican who herded for me when I was pardner to your uncle," said Beasley, and he sat down to put his huge gloved hands on his knees.

"Yes?" queried Helen, interrogatively.

"José rustled over from Magdalena, an' now I can back up my claim. . . . Miss Rayner, this hyar ranch ought to be mine an' is mine. It wasn't so big or so well stocked when Al Auchincloss beat me out of it. I reckon I'll allow for thet. I've papers, an' old José for witness. An' I calculate you'll pay me eighty thousand dollars, or else I'll take over the ranch."

Beasley spoke in an ordinary, matter-of-fact tone that certainly seemed sincere, and his manner was blunt, but perfectly natural.

"Mr. Beasley, your claim is no news to me," responded Helen, quietly. "I've heard about it. And I questioned my uncle. He swore on his death-bed that he did not owe you a dollar. Indeed, he claimed the indebtedness was yours to him. I could find nothing in his papers, so I must repudiate your claim. I will not take it seriously."

"Miss Rayner, I can't blame you for takin' Al's word against mine," said Beasley. "An' your stand is natural. But you're a stranger here an' you know nothin' of stock deals in these ranges. It ain't fair to speak bad of the dead, but the truth is thet Al Auchincloss got his start by stealin' sheep an' unbranded cattle. Thet was the start of every rancher I know. It was mine. An' we none of us ever thought of it as rustlin'."

Helen could only stare her surprise and doubt at this statement.

"Talk's cheap anywhere, an' in the West talk ain't much at all," continued Beasley. "I'm no talker. I jest want to tell my case an' make a deal if you'll have it. I can prove more in black an' white, an' with witness, than you can. Thet's my case. The deal I'd make is this. . . . Let's marry an' settle a bad deal thet way."

The man's direct assumption, absolutely without a qualifying consideration for her woman's attitude, was amazing, ignorant, and base; but Helen was so well prepared for it that she hid her disgust.

"Thank you, Mr. Beasley, but I can't accept your offer," she replied.

"Would you take time an' consider?" he asked, spreading wide his huge gloved hands.

"Absolutely no."

Beasley rose to his feet. He showed no disappointment or chagrin, but the bold pleasantness left his face, and, slight as that change was, it stripped him of the only redeeming quality he showed.

"Thet means I'll force you to pay me the eighty thousand or put you off," he said.

"Mr. Beasley, even if I owed you that, how could I raise so enormous a sum? I don't owe it. And I certainly won't be put off my property. You can't put me off."

"An' why can't I' he demanded, with lowering, dark gaze.

"Because your claim is dishonest. And I can prove it," declared Helen, forcibly.

"Who 're you goin' to prove it to - thet I'm dishonest?"

"To my men - to your men - to the people of Pine - to everybody. There's not a person who won't believe me."

He seemed curious, discomfited, surlily annoyed, and yet fascinated by her statement or else by the quality and appearance of her as she spiritedly defended her cause.

"An' how 're you goin' to prove all thet?" he growled.

"Mr. Beasley, do you remember last fall when you met Snake Anson with his gang up in the woods - and hired him to make off with me?" asked Helen, in swift, ringing words.

The dark olive of Beasley's bold face shaded to a dirty white.

"Wha-at?" he jerked out, hoarsely.

"I see you remember. Well, Milt Dale was hidden in the loft of that cabin where you met Anson. He heard every word of your deal with the outlaw."

Beasley swung his arm in sudden violence, so hard that he flung his glove to the floor. As he stooped to snatch it up he uttered a sibilant hiss. Then, stalking to the door, he jerked it open, and slammed it behind him. His loud voice, hoarse with passion, preceded the scrape and crack of hoofs.

Shortly after supper that day, when Helen was just recovering her composure, Carmichael presented himself at the open door. Bo was not there. In the dimming twilight Helen saw that the cowboy was pale, somber, grim.

"Oh, what's happened?" cried Helen.

"Roy's been shot. It come off in Turner's saloon But he ain't dead. We packed him over to Widow Cass's. An' he said for me to tell you he'd pull through."

"Shot! Pull through!" repeated Helen, in slow, unrealizing exclamation. She was conscious of a deep internal tumult and a cold checking of blood in all her external body.

"Yes, shot," replied Carmichael, fiercely.

"An', whatever he says, I reckon he won't pull through."

"0 Heaven, how terrible!" burst out Helen. "He was so good - such a man! What a pity! Oh, he must have met that in my behalf. Tell me, what happened? Who shot him?"

"Wal, I don't know. An' thet's what's made me hoppin' mad. I wasn't there when it come off. An' he won't tell me."

"Why not?"

"I don't know thet, either. I reckoned first it was because he wanted to get even. But, after thinkin' it over, I guess he doesn't want me lookin' up any one right now for fear I might get hurt. An' you're goin' to need your friends. Thet's all I can make of Roy."

Then Helen hurriedly related the event of Beasley's call on her that afternoon and all that had occurred.

"Wal, the half-breed son-of-a-greaser!" ejaculated Carmichael, in utter confoundment. "He wanted you to marry him!"

"He certainly did. I must say it was a - a rather abrupt proposal."

Carmichael appeared to be laboring with speech that had to be smothered behind his teeth. At last he let out an explosive breath.

"Miss Nell, I've shore felt in my bones thet I'm the boy slated to brand thet big bull."

"Oh, he must have shot Roy. He left here in a rage."

"I reckon you can coax it out of Roy. Fact is, all I could learn was thet Roy come in the saloon alone. Beasley was there, an' Riggs -"

"Riggs!" interrupted Helen.

"Shore, Riggs. He come back again. But he'd better keep out of my way. . . . An' Jeff Mulvey with his outfit. Turner told me he heard an argument an' then a shot. The gang cleared out, leavin' Roy on the floor. I come in a little later. Roy was still layin' there. Nobody

Zane Grey

was doin' anythin' for him. An' nobody had. I hold that against Turner. Wal, I got help an' packed Roy over to Widow Cass's. Roy seemed all right. But he was too bright an' talky to suit me. The bullet hit his lung, thet's shore. An' he lost a sight of blood before we stopped it. Thet skunk Turner might have lent a hand. An' if Roy croaks I reckon I'll -"

"Tom, why must you always be reckoning to kill somebody?" demanded Helen, angrily.

"'Cause somebody's got to be killed 'round here. Thet's why!" he snapped back.

"Even so - should you risk leaving Bo and me without a friend?" asked Helen, reproachfully.

At that Carmichael wavered and lost something of his sullen deadliness.

"Aw, Miss Nell, I'm only mad. If you'll just be patient with me - an' mebbe coax me. . . . But I can't see no other way out."

"Let's hope and pray," said Helen, earnestly. "You spoke of my coaxing Roy to tell who shot him. When can I see him?"

"To-morrow, I reckon. I'll come for you. Fetch Bo along with you. We've got to play safe from now on. An' what do you say to me an' Hal sleepin' here at the ranch-house?"

"Indeed I'd feel safer," she replied. "There are rooms. Please come."

"Allright. An' now I'll be goin' to fetch Hal. Shore wish I hadn't made you pale an' scared like this."

About ten o'clock next morning Carmichael drove Helen and Bo into Pine, and tied up the team before Widow Cass's cottage.

The peach- and apple-trees were mingling blossoms of pink and white; a drowsy hum of bees filled the fragrant air; rich, dark-green alfalfa covered the small orchard flat; a wood fire sent up a lazy column of blue smoke; and birds were singing sweetly.

Helen could scarcely believe that amid all this tranquillity a man lay perhaps fatally injured. Assuredly Carmichael had been somber and reticent enough to rouse the gravest fears.

Widow Cass appeared on the little porch, a gray, bent, worn, but cheerful old woman whom Helen had come to know as her friend.

"My land! I'm thet glad to see you, Miss Helen," she said. "An' you've fetched the little lass as I've not got acquainted with yet."

"Good morning, Mrs. Cass. How - how is Roy?" replied Helen, anxiously scanning the wrinkled face.

"Roy? Now don't you look so scared. Roy's 'most ready to git on his hoss an' ride home, if I let him. He knowed you was a-comin'. An' he made me hold a lookin'-glass for him to shave. How's thet fer a man with a bullet-hole through him! You can't kill them Mormons, nohow."

She led them into a little sitting-room, where on a couch underneath a window Roy Beeman lay. He was wide awake and smiling, but haggard. He lay partly covered with a blanket. His gray shirt was open at the neck, disclosing bandages.

"Mornin' - girls," he drawled. "Shore is good of you, now, comin' down."

Helen stood beside him, bent over him, in her earnestness, as she greeted him. She saw a shade of pain in his eyes and his immobility struck her, but he did not seem badly off. Bo was pale, round-eyed, and apparently too agitated to speak. Carmichael placed chairs beside the couch for the girls.

"Wal, what's ailin' you this nice mornin'?" asked Roy, eyes on the cowboy.

"Huh! Would you expect me to be wearin' the smile of 'a fellar goin' to be married?" retorted Carmichael.

"Shore you haven't made up with Bo yet," returned Roy.

Bo blushed rosy red, and the cowboy's face lost something of its somber hue.

"I allow it's none of your d - darn bizness if she ain't made up with me," he said.

"Las Vegas, you're a wonder with a hoss an' a rope, an' I reckon with a gun, but when it comes to girls you shore ain't there."

"I'm no Mormon, by golly! Come, Ma Cass, let's get

out of here, so they can talk."

"Folks, I was jest a-goin' to say thet Roy's got fever an' he oughtn't t' talk too much," said the old woman. Then she and Carmichael went into the kitchen and closed, the door.

Roy looked up at Helen with his keen eyes, more kindly piercing than ever.

"My brother John was here. He'd just left when you come. He rode home to tell my folks I'm not so bad hurt, an' then he's goin' to ride a bee-line into the mountains."

Helen's eyes asked what her lips refused to utter.

"He's goin' after Dale. I sent him. I reckoned we-all sorta needed sight of thet doggone hunter."

Roy had averted his gaze quickly to Bo.

"Don't you agree with me, lass?"

"I sure do," replied Bo, heartily.

All within Helen had been stilled for the moment of her realization; and then came swell and beat of heart, and inconceivable chafing of a tide at its restraint.

"Can John - fetch Dale out - when the snow's so deep?" she asked, unsteadily.

"Shore. He's takin' two hosses up to the snow-line. Then, if necessary, he'll go over the pass on snow-shoes. But I bet him Dale would ride out. Snow's about gone except on the north slopes an' on the peaks."

"Then - when may I - we expect to see Dale?"

"Three or four days, I reckon. I wish he was here now. . . . Miss Helen, there's trouble afoot."

"I realize that. I'm ready. Did Las Vegas tell you about Beasley's visit to me?"

"No. You tell me," replied Roy.

Briefly Helen began to acquaint him with the circumstances of that visit, and before she had finished she made sure Roy was swearing to himself.

"He asked you to marry him! Jerusalem! . . . Thet I'd never have reckoned. The - low-down coyote of a greaser! . . . Wal, Miss Helen, when I met up with Señor Beasley last night he was shore spoilin' from somethin'; now I see what thet was. An' I reckon I picked out the bad time."

"For what? Roy, what did you do?"

"Wal, I'd made up my mind awhile back to talk to Beasley the first chance I had. An' thet was it. I was in the store when I seen him go into Turner's. So I followed. It was 'most dark. Beasley an' Riggs an' Mulvey an' some more were drinkin' an' powwowin'. So I just braced him right then."

"Roy! Oh, the way you boys court danger!"

"But, Miss Helen, thet's the only way. To be afraid makes more danger. Beasley 'peared civil enough first off. Him an' me kept edgin' off, an' his pards kept edgin' after us, till we got over in a corner of the saloon. I don't know all I said to him. Shore I talked a heap. I told him what my old man thought. An' Beasley knowed as well as I thet my old man's not only the oldest inhabitant hereabouts, but he's the wisest, too. An' he wouldn't tell a lie. Wal, I used all his sayin's in my argument to show Beasley thet if he didn't haul up short he'd end almost as short. Beasley's thick-headed, an' powerful conceited. Vain as a peacock! He couldn't see, an' he got mad. I told him he was rich enough without robbin' you of your ranch, an' - wal, I shore put up a big talk for your side. By this time he an' his gang had me crowded in a corner, an' from their looks I begun to get cold feet. But I was in it an' had to make the best of it. The argument worked down to his pinnin' me to my word that I'd fight for you when thet fight come off. An' I shore told him for my own sake I wished it 'd come off quick. . . . Then - wal - then somethin' did come off quick!"

"Roy, then he shot you!" exclaimed Helen, passionately.

"Now, Miss Helen, I didn't say who done it," replied Roy, with his engaging smile.

"Tell me, then - who did?"

"Wal, I reckon I sha'n't tell you unless you promise not to tell Las Vegas. Thet cowboy is plumb off his head. He thinks he knows who shot me an' I've been lyin' somethin' scandalous. You see, if he learns - then he'll go gunnin'. An', Miss Helen, thet Texan is bad. He might get plugged as I did - an' there would be another man put off your side when the big trouble comes."

"Roy, I promise you I will not tell Las Vegas," replied Helen, earnestly.

"Wal, then - it was Riggs!" Roy grew still paler as he confessed this and his voice, almost a whisper, expressed shame and hate. "Thet four-flush did it. Shot me from behind Beasley! I had no chance. I couldn't even see him draw. But when I fell an' lay there an' the others dropped back, then I seen the smokin' gun in his hand. He looked powerful important. An' Beasley began to cuss him an' was cussin' him as they all run out."

"Oh, coward! the despicable coward!" cried Helen.

"No wonder Tom wants to find out!" exclaimed Bo, low and deep. "I'll bet he suspects Riggs."

Shore he does, but I wouldn't give him no satisfaction."

"Roy, you know that Riggs can't last out here."

"Wal, I hope he lasts till I get on my feet again."

"There you go! Hopeless, all you boys! You must spill blood!" murmured Helen, shudderingly.

"Dear Miss Helen, don't take on so. I'm like Dale - no man to hunt up trouble. But out here there's a sort of unwritten law - an eye for an eye - a tooth for a tooth. I believe in God Almighty, an' killin' is against my religion, but Riggs shot me - the same as shootin' me in the back."

"Roy, I'm only a woman - I fear, faint-hearted and unequal to this West."

"Wait till somethin' happens to you. 'Supposin' Beasley comes an' grabs you with his own dirty big paws an', after maulin' you some, throws you out of your home! Or supposin' Riggs chases you into a corner!"

Helen felt the start of all her physical being - a violent leap of blood. But she could only judge of her looks from the grim smile of the wounded man as he watched her with his keen, intent eyes.

"My friend, anythin' can happen," he said. "But let's hope it won't be the worst."

He had begun to show signs of weakness, and Helen, rising at once, said that she and Bo had better leave him then, but would come to see him the next day. At her call Carmichael entered again with Mrs. Cass, and after a few remarks the visit was terminated. Carmichael lingered in the doorway.

"Wal, Cheer up, you old Mormon!" he called.

"Cheer up yourself, you cross old bachelor!" retorted Roy, quite unnecessarily loud. "Can't you raise enough nerve to make up with Bo?"

Carmichael evacuated the doorway as if he had been spurred. He was quite red in the face while he unhitched the team, and silent during the ride up to the ranch-house. There he got down and followed the girls into the sitting room. He appeared still somber, though not sullen, and had fully regained his composure.

"Did you find out who shot Roy?" he asked, abruptly, of Helen.

"Yes. But I promised Roy I would not tell," replied Helen, nervously. She averted her eyes from his searching gaze, intuitively fearing his next query.

"Was it thet - Riggs?"

"Las Vegas, don't ask me. I will not break my promise."

He strode to the window and looked out a moment, and presently, when he turned toward Bo, he seemed a stronger, loftier, more impelling man, with all his emotions under control.

"Bo, will you listen to me - if I swear to speak the truth - as I know it?"

"Why, certainly," replied Bo, with the color coming swiftly to her face.

"Roy doesn't want me to know because he wants to meet thet fellar himself. An' I want to know because I want to stop him before he can do more dirt to us or our friends. Thet's Roy's reason an' mine. An' I'm askin' you to tell me."

"But, Tom - I oughtn't," replied Bo, haltingly.

"Did you promise Roy not to tell?"

"No."

"Or your sister?"

"No. I didn't promise either."

"Wal, then you tell me. I want you to trust me in this here matter. But not because I love you an' once had a wild dream you might care a little for me -"

"Oh - Tom!" faltered Bo.

"Listen. I want you to trust me because I'm the one who knows what's best. I wouldn't lie an' I wouldn't say so if I didn't know shore. I swear Dale will back me up. But he can't be here for some days. An' thet gang has got to be bluffed. You ought to see this. I reckon you've been quick in savvyin' Western ways. I couldn't pay you no higher compliment, Bo Rayner. . . Now will you tell me?"

"Yes, I will," replied Bo, with the blaze leaping to her eyes.

"Oh, Bo - please don't - please don't. Wait!" implored Helen.

"Bo - it's between you an' me," said Carmichael.

"Tom, I'll tell you," whispered Bo. "It was a lowdown, cowardly trick. . . . Roy was surrounded - and shot from behind Beasley - by that four-flush Riggs!"

CHAPTER XIX

The memory of a woman had ruined Milt Dale's peace, had confounded his philosophy of self-sufficient, lonely happiness in the solitude of the wilds, had forced him to come face to face with his soul and the fatal significance of life.

When he realized his defeat, that things were not as they seemed, that there was no joy for him in the coming of spring, that he had been blind in his free, sensorial, Indian relation to existence, he fell into an inexplicably strange state, a despondency, a gloom as deep as the silence of his home. Dale reflected that the stronger an animal, the keener its nerves, the higher its intelligence, the greater must be its suffering under restraint or injury. He thought of himself as a high order of animal whose great physical need was action, and now the incentive to action seemed dead. He grew lax. He did not want to move. He performed his diminishing duties under compulsion.

He watched for spring as a liberation, but not that he could leave the valley. He hated the cold, he grew weary of wind and snow; he imagined the warm sun, the park once more green with grass and bright with daisies, the return of birds and squirrels and deer to heir old haunts, would be the means whereby he could break this spell upon him. Then he might gradually return to past contentment, though it would never be the same.

But spring, coming early to Paradise Park, brought a fever to Dale's blood - a fire of unutterable longing. It was good, perhaps, that this was so, because he seemed driven to work, climb, tramp, and keep ceaselessly on the move from dawn till dark. Action strengthened his lax muscles and kept him from those motionless, senseless hours of brooding. He at least need not be ashamed of longing for that which could never be his - the sweetness of a woman - a home full of light, joy, hope, the meaning and beauty of children. But those dark moods were sinkings into a pit of hell.

Dale had not kept track of days and weeks. He did not know when the snow melted off three slopes of Paradise Park. All he knew was that an age had dragged over his head and that spring had come. During his restless waking hours, and even when he was asleep, there seemed always in the back of his mind a growing consciousness that soon he would emerge from this trial, a changed man, ready to sacrifice his chosen lot, to give up his lonely life of selfish indulgence in lazy affinity with nature, and to go wherever his strong hands might perform some real service to people. Nevertheless, he wanted to linger in this mountain fastness until his ordeal was over - until he could meet her, and the world, knowing himself more of a man than ever before.

One bright morning, while he was at his camp-fire, the tame cougar gave a low, growling warning. Dale was startled. Tom did not act like that because of a prowling grizzly or a straying stag. Presently Dale espied a horseman riding slowly out of the straggling spruces. And with that sight Dale's heart gave a leap, recalling to him a divination of his future relation to his kind. Never had he been so glad to see a man!

This visitor resembled one of the Beemans, judging from the way he sat his horse, and presently Dale recognized him to be John.

At this juncture the jaded horse was spurred into a trot, soon reaching the pines and the camp.

"Howdy, there, you ole b'ar-hunter!" called John, waving his hand.

For all his hearty greeting his appearance checked a like response from Dale. The horse was mud to his flanks and John was mud to his knees, wet, bedraggled, worn, and white. This hue of his face meant more than fatigue.

"Howdy, John?" replied Dale.

They shook hands. John wearily swung his leg over the pommel, but did not at once dismount. His clear gray eyes were wonderingly riveted upon the hunter.

"Milt - what 'n hell's wrong?" he queried.

"Why?"

"Bust me if you ain't changed so I hardly knowed you. You've been sick - all alone here!"

"Do I look sick?"

"Wal, I should smile. Thin an' pale an' down in the

mouth! Milt, what ails you?"

"I've gone to seed."

"You've gone off your head, jest as Roy said, livin' alone here. You overdid it, Milt. An' you look sick."

"John, my sickness is here," replied Dale, soberly, as he laid a hand on his heart.

"Lung trouble!" ejaculated John. "With thet chest, an' up in this air? . . . Get out!"

"No - not lung trouble," said Dale.

"I savvy. Had a hunch from Roy, anyhow."

"What kind of a hunch?"

"Easy now, Dale, ole man. . . . Don't you reckon I'm ridin' in on you pretty early? Look at thet hoss!" John slid off and waved a hand at the drooping beast, then began to unsaddle him. "Wal, he done great. We bogged some comin' over. An' I climbed the pass at night on the frozen snow."

"You're welcome as the flowers in May. John, what month is it?"

"By spades! are you as bad as thet? . . . Let's see. It's the twenty-third of March."

"March! Well, I'm beat. I've lost my reckonin' - an' a lot more, maybe."

"Thar!" declared John, slapping the mustang. "You can

jest hang up here till my next trip. Milt, how 're your hosses?"

"Wintered fine."

"Wal, thet's good. We'll need two big, strong hosses right off."

"What for?" queried Dale, sharply. He dropped a stick of wood and straightened up from the camp-fire.

"You're goin' to ride down to Pine with me - thet's what for."

Familiarly then came back to Dale the quiet, intent suggestiveness of the Beemans in moments foreboding trial.

At this certain assurance of John's, too significant to be doubted, Dale's though of Pine gave slow birth to a strange sensation, as if he had been dead and was vibrating back to life.

"Tell what you got to tell!" he broke out.

Quick as a flash the Mormon replied: "Roy's been shot. But he won't die. He sent for you. Bad deal's afoot. Beasley means to force Helen Rayner out an' steal her ranch."

A tremor ran all through Dale. It seemed another painful yet thrilling connection between his past and this vaguely calling future. His emotions had been broodings dreams, longings. This thing his friend said had the sting of real life.

"Then old Al's dead?" he asked.

"Long ago - I reckon around the middle of February. The property went to Helen. She's been doin' fine. An' many folks say it's a pity she'll lose it."

"She won't lose it," declared Dale. How strange his voice sounded to his own ears! It was hoarse and unreal, as if from disuse.

"Wal, we-all have our idees. I say she will. My father says so. Carmichael says so."

"Who's he?"

"Reckon you remember thet cow-puncher who came up with Roy an' Auchincloss after the girls - last fall?"

"Yes. They called him Las - Las Vegas. I liked his looks."

"Humph! You'll like him a heap when you know him. He's kept the ranch goin' for Miss Helen all along. But the deal's comin' to a head. Beasley's got thick with thet Riggs. You remember him?"

"Yes."

"Wal, he's been hangin' out at Pine all winter, watchin' for some chance to get at Miss Helen or Bo. Everybody's seen thet. An' jest lately he chased Bo on hossback - gave the kid a nasty fall. Roy says Riggs was after Miss Helen. But I think one or t'other of the girls would do thet varmint. Wal, thet sorta started goin's-on. Carmichael beat Riggs an' drove him out of town. But he come back. Beasley called on Miss Helen an' offered to marry her so's not to take the ranch from her, he said."

Dale awoke with a thundering curse.

"Shore!" exclaimed John. "I'd say the same - only I'm religious. Don't thet beady-eyed greaser's gall make you want to spit all over yourself? My Gawd! but Roy was mad! Roy's powerful fond of Miss Helen an' Bo. . . . Wal, then, Roy, first chance he got, braced Beasley an' give him some straight talk. Beasley was foamin' at the mouth, Roy said. It was then Riggs shot Roy. Shot him from behind Beasley when Roy wasn't lookin'! An' Riggs brags of bein' a gun-fighter. Mebbe thet wasn't a bad shot for him!"

"I reckon," replied Dale, as he swallowed hard. "Now, just what was Roy's message to me?"

"Wal, I can't remember all Roy said," answered John, dubiously. "But Roy shore was excited an' dead in earnest. He says: 'Tell Milt what's happened. Tell him Helen Rayner's in more danger than she was last fall. Tell him I've seen her look away acrost the mountains toward Paradise Park with her heart in her eyes. Tell him she needs him most of all!'"

Dale shook all over as with an attack of ague. He was seized by a whirlwind of passionate, terrible sweetness of sensation, when what he wildly wanted was to curse Roy and John for their simple-minded conclusions.

"Roy's - crazy!" panted Dale.

"Wal, now, Milt - thet's downright surprisin' of you. Roy's the level-headest of any fellars I know."

"Man! if he made me believe him - an' it turned out untrue - I'd - I'd kill him," replied Dale.

"Untrue! Do you think Roy Beeman would lie?"

"But, John - you fellows can't see my case. Nell Rayner wants me - needs me! . . . It can't be true!"

"Wal, my love-sick pard - it jest is true!" exclaimed John, feelingly. "Thet's the hell of life - never knowin'. But here it's joy for you. You can believe Roy Beeman about women as quick as you'd trust him to track your lost hoss. Roy's married three girls. I reckon he'll marry some more. Roy's only twenty-eight an' he has two big farms. He said he'd seen Nell Rayner's heart in her eyes, lookin' for you - an' you can jest bet your life thet's true. An' he said it because he means you to rustle down there an' fight for thet girl."

"I'll - go," said Dale, in a shaky whisper, as he sat down on a pine log near the fire. He stared unseeingly at the bluebells in the grass by his feet while storm after storm possessed his breast. They were fierce and brief because driven by his will. In those few moments of contending strife Dale was immeasurably removed from that dark gulf of self which had made his winter a nightmare. And when he stood erect again it seemed that the old earth had a stirring, electrifying impetus for his feet. Something black, bitter, melancholy, and morbid, always unreal to him, had passed away forever. The great moment had been forced upon him. He did not believe Roy Beeman's preposterous hint regarding Helen; but he had gone back or soared onward, as if by magic, to his old true self.

Mounted on Dale's strongest horses, with only a light

pack, an ax, and their weapons, the two men had reached the snow-line on the pass by noon that day. Tom, the tame cougar, trotted along in the rear.

The crust of the snow, now half thawed by the sun, would not hold the weight of a horse, though it upheld the men on foot. They walked, leading the horses. Travel was not difficult until the snow began to deepen; then progress slackened materially. John had not been able to pick out the line of the trail, so Dale did not follow his tracks. An old blaze on the trees enabled Dale to keep fairly well to the trail; and at length the height of the pass was reached, where the snow was deep. Here the horses labored, plowing through foot by foot. When, finally, they sank to their flanks, they had to be dragged and goaded on, and helped by thick flat bunches of spruce boughs placed under their hoofs. It took three hours of breaking toil to do the few hundred yards of deep snow on the height of the pass. The cougar did not have great difficulty in following, though it was evident he did not like such traveling.

That behind them, the horses gathered heart and worked on to the edge of the steep descent, where they had all they could do to hold back from sliding and rolling. Fast time was made on this slope, at the bottom of which began a dense forest with snow still deep in places and windfalls hard to locate. The men here performed Herculean labors, but they got through to a park where the snow was gone. The ground, however, soft and boggy, in places was more treacherous than the snow; and the travelers had to skirt the edge of the park to a point opposite, and then go on through the forest. When they reached bare and solid ground, just before dark that night, it was high time, for the horses were ready to drop, and the men likewise.

Camp was made in an open wood. Darkness fell and the men were resting on bough beds, feet to the fire, with Tom curled up close by, and the horses still drooping where they had been unsaddled. Morning, however, discovered them grazing on the long, bleached grass. John shook his head when he looked at them.

"You reckoned to make Pine by nightfall. How far is it - the way you'll go?"

"Fifty mile or thereabouts," replied Dale.

"Wal, we can't ride it on them critters."

"John, we'd do more than that if we had to."

They were saddled and on the move before sunrise, leaving snow and bog behind. Level parks and level forests led one after another to long slopes and steep descents, all growing sunnier and greener as the altitude diminished. Squirrels and grouse, turkeys and deer, and less tame denizens of the forest grew more abundant as the travel advanced. In this game zone, however, Dale had trouble with Tom. The cougar had to be watched and called often to keep him off of trails.

"Tom doesn't like a long trip," said Dale. "But I'm goin' to take him. Some way or other he may come in handy."

"Sic him onto Beasley's gang," replied John. "Some men are powerful scared of cougars. But I never was."

"Nor me. Though I've had cougars give me a darn uncanny feelin'."

The men talked but little. Dale led the way, with Tom trotting noiselessly beside his horse. John followed close behind. They loped the horses across parks, trotted through the forests, walked slow up what few inclines they met, and slid down the soft, wet, pine-matted descents. So they averaged from six to eight miles an hour. The horses held up well under that steady travel, and this without any rest at noon.

Dale seemed to feel himself in an emotional trance. Yet, despite this, the same old sensorial perceptions crowded thick and fast upon him, strangely sweet and vivid after the past dead months when neither sun nor wind nor cloud nor scent of pine nor anything in nature could stir him. His mind, his heart, his soul seemed steeped in an intoxicating wine of expectation, while his eyes and ears and nose had never been keener to register the facts of the forest-land. He saw the black thing far ahead that resembled a burned stump, but he knew was a bear before it vanished; he saw gray flash of deer and wolf and coyote, and the red of fox, and the small, wary heads of old gobblers just sticking above the grass; and he saw deep tracks of game as well as the slow-rising blades of bluebells where some soft-footed beast had just trod. And he heard the melancholy notes of birds, the twitter of grouse, the sough of the wind, the light dropping of pine-cones, the near and distant bark of squirrels, the deep gobble of a turkey close at hand and the challenge from a rival far away, the cracking of twigs in the thickets, the murmur of running water, the scream of an eagle and the shrill cry of a hawk, and always the soft, dull, steady pads of the hoofs of the horses.

The smells, too, were the sweet, stinging ones of spring, warm and pleasant - the odor of the clean, fresh earth cutting its way through that thick, strong fragrance of pine, the smell of logs rotting in the sun, and of fresh new grass and flowers along a brook of snow-water.

"I smell smoke," said Dale, suddenly, as he reined in, and turned for corroboration from his companion.

John sniffed the warm air.

"Wal, you're more of an Injun than me," he replied, shaking his head.

They traveled on, and presently came out upon the rim of the last slope. A long league of green slanted below them, breaking up into straggling lines of trees and groves that joined the cedars, and these in turn stretched on and down in gray-black patches to the desert, that glittering and bare, with streaks of somber hue, faded in the obscurity of distance.

The village of Pine appeared to nestle in a curve of the edge of the great forest, and the cabins looked like tiny white dots set in green.

"Look there," said Dale, pointing.

Some miles to the right a gray escarpment of rock cropped out of the slope, forming a promontory; and from it a thin, pale column of smoke curled upward to be lost from sight as soon as it had no background of green.

"Thet's your smoke, shore enough," replied John,

thoughtfully. "Now, I jest wonder who's campin' there. No water near or grass for hosses."

"John, that point's been used for smoke signals many a time."

"Was jest thinkin' of thet same. Shall we ride around there an' take a peek?"

"No. But we'll remember that. If Beasley's got his deep scheme goin', he'll have Snake Anson's gang somewhere close."

"Roy said thet same. Wal, it's some three hours till sundown. The hosses keep up. I reckon I'm fooled, for we'll make Pine all right. But old Tom there, he's tired or lazy."

The big cougar was lying down, panting, and his half-shut eyes were on Dale.

"Tom's only lazy an' fat. He could travel at this gait for a week. But let's rest a half-hour an' watch that smoke before movin' on. We can make Pine before sundown."

When travel had been resumed, half-way down the slope Dale's sharp eyes caught a broad track where shod horses had passed, climbing in a long slant toward the promontory. He dismounted to examine it, and John, coming up, proceeded with alacrity to get off and do likewise. Dale made his deductions, after which he stood in a brown study beside his horse, waiting for John.

"Wal, what 'd you make of these here tracks?" asked that worthy.

"Some horses an' a pony went along here yesterday, an' to-day a single horse made, that fresh track."

"Wal, Milt, for a hunter you ain't so bad at hoss tracks," observed John, "But how many hosses went yesterday ?"

"I couldn't make out - several - maybe four or five."

"Six hosses an' a colt or little mustang, unshod, to be strict-correct. Wal, supposin' they did. What 's it mean to us?"

"I don't know as I'd thought anythin' unusual, if it hadn't been for that smoke we saw off the rim, an' then this here fresh track made along to-day. Looks queer to me."

"Wish Roy was here," replied John, scratching his head. "Milt, I've a hunch, if he was, he'd foller them tracks."

"Maybe. But we haven't time for that. We can backtrail them, though, if they keep clear as they are here. An' we'll not lose any time, either."

That broad track led straight toward Pine, down to the edge of the cedars, where, amid some jagged rocks, evidences showed that men had camped there for days. Here it ended as a broad trail. But from the north came the single fresh track made that very day, and from the east, more in a line with Pine, came two tracks made the day before. And these were imprints of big and little hoofs. Manifestly these interested John more than they did Dale, who had to wait for his companion.

"Milt, it ain't a colt's - thet little track," avowed John.

"Why not - an' what if it isn't?" queried Dale.

"Wal, it ain't, because a colt always straggles back, an' from one side to t'other. This little track keeps close to the big one. An', by George! it was made by a led mustang."

John resembled Roy Beeman then with that leaping, intent fire in his gray eyes. Dale's reply was to spur his horse into a trot and call sharply to the lagging cougar.

When they turned into the broad, blossom-bordered road that was the only thoroughfare of Pine the sun was setting red and gold behind the mountains. The horses were too tired for any more than a walk. Natives of the village, catching sight of Dale and Beeman, and the huge gray cat following like a dog, called excitedly to one another. A group of men in front of Turner's gazed intently down the road, and soon manifested signs of excitement. Dale and his comrade dismounted in front of Widow Cass's cottage. And Dale called as he strode up the little path. Mrs. Cass came out. She was white and shaking, but appeared calm. At sight of her John Beeman drew a sharp breath.

"Wal, now -" he began, hoarsely, and left off.

"How's Roy?" queried Dale.

"Lord knows I'm glad to see you, boys! Milt, you're thin an' strange-lookin'. Roy's had a little setback. He got a shock to-day an' it throwed him off. Fever - an' now he's out of his head. It won't do no good for you to waste time seein' him. Take my word for it he's all right. But there's others as - For the land's sakes, Milt Dale, you fetched thet cougar back! Don't let him near me!"

"Tom won't hurt you, mother," said Dale, as the cougar came padding up the path. "You were sayin' somethin' - about others. Is Miss Helen safe? Hurry!"

"Ride up to see her - an' waste no more time here."

Dale was quick in the saddle, followed by John, but the horses had to be severely punished to force them even to a trot. And that was a lagging trot, which now did not leave Torn behind.

The ride up to Auchincloss's ranch-house seemed endless to Dale. Natives came out in the road to watch after he had passed. Stern as Dale was in dominating his feelings, he could not wholly subordinate his mounting joy to a waiting terrible anticipation of catastrophe. But no matter what awaited - nor what fateful events might hinge upon this nameless circumstance about to be disclosed, the wonderful and glorious fact of the present was that in a moment he would see Helen Rayner.

There were saddled horses in the courtyard, but no riders. A Mexican boy sat on the porch bench, in the seat where Dale remembered he had encountered Al Auchincloss. The door of the big sitting-room was open. The scent of flowers, the murmur of bees, the pounding of hoofs came vaguely to Dale. His eyes dimmed, so that the ground, when he slid out of his saddle, seemed far below him. He stepped upon the porch. His sight suddenly cleared. A tight fullness at his throat made incoherent the words he said to the

Mexican boy. But they were understood, as the boy ran back around the house. Dale knocked sharply and stepped over the threshold.

Outside, John, true to his habits, was thinking, even in that moment of suspense, about the faithful, exhausted horses. As he unsaddled them he talked: "Fer soft an' fat hosses, winterin' high up, wal, you've done somethin'!"

Then Dale heard a voice in another room, a step, a creak of the door. It opened. A woman in white appeared. He recognized Helen. But instead of the rich brown bloom and dark-eyed beauty so hauntingly limned on his memory, he saw a white, beautiful face, strained and quivering in anguish, and eyes that pierced his heart. He could not speak.

"Oh! my friend - you've come!" she whispered.

Dale put out a shaking hand. But she did not see it. She clutched his shoulders, as if to feel whether or not he was real, and then her arms went up round his neck.

"Oh, thank God! I knew you would come!" she said, and her head sank to his shoulder.

Dale divined what he had suspected. Helen's sister had been carried off. Yet, while his quick mind grasped Helen's broken spirit - the unbalance that was reason for this marvelous and glorious act - he did not take other meaning of the embrace to himself. He just stood there, transported, charged like a tree struck by lightning, making sure with all his keen senses, so that he could feel forever, how she was clinging round his neck, her face over his bursting heart, her quivering form close pressed to his.

"It's - Bo," he said, unsteadily.

"She went riding yesterday - and - never - came - back!" replied Helen, brokenly.

"I've seen her trail. She's been taken into the woods. I'll find her. I'll fetch her back," he replied, rapidly.

With a shock she seemed to absorb his meaning. With another shock she raised her face - leaned back a little to look at him.

"You'll find her - fetch her back?"

"Yes," he answered, instantly.

With that ringing word it seemed to Dale she realized how she was standing. He felt her shake as she dropped her arms and stepped back, while the white anguish of her face was flooded out by a wave of scarlet. But she was brave in her confusion. Her eyes never fell, though they changed swiftly, darkening with shame, amaze, and with feelings he could not read.

"I'm almost - out of my head," she faltered.

"No wonder. I saw that. . . . But now you must get clear-headed. I've no time to lose."

He led her to the door.

"John, it's Bo that's gone," he called. "Since yesterday. . . . Send the boy to get me a bag of meat an' bread.

You run to the corral an' get me a fresh horse. My old horse Ranger if you can find him quick. An' rustle."

Without a word John leaped bareback on one of the horses he had just unsaddled and spurred him across the courtyard.

Then the big cougar, seeing Helen, got up from where he lay on the porch and came to her.

"Oh, it's Tom!" cried Helen, and as he rubbed against her knees she patted his head with trembling hand. "You big, beautiful pet! Oh, how I remember! Oh, how Bo would love to -"

"Where's Carmichael?" interrupted Dale. "Out huntin' Bo?"

"Yes. It was he who missed her first. He rode everywhere yesterday. Last night when he came back he was wild. I've not seen him to-day. He made all the other men but Hal and Joe stay home on the ranch."

"Right. An' John must stay, too, declared Dale. "But it's strange. Carmichael ought to have found the girl's tracks. She was ridin' a pony?"

"Bo rode Sam. He's a little bronc, very strong and fast."

"I come across his tracks. How'd Carmichael miss them?"

"He didn't. He found them - trailed them all along the north range. That's where he forbade Bo to go. You see, they're in love with each other. They've been at odds. Neither will give in. Bo disobeyed him. There's hard ground off the north range, so he said. He was able to follow her tracks only so far."

"Were there any other tracks along with hers?"

"No."

"Miss Helen, I found them 'way southeast of Pine up on the slope of the mountain. There were seven other horses makin' that trail - when we run across it. On the way down we found a camp where men had waited. An' Bo's pony, led by a rider on a big horse, come into that camp from the east - maybe north a little. An' that tells the story."

"Riggs ran her down - made off with her!" cried Helen, passionately. "Oh, the villain! He had men in waiting. That's Beasley's work. They were after me."

"It may not be just what you said, but that's close enough. An' Bo's in a bad fix. You must face that an' try to bear up under - fears of the worst."

"My friend! You will save her!"

"I'll fetch her back, alive or dead."

"Dead! Oh, my God!" Helen cried, and closed her eyes an instant, to open them burning black. "But Bo isn't dead. I know that - I feel it. She'll not die very easy. She's a little savage. She has no fear. She'd fight like a tigress for her life. She's strong. You remember how strong. She can stand anything. Unless they murder her outright she'll live - a long time - through any ordeal .... So I beg you, my friend, don't lose an hour -

don't ever give up!"

Dale trembled under the clasp of her hands. Loosing his own from her clinging hold, he stepped out on the porch At that moment John appeared on Ranger, coming at a gallop.

"Nell, I'll never come back without her," said Dale. "I reckon you can hope - only be prepared. That's all. It's hard. But these damned deals are common out here in the West."

"Suppose Beasley comes - here!" exclaimed Helen, and again her hand went out toward him.

"If he does, you refuse to get off ," replied Dale. "But don't let him or his greasers put a dirty hand on you. Should he threaten force - why, pack some clothes - an' your valuables - an' go down to Mrs. Cass's. An' wait till I come back!"

"Wait - till you - come back!" she faltered, slowly turning white again. Her dark eyes dilated. "Milt - you're like Las Vegas. You'll kill Beasley!"

Dale heard his own laugh, very cold and strange, foreign to his ears. A grim, deadly hate of Beasley vied with the tenderness and pity he felt for this distressed girl. It was a sore trial to see her leaning there against the door - to be compelled to leave her alone. Abruptly be stalked off the porch. Tom followed him. The black horse whinnied his recognition of Dale and snorted at sight of the cougar. Just then the Mexican boy returned with a bag. Dale tied this, with the small pack, behind the saddle.

"John, you stay here with Miss Helen," said Dale. "An' if Carmichael comes back, keep him, too! An' to-night, if any one rides into Pine from the way we come, you be sure to spot him."

"I'll do thet, Milt," responded John.

Dale mounted, and, turning for a last word to Helen, he felt the words of cheer halted on his lips as he saw her standing white and broken-hearted, with her hands to her bosom. He could not look twice.

"Come on there, you Tom," he called to the cougar. Reckon on this track you'll pay me for all my trainin' of you"

"Oh, my friend!" came Helen's sad voice, almost a whisper to his throbbing ears. "Heaven help you - to save her! I -"

Then Ranger started and Dale heard no more. He could not look back. His eyes were full of tears and his breast ached. By a tremendous effort he shifted that emotion - called on all the spiritual energy of his being to the duty of this grim task before him.

He did not ride down through the village, but skirted the northern border, and worked round to the south, where, coming to the trail he had made an hour past, he headed on it, straight for the slope now darkening in the twilight. The big cougar showed more willingness to return on this trail than he had shown in the coming. Ranger was fresh and wanted to go, but Dale held him in.

A cool wind blew down from the mountain with the

coming of night. Against the brightening stars Dale saw the promontory lift its bold outline. It was miles away. It haunted him, strangely calling. A night, and perhaps a day, separated him from the gang that held Bo Rayner prisoner. Dale had no plan as yet. He had only a motive as great as the love he bore Helen Rayner.

Beasley's evil genius had planned this abduction. Riggs was a tool, a cowardly knave dominated by a stronger will. Snake Anson and his gang had lain in wait at that cedar camp; had made that broad hoof track leading up the mountain. Beasley had been there with them that very day. All this was as assured to Dale as if he had seen the men.

But the matter of Dale's recovering the girl and doing it speedily strung his mental strength to its highest pitch. Many outlines of action flashed through his mind as he rode on, peering keenly through the night, listening with practised ears. All were rejected. And at the outset of every new branching of thought he would gaze down at the gray form of the cougar, long, graceful, heavy, as he padded beside the horse. From the first thought of returning to help Helen Rayner he had conceived an undefined idea of possible value in the qualities of his pet. Tom had performed wonderful feats of trailing, but he had never been tried on men. Dale believed he could make him trail anything, yet he had no proof of this. One fact stood out of all Dale's conjectures, and it was that he had known men, and brave men, to fear cougars.

Far up on the slope, in a little hollow where water ran and there was a little grass for Ranger to pick, Dale haltered him and made ready to spend the night. He was sparing with his food, giving Tom more than he took himself. Curled close up to Dale, the big cat went to sleep.

But Dale lay awake for long.

The night was still, with only a faint moan of wind on this sheltered slope. Dale saw hope in the stars. He did not seem to have promised himself or Helen that he could save her sister, and then her property. He seemed to have stated something unconsciously settled, outside of his thinking. Strange how this certainty was not vague, yet irreconcilable with any plans he created! Behind it, somehow nameless with inconceivable power, surged all his wonderful knowledge of forest, of trails, of scents, of night, of the nature of men lying down to sleep in the dark, lonely woods, of the nature of this great cat that lived its every action in accordance with his will.

He grew sleepy, and gradually his mind stilled, with his last conscious thought a portent that he would awaken to accomplish his desperate task.

CHAPTER XX

Young Burt possessed the keenest eyes of any man in Snake Anson's gang, for which reason he was given the post as lookout from the lofty promontory. His instructions were to keep sharp watch over the open slopes below and to report any sight of a horse.

A cedar fire with green boughs on top of dead wood sent up a long, pale column of smoke. This signal-fire had been kept burning since sunrise.

The preceding night camp had been made on a level spot in the cedars back of the promontory. But manifestly Anson did not expect to remain there long. For, after breakfast, the packs had been made up and the horses stood saddled and bridled. They were restless and uneasy, tossing bits and fighting flies. The sun, now half-way to meridian, was hot and no breeze blew in that sheltered spot.

Shady Jones had ridden off early to fill the water-bags, and had not yet returned. Anson, thinner and scalier and more snakelike than ever, was dealing a greasy, dirty deck of cards, his opponent being the square-shaped, black-visaged Moze. In lieu of money the gamblers wagered with cedar-berries, each of which berries represented a pipeful of tobacco. Jim Wilson brooded under a cedar-tree, his unshaven face a dirty dust-hue, a smoldering fire in his light eyes, a sullen set to his jaw. Every little while he would raise his eyes to glance at Riggs, and it seemed that a quick glance was enough. Riggs paced to and fro in the open, coatless and hatless, his black-broadcloth trousers and embroidered vest dusty and torn. An enormous gun bumped awkwardly in its sheath swinging below his hip. Riggs looked perturbed. His face was sweating freely, yet it was far from red in color. He did not appear to mind the sun or the flies. His eyes were staring, dark, wild, shifting in gaze from everything they encountered. But often that gaze shot back to the captive girl sitting under a cedar some yards from the man.

Bo Rayner's little, booted feet were tied together with one end of a lasso and the other end trailed off over the ground. Her hands were free. Her riding-habit was dusty and disordered. Her eyes blazed defiantly out of a small, pale face.

"Harve Riggs, I wouldn't be standing in those cheap boots of yours for a million dollars," she said, sarcastically. Riggs took no notice of her words.

"You pack that gun-sheath wrong end out. What have you got the gun for, anyhow?" she added, tauntingly.

Snake Anson let out a hoarse laugh and Moze's black visage opened in a huge grin. Jim Wilson seemed to drink in the girl's words. Sullen and somber, he bent his lean head, very still, as if listening.

"You'd better shut up," said Riggs, darkly.

"I will not shut up," declared Bo.

"Then I'll gag you," he threatened.

"Gag me! Why, you dirty, low-down, two-bit of a bluff!" she exclaimed, hotly, "I'd like to see you try it. I'll tear that long hair of yours right off your head."

Riggs advanced toward her with his hands clutching, as if eager to throttle her. The girl leaned forward, her face reddening, her eyes fierce.

"You damned little cat!" muttered Riggs, thickly. "I'll gag you - if you don't stop squallin'."

"Come on. I dare you to lay a hand on me. . . . Harve Riggs, I'm not the least afraid of you. Can't you savvy that? You're a liar, a four-flush, a sneak! Why, you're not fit to wipe the feet of any of these outlaws."

Riggs took two long strides and bent over her, his teeth protruding in a snarl, and he cuffed her hard on the side of the head.

Bo's head jerked back with the force of the blow, but she uttered no cry.

"Are you goin' to keep your jaw shut?" he demanded, stridently, and a dark tide of blood surged up into his neck.

"I should smile I'm not," retorted Bo, in cool, deliberate anger of opposition. "You've roped me - and you've struck me! Now get a club - stand off there - out of my reach - and beat me! Oh, if I only knew cuss words fit for you - I'd call you them!"

Snake Anson had stopped playing cards, and was

watching, listening, with half-disgusted, half-amused expression on his serpent-like face. Jim Wilson slowly rose to his feet. If any one had observed him it would have been to note that he now seemed singularly fascinated by this scene, yet all the while absorbed in himself. Once he loosened the neck-band of his blouse.

Riggs swung his arm more violently at the girl. But she dodged.

"You dog!" she hissed. "Oh, if I only had a gun!"

Her face then, with its dead whiteness and the eyes of flame, held a tragic, impelling beauty that stung Anson into remonstrance.

"Aw, Riggs, don't beat up the kid," he protested. "Thet won't do any good. Let her alone."

"But she's got to shut up," replied Riggs.

"How 'n hell air you goin' to shet her up? Mebbe if you get out of her sight she'll be quiet. . . . How about thet, girl?"

Anson gnawed his drooping mustache as he eyed Bo.

"Have I made any kick to you or your men yet?" she queried.

"It strikes me you 'ain't," replied Anson.

"You won't hear me make any so long as I'm treated decent," said Bo. "I don't know what you've got to do with Riggs. He ran me down - roped me - dragged me to your camp. Now I've a hunch you're waiting for Beasley."

"Girl, your hunch 's correct," said Anson.

"Well, do you know I'm the wrong girl?"

"What's thet? I reckon you're Nell Rayner, who got left all old Auchincloss's property."

"No. I'm Bo Rayner. Nell is my sister. She owns the ranch. Beasley wanted her."

Anson cursed deep and low. Under his sharp, bristling eyebrows he bent cunning green eyes upon Riggs.

"Say, you! Is what this kid says so?"

"Yes. She's Nell Rayner's sister," replied Riggs, doggedly.

"A-huh! Wal, why in the hell did you drag her into my camp an' off up here to signal Beasley? He ain't wantin' her. He wants the girl who owns the ranch. Did you take one fer the other - same as thet day we was with you?"

"Guess I must have," replied Riggs, sullenly.

"But you knowed her from her sister afore you come to my camp?"

Riggs shook his head. He was paler now and sweating more freely. The dank hair hung wet over his forehead. His manner was that of a man suddenly realizing he had gotten into a tight place.

"Oh, he's a liar!" exclaimed Bo, with contemptuous ring in her voice. "He comes from my country. He has known Nell and me for years."

Snake Anson turned to look at Wilson.

"Jim, now hyar's a queer deal this feller has rung in on us. I thought thet kid was pretty young. Don't you remember Beasley told us Nell Rayner was a handsome woman?"

"Wal, pard Anson, if this heah gurl ain't handsome my eyes have gone pore," drawled Wilson.

"A-huh! So your Texas chilvaree over the ladies is some operatin'," retorted Anson, with fine sarcasm. "But thet ain't tellin' me what you think?"

"Wal, I ain't tellin' you what I think yet. But I know thet kid ain't Nell Rayner. For I've seen her."

Anson studied his right-hand man for a moment, then, taking out his tobacco-pouch, he sat himself down upon a stone and proceeded leisurely to roll a cigarette. He put it between his thin lips and apparently forgot to light it. For a few moments he gazed at the yellow ground and some scant sage-brush. Riggs took to pacing up and down. Wilson leaned as before against the cedar. The girl slowly recovered from her excess of anger.

"Kid, see hyar," said Anson, addressing the girl; "if Riggs knowed you wasn't Nell an' fetched you along anyhow - what 'd he do thet fur?"

"He chased me - caught me. Then he saw some one

after us and he hurried to your camp. He was afraid - the cur!"

Riggs heard her reply, for he turned a malignant glance upon her.

"Anson, I fetched her because I know Nell Rayner will give up anythin' on earth for her," he said, in loud voice.

Anson pondered this statement with an air of considering its apparent sincerity.

"Don't you believe him," declared Bo Rayner, bluntly. "He's a liar. He's double-crossing Beasley and all of you."

Riggs raised a shaking hand to clench it at her. "Keep still or it 'll be the worse for you."

"Riggs, shut up yourself," put in Anson, as he leisurely rose. "Mebbe it 'ain't occurred to you thet she might have some talk interestin' to me. An' I'm runnin' this hyar camp. . . . Now, kid, talk up an' say what you like."

"I said he was double-crossing you all," replied the girl, instantly. "Why, I'm surprised you'd be caught in his company! My uncle Al and my sweetheart Carmichael and my friend Dale - they've all told me what Western men are, even down to outlaws, robbers, cutthroat rascals like you. And I know the West well enough now to be sure that four-flush doesn't belong here and can't last here. He went to Dodge City once and when he came back he made a bluff at being a bad man. He was a swaggering, bragging, drinking gun-fighter. He talked of the men he'd shot, of the fights he'd had. He dressed like some of those gun-throwing gamblers. . . . He was in love with my sister Nell. She hated him. He followed us out West and he has hung on our actions like a sneaking Indian. Why, Nell and I couldn't even walk to the store in the village. He rode after me out on the range - chased me. . . . For that Carmichael called Riggs's bluff down in Turner's saloon. Dared him to draw! Cussed him every name on the range! Slapped and beat and kicked him! Drove him out of Pine! . . . And now, whatever he has said to Beasley or you, it's a dead sure bet he's playing his own game. That's to get hold of Nell, and if not her - then me! . . . Oh, I'm out of breath - and I'm out of names to call him. If I talked forever - I'd never be - able to - do him justice. But lend me - a gun - a minute!"

Jim Wilson's quiet form vibrated with a start. Anson with his admiring smile pulled his gun and, taking a couple of steps forward, held it out butt first. She stretched eagerly for it and he jerked it away.

"Hold on there!" yelled Riggs, in alarm.

"Damme, Jim, if she didn't mean bizness!" exclaimed the outlaw.

"Wal, now - see heah, Miss. Would you bore him - if you hed a gun?" inquired Wilson, with curious interest. There was more of respect in his demeanor than admiration.

"No. I don't want his cowardly blood on my hands," replied the girl. "But I'd make him dance - I'd make him run."

"Shore you can handle a gun?"

She nodded her answer while her eyes flashed hate and her resolute lips twitched.

Then Wilson made a singularly swift motion and his gun was pitched butt first to within a foot of her hand. She snatched it up, cocked it, aimed it, all before Anson could move. But he yelled:

"Drop thet gun, you little devil!"

Riggs turned ghastly as the big blue gun lined on him. He also yelled, but that yell was different from Anson's.

"Run or dance!" cried the girl.

The big gun boomed and leaped almost out of her hand. She took both hands, and called derisively as she fired again. The second bullet hit at Riggs's feet, scattering the dust and fragments of stone all over him. He bounded here - there - then darted for the rocks. A third time the heavy gun spoke and this bullet must have ticked Riggs, for he let out a hoarse bawl and leaped sheer for the protection of a rock.

"Plug him! Shoot off a leg!" yelled Snake Anson, whooping and stamping, as Riggs got out of sight.

Jim Wilson watched the whole performance with the same quietness that had characterized his manner toward the girl. Then, as Riggs disappeared, Wilson stepped forward and took the gun from the girl's trembling hands. She was whiter than ever, but still resolute and defiant. Wilson took a glance over in the direction Riggs had hidden and then proceeded to reload the gun. Snake Anson's roar of laughter ceased rather suddenly.

"Hyar, Jim, she might have held up the whole gang with thet gun," he protested.

"I reckon she 'ain't nothin' ag'in' us," replied Wilson.

"A-huh! You know a lot about wimmen now, don't you? But thet did my heart good. Jim, what 'n earth would you have did if thet 'd been you instead of Riggs?"

The query seemed important and amazing. Wilson pondered.

"Shore I'd stood there - stock-still - an' never moved an eye-winker."

"An' let her shoot!" ejaculated Anson, nodding his long head. "Mc, too!"

So these rough outlaws, inured to all the violence and baseness of their dishonest calling, rose to the challenging courage of a slip of a girl. She had the one thing they respected - nerve.

Just then a halloo, from the promontory brought Anson up with a start. Muttering to himself, he strode out toward the jagged rocks that hid the outlook. Moze shuffled his burly form after Anson.

"Miss, it shore was grand - thet performance of Mister Gunman Riggs," remarked Jim Wilson, attentively studying the girl.

"Much obliged to you for lending me your gun," she replied. "I - I hope I hit him - a little."

"Wal, if you didn't sting him, then Jim Wilson knows nothin' about lead."

"Jim Wilson? Are you the man - the outlaw my uncle Al knew?"

"Reckon I am, miss. Fer I knowed Al shore enough. What 'd he say aboot me?"

"I remember once he was telling me about Snake Anson's gang. He mentioned you. Said you were a real gun-fighter. And what a shame it was you had to be an outlaw."

"Wal! An' so old Al spoke thet nice of me. . . . It's tolerable likely I'll remember. An' now, miss, can I do anythin' for you?"

Swift as a flash she looked at him.

"What do you mean?"

"Wal, shore I don't mean much, I'm sorry to say. Nothin' to make you look like thet. . . . I hev to be an outlaw, shore as you're born. But - mebbe there's a difference in outlaws."

She understood him and paid him the compliment not to voice her sudden upflashing hope that he might be one to betray his leader.

"Please take this rope off my feet. Let me walk a little.

Let me have a - a little privacy. That fool watched every move I made. I promise not to run away. And, oh! I'm thirsty."

"Shore you've got sense." He freed her feet and helped her get up. "There'll be some fresh water any minit now, if you'll wait."

Then he turned his back and walked over to where Riggs sat nursing a bullet-burn on his leg.

"Say, Riggs, I'm takin' the responsibility of loosin' the girl for a little spell. She can't get away. An' there ain't any sense in bein' mean."

Riggs made no reply, and went on rolling down his trousers leg, lapped a fold over at the bottom and pulled on his boot. Then he strode out toward the promontory. Half-way there he encountered Anson tramping back.

"Beasley's comin' one way an' Shady's comin' another. We'll be off this hot point of rock by noon," said the outlaw leader.

Riggs went on to the promontory to look for himself.

"Where's the girl?" demanded Anson, in surprise, when he got back to the camp.

"Wal, she's walkin' 'round between heah an' Pine," drawled Wilson.

"Jim, you let her loose?"

"Shore I did. She's been hawg-tied all the time. An' she

said she'd not run off. I'd take thet girl's word even to a sheep-thief."

"A-huh. So would I, for all of thet. But, Jim, somethin's workin' in you. Ain't you sort of remem-berin' a time when you was young - an' mebbe knowed pretty kids like this one?"

"Wal, if I am it 'll shore turn out bad fer somebody."

Anson gave him a surprised stare and suddenly lost the bantering tone.

"A-huh! So thet's how it's workin'," he replied, and flung himself down in the shade.

Young Burt made his appearance then, wiping his sallow face. His deep-set, hungry eyes, upon which his comrades set such store, roved around the camp.

"Whar's the gurl?" he queried.

"Jim let her go out fer a stroll," replied Anson.

"I seen Jim was gittin' softy over her. Haw! Haw! Haw!"

But Snake Anson did not crack a smile. The atmosphere appeared not to be congenial for jokes, a fact Burt rather suddenly divined. Riggs and Moze returned from the promontory, the latter reporting that Shady Jones was riding up close. Then the girl walked slowly into sight and approached to find a seat within ten yards of the group. They waited in silence until the expected horseman rode up with water-bottles slung on both sides of his saddle. His advent was welcome. All the men were thirsty. Wilson took water to the girl before drinking himself.

"Thet's an all-fired hot ride fer water," declared the outlaw Shady, who somehow fitted his name in color and impression. "An', boss, if it's the same to you I won't take it ag'in."

"Cheer up, Shady. We'll be rustlin' back in the mountains before sundown," said Anson.

"Hang me if that ain't the cheerfulest news I've hed in some days. Hey, Moze?"

The black-faced Moze nodded his shaggy head.

"I'm sick an' sore of this deal," broke out Burt, evidently encouraged by his elders. "Ever since last fall we've been hangin' 'round - till jest lately freezin' in camps - no money - no drink - no grub wuth havin'. All on promises!"

Not improbably this young and reckless member of the gang had struck the note of discord. Wilson seemed most detached from any sentiment prevailing there. Some strong thoughts were revolving in his brain.

"Burt, you ain't insinuatin' thet I made promises?" inquired Anson, ominously.

"No, boss, I ain't. You allus said we might hit it rich. But them promises was made to you. An' it 'd be jest like thet greaser to go back on his word now we got the gurl."

"Son, it happens we got the wrong one. Our

long-haired pard hyar - Mister Riggs - him with the big gun - he waltzes up with this sassy kid instead of the woman Beasley wanted."

Burt snorted his disgust while Shady Jones, roundly swearing, pelted the smoldering camp-fire with stones. Then they all lapsed into surly silence. The object of their growing scorn, Riggs, sat a little way apart, facing none of them, but maintaining as bold a front as apparently he could muster.

Presently a horse shot up his ears, the first indication of scent or sound imperceptible to the men. But with this cue they all, except Wilson, sat up attentively. Soon the crack of iron-shod hoofs on stone broke the silence. Riggs nervously rose to his feet. And the others, still excepting Wilson, one by one followed suit. In another moment a rangy bay horse trotted out of the cedars, up to the camp, and his rider jumped off nimbly for so heavy a man.

"Howdy, Beasley?" was Anson's greeting.

"Hello, Snake, old man!" replied Beasley, as his bold, snapping black eyes swept the group. He was dusty and hot, and wet with sweat, yet evidently too excited to feel discomfort. "I seen your smoke signal first off an' jumped my hoss quick. But I rode north of Pine before I headed 'round this way. Did you corral the girl or did Riggs? Say! - you look queer! . . . What's wrong here? You haven't signaled me for nothin'?

Snake Anson beckoned to Bo.

"Come out of the shade. Let him look you over."

The girl walked out from under the spreading cedar that had hidden her from sight.

Beasley stared aghast - his jaw dropped.

"Thet's the kid sister of the woman I wanted!" he ejaculated.

"So we've jest been told."

Astonishment still held Beasley.

"Told?" he echoed. Suddenly his big body leaped with a start. "Who got her? , Who fetched her?"

"Why, Mister Gunman Riggs hyar," replied Anson, with a subtle scorn.

"Riggs, you got the wrong girl," shouted Beasley. "You made thet mistake once before. What're you up to?"

"I chased her an' when I got her, seein' it wasn't Nell Rayner - why - I kept her, anyhow," replied Riggs. "An' I've got a word for your ear alone."

"Man, you're crazy - queerin' my deal thet way!" roared Beasley. "You heard my plans. . . . Riggs, this girl-stealin' can't be done twice. Was you drinkin' or locoed or what?"

"Beasley, he was giving you the double-cross," cut in Bo Rayner's cool voice.

The rancher stared speechlessly at her, then at Anson, then at Wilson, and last at Riggs, when his brown visage shaded dark with rush of purple blood. With one lunge he knocked Riggs flat, then stood over him with a convulsive hand at his gun.

"You white-livered card-sharp! I've a notion to bore you. . . . They told me you had a deal of your own, an' now I believe it."

"Yes - I had," replied Riggs, cautiously getting up. He was ghastly. "But I wasn't double-crossin' you. Your deal was to get the girl away from home so you could take possession of her property. An' I wanted her."

"What for did you fetch the sister, then?" demanded Beasley, his big jaw bulging.

"Because I've a plan to -"

"Plan hell! You've spoiled my plan an' I've seen about enough of you." Beasley breathed hard; his lowering gaze boded an uncertain will toward the man who had crossed him; his hand still hung low and clutching.

"Beasley, tell them to get my horse. I want to go home," said Bo Rayner.

Slowly Beasley turned. Her words enjoined a silence. What to do with her now appeared a problem.

"I had nothin' to do with fetchin' you here an' I'll have nothin' to do with sendin' you back or whatever's done with you," declared Beasley.

Then the girl's face flashed white again and her eyes changed to fire.

"You're as big a liar as Riggs," she cried, passionately. "And you're a thief, a bully who picks on defenseless girls. Oh, we know your game! Milt Dale heard your plot with this outlaw Anson to steal my sister. You ought to be hanged - you half-breed greaser!"

"I'll cut out your tongue!" hissed Beasley.

"Yes, I'll bet you would if you had me alone. But these outlaws - these sheep-thieves - these tools you hire are better than you and Riggs. . . . What do you suppose Carmichael will do to you? Carmichael! He's my sweetheart - that cowboy. You know what he did to Riggs. Have you brains enough to know what he'll do to you?"

"He'll not do much," growled Beasley. But the thick purplish blood was receding from his face. "Your cowpuncher -"

"Bah!" she interrupted, and she snapped her fingers in his face. "He's from Texas! He's from Texas!"

"Supposin' he is from Texas?" demanded Beasley, in angry irritation. "What's thet? Texans are all over. There's Jim Wilson, Snake Anson's right-hand man. He's from Texas. But thet ain't scarin' any one."

He pointed toward Wilson, who shifted uneasily from foot to foot. The girl's flaming glance followed his hand.

"Are you from Texas?" she asked.

"Yes, Miss, I am - an' I reckon I don't deserve it," replied Wilson. It was certain that a vague shame attended his confession.

"Oh! I believed even a bandit from Texas would fight for a helpless girl!" she replied, in withering scorn of disappointment.

Jim Wilson dropped his head. If any one there suspected a serious turn to Wilson's attitude toward that situation it was the keen outlaw leader.

"Beasley, you're courtin' death," he broke in.

"You bet you are!" added Bo, with a passion that made her listeners quiver. "You've put me at the mercy of a gang of outlaws! You may force my sister out of her home! But your day will come.' Tom Carmichael will kill you."

Beasley mounted his horse. Sullen, livid, furious, he sat shaking in the saddle, to glare down at the outlaw leader.

"Snake, thet's no fault of mine the deal's miscarried. I was square. I made my offer for the workin' out of my plan. It 'ain't been done. Now there's hell to pay an' I'm through."

"Beasley, I reckon I couldn't hold you to anythin'," replied Anson, slowly. "But if you was square you ain't square now. We've hung around an' tried hard. My men are all sore. An' we're broke, with no outfit to speak of. Me an' you never fell out before. But I reckon we might."

"Do I owe you any money - accordin' to the deal?" demanded Beasley.

"No, you don't," responded Anson, sharply.

"Then thet's square. I wash my hands of the whole deal. Make Riggs pay up. He's got money an' he's got plans. Go in with him."

With that Beasley spurred his horse, wheeled and rode away. The outlaws gazed after him until he disappeared in the cedars.

"What'd you expect from a greaser?" queried Shady Jones.

"Anson, didn't I say so?" added Burt.

The black-visaged Moze rolled his eyes like a mad bull and Jim Wilson studiously examined a stick he held in his hands. Riggs showed immense relief.

"Anson, stake me to some of your outfit an' I'll ride off with the girl," he said, eagerly.

"Where'd you go now?" queried Anson, curiously.

Riggs appeared at a loss for a quick answer; his wits were no more equal to this predicament than his nerve.

"You're no woodsman. An' onless you're plumb locoed you'd never risk goin' near Pine or Show Down. There'll be real trackers huntin' your trail."

The listening girl suddenly appealed to Wilson.

"Don't let him take me off - alone - in the woods!" she faltered. That was the first indication of her weakening.

Jim Wilson broke into gruff reply. "I'm not bossin' this gang."

"But you're a man!" she importuned.

"Riggs, you fetch along your precious firebrand an' come with us," said Anson, craftily. "I'm particular curious to see her brand you."

"Snake, lemme take the girl back to Pine," said Jim Wilson.

Anson swore his amaze.

"It's sense," continued Wilson. "We've shore got our own troubles, an' keepin' her 'll only add to them. I've a hunch. Now you know I ain't often givin' to buckin' your say-so. But this deal ain't tastin' good to me. Thet girl ought to be sent home."

"But mebbe there's somethin' in it for us. Her sister 'd pay to git her back."

"Wal, I shore hope you'll recollect I offered - thet's all," concluded Wilson.

"Jim, if we wanted to git rid of her we'd let Riggs take her off," remonstrated the outlaw leader. He was perturbed and undecided. Wilson worried him.

The long Texan veered around full faced. What subtle transformation in him!

"Like hell we would!" he said.

It could not have been the tone that caused Anson to

quail. He might have been leader here, but he was not the greater man. His face clouded.

"Break camp," he ordered.

Riggs had probably not heard that last exchange between Anson and Wilson, for he had walked a few rods aside to get his horse.

In a few moments when they started off, Burt, Jones, and Moze were in the lead driving the pack-horses, Anson rode next, the girl came between him and Riggs, and significantly, it seemed, Jim Wilson brought up the rear.

This start was made a little after the noon hour. They zigzagged up the slope, took to a deep ravine, and followed it up to where it headed in the level forest. From there travel was rapid, the pack-horses being driven at a jogtrot. Once when a troop of deer burst out of a thicket into a glade, to stand with ears high, young Burt halted the cavalcade. His well-aimed shot brought down a deer. Then the men rode on, leaving him behind to dress and pack the meat. The only other halt made was at the crossing of the first water, a clear, swift brook, where both horses and men drank thirstily. Here Burt caught up with his comrades.

They traversed glade and park, and wended a crooked trail through the deepening forest, and climbed, bench after bench, to higher ground, while the sun sloped to the westward, lower and redder. Sunset had gone, and twilight was momentarily brightening to the afterglow when Anson, breaking his silence of the afternoon, ordered a halt.

The place was wild, dismal, a shallow vale between dark slopes of spruce. Grass, fire-wood, and water were there in abundance. All the men were off, throwing saddles and packs, before the tired girl made an effort to get down. Riggs, observing her, made a not ungentle move to pull her off. She gave him a sounding slap with her gloved hand.

"Keep your paws to yourself," she said. No evidence of exhaustion was there in her spirit.

Wilson had observed this by-play, but Anson had not.

"What come off?" he asked.

"Wal, the Honorable Gunman Riggs jest got caressed by the lady - as he was doin' the elegant," replied Moze, who stood nearest.

"Jim, was you watchin'?" queried Anson. His curiosity had held through the afternoon.

"He tried to yank her off an' she biffed him," replied Wilson.

"That Riggs is jest daffy or plain locoed," said Snake, in an aside to Moze.

"Boss, you mean plain cussed. Mark my words, he'll hoodoo this outfit. Jim was figgerin' correct."

"Hoodoo -" cursed Anson, under his breath.

Many hands made quick work. In a few moments a fire was burning brightly, water was boiling, pots were steaming, the odor of venison permeated the cool air.

The girl had at last slipped off her saddle to the ground, where she sat while Riggs led the horse away. She sat there apparently forgotten, a pathetic droop to her head.

Wilson had taken an ax and was vigorously wielding it among the spruces. One by one they fell with swish and soft crash. Then the sliding ring of the ax told how he was slicing off the branches with long sweeps. Presently he appeared in the semi-darkness, dragging half-trimmed spruces behind him. He made several trips, the last of which was to stagger under a huge burden of spruce boughs. These he spread under a low, projecting branch of an aspen. Then he leaned the bushy spruces slantingly against this branch on both sides, quickly improvising a V-shaped shelter with narrow aperture in front. Next from one of the packs he took a blanket and threw that inside the shelter. Then, touching the girl on the shoulder, he whispered:

"When you're ready, slip in there. An' don't lose no sleep by worryin', fer I'll be layin' right here."

He made a motion to indicate his length across the front of the narrow aperture.

"Oh, thank you! Maybe you really are a Texan," she whispered back.

"Mebbe," was his gloomy reply.

CHAPTER XXI

The girl refused to take food proffered her by Riggs, but she ate and drank a little that Wilson brought her, then she disappeared in the spruce lean-to.

Whatever loquacity and companionship had previously existed in Snake Anson's gang were not manifest in this camp. Each man seemed preoccupied, as if pondering the dawn in his mind of an ill omen not clear to him yet and not yet dreamed of by his fellows. They all smoked. Then Moze and Shady played cards awhile by the light of the fire, but it was a dull game, in which either seldom spoke. Riggs sought his blanket first, and the fact was significant that he lay down some distance from the spruce shelter which contained Bo Rayner. Presently young Burt went off grumbling to his bed. And not long afterward the card-players did likewise.

Snake Anson and Jim Wilson were left brooding in silence beside the dying camp-fire.

The night was dark, with only a few stars showing. A fitful wind moaned unearthly through the spruce. An occasional thump of hoof sounded from the dark woods. No cry of wolf or coyote or cat gave reality to the wildness of forest-land.

By and by those men who had rolled in their blankets

were breathing deep and slow in heavy slumber.

"Jim, I take it this hyar Riggs has queered our deal," said Snake Anson, in low voice.

"I reckon," replied Wilson.

"An' I'm feared he's queered this hyar White Mountain country fer us."

"Shore I 'ain't got so far as thet. What d' ye mean, Snake?"

"Damme if I savvy," was the gloomy reply. "I only know what was bad looks growin' wuss. Last fall - an' winter - an' now it's near April. We've got no outfit to make a long stand in the woods. . . . Jim, jest how strong is thet Beasley down in the settlements?"

"I've a hunch he ain't half as strong as he bluffs."

"Me, too. I got thet idee yesterday. He was scared of the kid - when she fired up an' sent thet hot-shot about her cowboy sweetheart killin' him. He'll do it, Jim. I seen that Carmichael at Magdalena some years ago. Then he was only a youngster. But, whew! Mebbe he wasn't bad after toyin' with a little red liquor."

"Shore. He was from Texas, she said."

"Jim, I savvied your feelin's was hurt - by thet talk about Texas - an' when she up an' asked you."

Wilson had no rejoinder for this remark.

"Wal, Lord knows, I ain't wonderin'. You wasn't a

hunted outlaw all your life. An' neither was I. . . .
Wilson, I never was keen on this girl deal - now,
was I?"

"I reckon it's honest to say no to thet," replied Wilson.
But it's done. Beasley 'll get plugged sooner or later.
Thet won't help us any. Chasin' sheep-herders out of
the country an' stealin' sheep - thet ain't stealin' gurls
by a long sight. Beasley 'll blame that on us, an' be
greaser enough to send some of his men out to hunt us.
For Pine an' Show Down won't stand thet long. There's
them Mormons. They'll be hell when they wake up.
Suppose Carmichael got thet hunter Dale an' them
hawk-eyed Beemans on our trail?"

"Wal, we'd cash in - quick," replied Anson, gruffly.

"Then why didn't you let me take the gurl back home?"

"Wal, come to think of thet, Jim, I'm sore, an' I need
money - an' I knowed you'd never take a dollar from
her sister. An' I've made up my mind to git somethin'
out of her."

"Snake, you're no fool. How 'll you do thet same an' do
it quick?"

"'Ain't reckoned it out yet."

"Wal, you got aboot to-morrer an' thet's all," returned
Wilson, gloomily.

"Jim, what's ailin' you?"

"I'll let you figger thet out."

"Wal, somethin' ails the whole gang," declared Anson, savagely. "With them it's nothin' to eat - no whisky - no money to bet with - no tobacco!. . . But thet's not what's ailin' you, Jim Wilson, nor me!"

"Wal, what is, then?" queried Wilson.

"With me it's a strange feelin' thet my day's over on these ranges. I can't explain, but it jest feels so. Somethin' in the air. I don't like them dark shadows out there under the spruces. Savvy? . . . An' as fer you, Jim - wal, you allus was half decent, an' my gang's got too lowdown fer you."

"Snake, did I ever fail you?"

"No, you never did. You're the best pard I ever knowed. In the years we've rustled together we never had a contrary word till I let Beasley fill my ears with his promises. Thet's my fault. But, Jim, it's too late."

"It mightn't have been too late yesterday."

"Mebbe not. But it is now, an' I'll hang on to the girl or git her worth in gold," declared the outlaw, grimly.

"Snake, I've seen stronger gangs than yours come an' go. Them Big Bend gangs in my country - them rustlers - they were all bad men. You have no likes of them gangs out heah. If they didn't get wiped out by Rangers or cowboys, why they jest naturally wiped out themselves. Thet's a law I recognize in relation to gangs like them. An' as for yours - why, Anson, it wouldn't hold water against one real gun-slinger."

"A-huh' Then if we ran up ag'in' Carmichael or some

such fellar - would you be suckin' your finger like a baby?"

"Wal, I wasn't takin' count of myself. I was takin' generalities."

"Aw, what 'n hell are them?" asked Anson, disgustedly. Jim, I know as well as you thet this hyar gang is hard put. We're goin' to be trailed an' chased. We've got to hide - be on the go all the time - here an' there - all over, in the roughest woods. An' wait our chance to work south."

"Shore. But, Snake, you ain't takin' no count of the feelin's of the men - an' of mine an' yours. . . . I'll bet you my hoss thet in a day or so this gang will go to pieces."

"I'm feared you spoke what's been crowdin' to git in my mind," replied Anson. Then he threw up his hands in a strange gesture of resignation. The outlaw was brave, but all men of the wilds recognized a force stronger than themselves. He sat there resembling a brooding snake with basilisk eyes upon the fire. At length he arose, and without another word to his comrade he walked wearily to where lay the dark, quiet forms of the sleepers.

Jim Wilson remained beside the flickering fire. He was reading something in the red embers, perhaps the past. Shadows were on his face, not all from the fading flames or the towering spruces. Ever and anon he raised his head to listen, not apparently that he expected any unusual sound, but as if involuntarily. Indeed, as Anson had said, there was something nameless in the air. The black forest breathed heavily, in fitful moans of wind. It had its secrets. The glances Wilson threw on all sides betrayed that any hunted man did not love the dark night, though it hid him. Wilson seemed fascinated by the life inclosed there by the black circle of spruce. He might have been reflecting on the strange reaction happening to every man in that group, since a girl had been brought among them. Nothing was clear, however; the forest kept its secret, as did the melancholy wind; the outlaws were sleeping like tired beasts, with their dark secrets locked in their hearts.

After a while Wilson put some sticks on the red embers, then pulled the end of a log over them. A blaze sputtered up, changing the dark circle and showing the sleepers with their set, shadowed faces upturned. Wilson gazed on all of them, a sardonic smile on his lips, and then his look fixed upon the sleeper apart from the others - Riggs. It might have been the false light of flame and shadow that created Wilson's expression of dark and terrible hate. Or it might have been the truth, expressed in that lonely, unguarded hour, from the depths of a man born in the South - a man who by his inheritance of race had reverence for all womanhood - by whose strange, wild, outlawed bloody life of a gun-fighter he must hate with the deadliest hate this type that aped and mocked his fame.

It was a long gaze Wilson rested upon Riggs - as strange and secretive as the forest wind moaning down the great aisles - and when that dark gaze was withdrawn Wilson stalked away to make his bed with the stride of one ill whom spirit had liberated force.

He laid his saddle in front of the spruce shelter where the girl had entered, and his tarpaulin and blankets likewise and then wearily stretched his long length to rest.

The camp-fire blazed up, showing the exquisite green. and brown-flecked festooning of the spruce branches, symmetrical and perfect, yet so irregular, and then it burned out and died down, leaving all in the dim gray starlight. The horses were not moving around; the moan of night wind had grown fainter; the low hum of insects, was dying away; even the tinkle of the brook had diminished. And that growth toward absolute silence continued, yet absolute silence was never attained. Life abided in the forest; only it had changed its form for the dark hours.

Anson's gang did not bestir themselves at the usual early sunrise hour common to all woodsmen, hunters, or outlaws, to whom the break of day was welcome. These companions - Anson and Riggs included - might have hated to see the dawn come. It meant only another meager meal, then the weary packing and the long, long ride to nowhere in particular, and another meager meal - all toiled for without even the necessities of satisfactory living, and assuredly without the thrilling hopes that made their life significant, and certainly with a growing sense of approaching calamity.

The outlaw leader rose surly and cross-grained. He had to boot Burt to drive him out for the horses. Riggs followed him. Shady Jones did nothing except grumble. Wilson, by common consent, always made the sour-dough bread, and he was slow about it this morning. Anson and Moze did the rest of the work, without alacrity. The girl did not appear.

"Is she dead?" growled Anson.

"No, she ain't," replied Wilson, looking up. "She's sleepin'. Let her sleep. She'd shore be a sight better off if she was daid."

"A-huh! So would all of this hyar outfit," was Anson's response.

"Wal, Sna-ake, I shore reckon we'll all be thet there soon," drawled Wilson, in his familiar cool and irritating tone that said so much more than the content of the words.

Anson did not address the Texas member of his party again.

Burt rode bareback into camp, driving half the number of the horses; Riggs followed shortly with several more. But three were missed, one of them being Anson's favorite. He would not have budged without that horse. During breakfast he growled about his lazy men, and after the meal tried to urge them off. Riggs went unwillingly. Burt refused to go at all.

"Nix. I footed them hills all I'm a-goin' to," he said. "An' from now on I rustle my own hoss."

The leader glared his reception of this opposition. Perhaps his sense of fairness actuated him once more, for he ordered Shady and Moze out to do their share.

"Jim, you're the best tracker in this outfit. Suppose you go," suggested Anson. "You allus used to be the first one off."

"Times has changed, Snake," was the imperturbable reply.

"Wal, won't you go?" demanded the leader, impatiently.

"I shore won't."

Wilson did not look or intimate in any way that he would not leave the girl in camp with one or any or all of Anson's gang, but the truth was as significant as if he had shouted it. The slow-thinking Moze gave Wilson a sinister look.

"Boss, ain't it funny how a pretty wench -?" began Shady Jones, sarcastically.

"Shut up, you fool!" broke in Anson. "Come on, I'll help rustle them hosses."

After they had gone Burt took his rifle and strolled off into the forest. Then the girl appeared. Her hair was down, her face pale, with dark shadows. She asked for water to wash her face. Wilson pointed to the brook, and as she walked slowly toward it he took a comb and a clean scarf from his pack and carried them to her.

Upon her return to the camp-fire she looked very different with her hair arranged and the red stains in her cheeks.

"Miss, air you hungry?" asked Wilson.

"Yes, I am," she replied.

He helped her to portions of bread, venison and gravy,

and a cup of coffee. Evidently she relished the meat, but she had to force down the rest.

"Where are they all?" she asked.

"Rustlin' the hosses."

Probably she divined that he did not want to talk, for the fleeting glance she gave him attested to a thought that his voice or demeanor had changed. Presently she sought a seat under the aspen-tree, out of the sun, and the smoke continually blowing in her face; and there she stayed, a forlorn little figure, for all the resolute lips and defiant eyes.

The Texan paced to and fro beside the camp-fire with bent head, and hands locked behind him. But for the swinging gun he would have resembled a lanky farmer, coatless and hatless, with his brown vest open, his trousers stuck in the top of the high boots.

And neither he nor the girl changed their positions relatively for a long time. At length, however, after peering into the woods, and listening, he remarked to the girl that he would be back in a moment, and then walked off around the spruces.

No sooner had he disappeared - in fact, so quickly after-ward that it presupposed design instead of accident - than Riggs came running from the opposite side of the glade. He ran straight to the girl, who sprang to her feet.

"I hid - two of the - horses," he panted, husky with excitement. "I'll take - two saddles. You grab some grub. We'll run for it."

"No," she cried, stepping back.

"But it's not safe - for us - here," he said, hurriedly, glancing all around. "I'll take you - home. I swear. . . . Not safe - I tell you - this gang's after me. Hurry!"

He laid hold of two saddles, one with each hand. The moment had reddened his face, brightened his eyes, made his action strong.

"I'm safer - here with this outlaw gang," she replied.

"You won't come!" His color began to lighten then, and his face to distort. He dropped his hold on the saddles.

"Harve Riggs, I'd rather become a toy and a rag for these ruffians than spend an hour alone with you," she flashed at him, in unquenchable hate.

"I'll drag you!"

He seized her, but could not hold her. Breaking away, she screamed.

"Help!"

That whitened his face, drove him to frenzy. Leaping forward, he struck her a hard blow across the mouth. It staggered her, and, tripping on a saddle, she fell. His hands flew to her throat, ready to choke her. But she lay still and held her tongue. Then he dragged her to her feet.

"Hurry now - grab that pack - an' follow me." Again Riggs laid hold of the two saddles. A desperate gleam, baleful and vainglorious, flashed over his face. He was living his one great adventure.

The girl's eyes dilated. They looked beyond him. Her lips opened.

"Scream again an' I'll kill you!" he cried, hoarsely and swiftly. The very opening of her lips had terrified Riggs.

"Reckon one scream was enough," spoke a voice, slow, but without the drawl, easy and cool, yet incalculable in some terrible sense.

Riggs wheeled with inarticulate cry. Wilson stood a few paces off, with his gun half leveled, low down. His face seemed as usual, only his eyes held a quivering, light intensity, like boiling molten silver.

"Girl, what made thet blood on your mouth?"

"Riggs hit me!" she whispered. Then at something she feared or saw or divined she shrank back, dropped on her knees, and crawled into the spruce shelter.

"Wal, Riggs, I'd invite you to draw if thet 'd be any use," said Wilson. This speech was reflective, yet it hurried a little.

Riggs could not draw nor move nor speak. He seemed turned to stone, except his jaw, which slowly fell.

"Harve Riggs, gunman from down Missouri way," continued the voice of incalculable intent, "reckon you've looked into a heap of gun-barrels in your day. Shore! Wal, look in this heah one!"

Wilson deliberately leveled the gun on a line with Riggs's starting eyes.

"Wasn't you heard to brag in Turner's saloon - thet you could see lead comin' - an' dodge it? Shore you must be swift! . . . Dodge this heah bullet!"

The gun spouted flame and boomed. One of Riggs's starting, popping eyes - the right one - went out, like a lamp. The other rolled horribly, then set in blank dead fixedness. Riggs swayed in slow motion until a lost balance felled him heavily, an inert mass.

Wilson bent over the prostrate form. Strange, violent contrast to the cool scorn of the preceding moment! Hissing, spitting, as if poisoned by passion, he burst with the hate that his character had forbidden him to express on a living counterfeit. Wilson was shaken, as if by a palsy. He choked over passionate, incoherent invective. It was class hate first, then the hate of real manhood for a craven, then the hate of disgrace for a murder. No man so fair as a gun-fighter in the Western creed of an "even break"!

Wilson's terrible cataclysm of passion passed. Straightening up, he sheathed his weapon and began a slow pace before the fire. Not many moments afterward he jerked his head high and listened. Horses were softly thudding through the forest. Soon Anson rode into sight with his men and one of the strayed horses. It chanced, too, that young Burt appeared on the other side of the glade. He walked quickly, as one who anticipated news.

Snake Anson as he dismounted espied the dead man.

"Jim - I thought I heard a shot."

The others exclaimed and leaped off their horses to view the prostrate form with that curiosity and strange fear common to all men confronted by sight of sudden death.

That emotion was only momentary.

"Shot his lamp out!" ejaculated Moze.

"Wonder how Gunman Riggs liked thet plumb center peg!" exclaimed Shady Jones, with a hard laugh.

"Back of his head all gone!" gasped young Burt. Not improbably he had not seen a great many bullet-marked men.

"Jim! - the long-haired fool didn't try to draw on you!" exclaimed Snake Anson, astounded.

Wilson neither spoke nor ceased his pacing.

"What was it over?" added Anson, curiously.

"He hit the gurl," replied Wilson.

Then there were long-drawn exclamations all around, and glance met glance.

"Jim, you saved me the job," continued the outlaw leader. "An' I'm much obliged. . . . Fellars, search Riggs an' we'll divvy. . . . Thet all right, Jim?"

"Shore, an' you can have my share."

They found bank-notes in the man's pocket and considerable gold worn in a money-belt around his waist. Shady Jones appropriated his boots, and Moze his gun. Then they left him as he had fallen.

"Jim, you'll have to track them lost hosses. Two still missin' an' one of them's mine," called Anson as Wilson paced to the end of his beat.

The girl heard Anson, for she put her head out of the spruce shelter and called: "Riggs said he'd hid two of the horses. They must be close. He came that way."

"Howdy, kid! Thet's good news," replied Anson. His spirits were rising. "He must hev wanted you to slope with him?"

"Yes. I wouldn't go."

"An' then he hit you?"

"Yes."

"Wal, recallin' your talk of yestiddy, I can't see as Mister Riggs lasted much longer hyar than he'd hev lasted in Texas. We've some of thet great country right in our outfit."

The girl withdrew her white face.

"It's break camp, boys," was the leader's order. "A couple of you look up them hosses. They'll be hid in some thick spruces. The rest of us 'll pack."

Soon the gang was on the move, heading toward the height of land, and swerving from it only to find soft and grassy ground that would not leave any tracks.

They did not travel more than a dozen miles during the afternoon, but they climbed bench after bench until they reached the timbered plateau that stretched in sheer black slope up to the peaks. Here rose the great and gloomy forest of firs and pines, with the spruce overshadowed and thinned out. The last hour of travel was tedious and toilsome, a zigzag, winding, breaking, climbing hunt for the kind of camp-site suited to Anson's fancy. He seemed to be growing strangely irrational about selecting places to camp. At last, for no reason that could have been manifest to a good woodsman, he chose a gloomy bowl in the center of the densest forest that had been traversed. The opening, if such it could have been called, was not a park or even a glade. A dark cliff, with strange holes, rose to one side, but not so high as the lofty pines that brushed it. Along its base babbled a brook, running over such formation of rock that from different points near at hand it gave forth different sounds, some singing, others melodious, and one at least of a hollow, weird, deep sound, not loud, but strangely penetrating.

"Sure spooky I say," observed Shady, sentiently.

The little uplift of mood, coincident with the rifling of Riggs's person, had not worn over to this evening camp. What talk the outlaws indulged in was necessary and conducted in low tones. The place enjoined silence.

Wilson performed for the girl very much the same service as he had the night before. Only he advised her not to starve herself; she must eat to keep up her strength. She complied at the expense of considerable effort.

As it had been a back-breaking day, in which all of them, except the girl, had climbed miles on foot, they did not linger awake long enough after supper to learn what a wild, weird, and pitch-black spot the outlaw leader had chosen. The little spaces of open ground between the huge-trunked pine-trees had no counterpart up in the lofty spreading foliage. Not a star could blink a wan ray of light into that Stygian pit. The wind, cutting down over abrupt heights farther up, sang in the pine-needles as if they were strings vibrant with chords. Dismal creaks were audible. They were the forest sounds of branch or tree rubbing one another, but which needed the corrective medium of daylight to convince any human that they were other than ghostly. Then, despite the wind and despite the changing murmur of the brook, there seemed to be a silence insulating them, as deep and impenetrable as the darkness.

But the outlaws, who were fugitives now, slept the sleep of the weary, and heard nothing. They awoke with the sun, when the forest seemed smoky in a golden gloom, when light and bird and squirrel proclaimed the day.

The horses had not strayed out of this basin during the night, a circumstance that Anson was not slow to appreciate.

"It ain't no cheerful camp, but I never seen a safer place to hole up in," he remarked to Wilson.

"Wal, yes - if any place is safe," replied that ally, dubiously.

"We can watch our back tracks. There ain't any other way to git in hyar thet I see."

"Snake, we was tolerable fair sheep-rustlers, but we're no good woodsmen."

Anson grumbled his disdain of this comrade who had once been his mainstay. Then he sent Burt out to hunt fresh meat and engaged his other men at cards. As they now had the means to gamble, they at once became absorbed. Wilson smoked and divided his thoughtful gaze between the gamblers and the drooping figure of the girl. The morning air was keen, and she, evidently not caring to be near her captors beside the camp-fire, had sought the only sunny spot in this gloomy dell. A couple of hours passed; the sun climbed high; the air grew warmer. Once the outlaw leader raised his head to scan the heavy-timbered slopes that inclosed the camp.

"Jim, them hosses are strayin' off ," he observed.

Wilson leisurely rose and stalked off across the small, open patches, in the direction of the horses. They had grazed around from the right toward the outlet of the brook. Here headed a ravine, dense and green. Two of the horses had gone down. Wilson evidently heard them, though they were not in sight, and he circled somewhat so as to get ahead of them and drive them back. The invisible brook ran down over the rocks with murmur and babble. He halted with instinctive action. He listened. Forest sounds, soft, lulling, came on the warm, pine-scented breeze. It would have taken no keen ear to hear soft and rapid padded footfalls. He moved on cautiously and turned into a little open, mossy spot, brown-matted and odorous, full of ferns and bluebells. In the middle of this, deep in the moss, he espied a huge round track of a cougar. He bent over it. Suddenly he stiffened, then straightened guardedly. At that instant he received a hard prod in the back. Throwing up his hands, he stood still, then slowly turned. A tall hunter in gray buckskin, gray-eyed and square-jawed, had him covered with a cocked rifle. And beside this hunter stood a monster cougar, snarling and blinking.

CHAPTER XXII

"Howdy, Dale," drawled Wilson. "Reckon you're a little previous on me."

"Sssssh! Not so loud," said the hunter, in low voice. "You're Jim Wilson?"

"Shore am. Say, Dale, you showed up soon. Or did you jest happen to run acrost us?"

"I've trailed you. Wilson, I'm after the girl."

"I knowed thet when I seen you!"

The cougar seemed actuated by the threatening position of his master, and he opened his mouth, showing great yellow fangs, and spat at Wilson. The outlaw apparently had no fear of Dale or the cocked rifle, but that huge, snarling cat occasioned him uneasiness.

"Wilson, I've heard you spoken of as a white outlaw," said Dale.

"Mebbe I am. But shore I'll be a scared one in a minit. Dale, he's goin' to jump me!"

"The cougar won't jump you unless I make him. Wilson, if I let you go will you get the girl for me?"

Zane Grey

"Wal, lemme see. Supposin' I refuse?" queried Wilson, shrewdly.

"Then, one way or another, it's all up with you."

"Reckon I 'ain't got much choice. Yes, I'll do it. But, Dale, are you goin' to take my word for thet an' let me go back to Anson?"

"Yes, I am. You're no fool. An' I believe you're square. I've got Anson and his gang corralled. You can't slip me - not in these woods. I could run off your horses - pick you off one by one - or turn the cougar loose on you at night."

"Shore. It's your game. Anson dealt himself this hand. . . . Between you an' me, Dale, I never liked the deal."

"Who shot Riggs? . . . I found his body."

"Wal, yours truly was around when thet come off," replied Wilson, with an involuntary little shudder. Some thought made him sick.

"The girl? Is she safe - unharmed?" queried Dale, hurriedly.

"She's shore jest as safe an' sound as when she was home. Dale, she's the gamest kid thet ever breathed! Why, no one could hev ever made me believe a girl, a kid like her, could hev the nerve she's got. Nothin's happened to her 'cept Riggs hit her in the mouth. . . . I killed him for thet. . . . An', so help me, God, I believe it's been workin' in me to save her somehow! Now it'll not be so hard."

"But how?" demanded Dale.

"Lemme see. . . . Wal, I've got to sneak her out of camp an' meet you. Thet's all."

"It must be done quick."

"But, Dale, listen," remonstrated Wilson, earnestly. "Too quick 'll be as bad as too slow. Snake is sore these days, gittin' sorer all the time. He might savvy somethin', if I ain't careful, an' kill the girl or do her harm. I know these fellars. They're all ready to go to pieces. An' shore I must play safe. Shore it'd be safer to have a plan."

Wilson's shrewd, light eyes gleamed with an idea. He was about to lower one of his upraised hands, evidently to point to the cougar, when he thought better of that.

"Anson's scared of cougars. Mebbe we can scare him an' the gang so it 'd be easy to sneak the girl off. Can you make thet big brute do tricks? Rush the camp at night an' squall an' chase off the horses?"

"I'll guarantee to scare Anson out of ten years' growth," replied Dale.

"Shore it's a go, then," resumed Wilson, as if glad. "I'll post the girl - give her a hunch to do her part. You sneak up to-night jest before dark. I'll hev the gang worked up. An' then you put the cougar to his tricks, whatever you want. When the gang gits wild I'll grab the girl an' pack her off down heah or somewheres aboot an' whistle fer you. . . . But mebbe thet ain't so good. If thet cougar comes pilin' into camp he might jump me instead of one of the gang. An' another hunch. He, might slope up on me in the dark when I was tryin' to find you. Shore thet ain't appealin' to me."

"Wilson, this cougar is a pet," replied Dale. "You think he's dangerous, but he's not. No more than a kitten. He only looks fierce. He has never been hurt by a person an' he's never fought anythin' himself but deer an' bear. I can make him trail any scent. But the truth is I couldn't make him hurt you or anybody. All the same, he can be made to scare the hair off any one who doesn't know him."

"Shore thet settles me. I'll be havin' a grand joke while them fellars is scared to death. . . . Dale, you can depend on me. An' I'm beholdin' to you fer what 'll square me some with myself. . . . To-night, an' if it won't work then, to-morrer night shore!"

Dale lowered the rifle. The big cougar spat again. Wilson dropped his hands and, stepping forward, split the green wall of intersecting spruce branches. Then he turned up the ravine toward the glen. Once there, in sight of his comrades, his action and expression changed.

"Hosses all thar, Jim?" asked Anson, as he picked up, his cards.

"Shore. They act awful queer, them hosses," replied. Wilson. "They're afraid of somethin'."

"A-huh! Silvertip mebbe," muttered Anson. "Jim, You jest keep watch of them hosses. We'd be done if some tarnal varmint stampeded them."

"Reckon I'm elected to do all the work now," complained Wilson, "while you card-sharps cheat each other." Rustle the hosses - an' water an' fire-wood. Cook an' wash. Hey?"

"No one I ever seen can do them camp tricks any better 'n Jim Wilson," replied Anson.

"Jim, you're a lady's man an' thar's our pretty hoodoo over thar to feed an' amoose," remarked Shady Jones, with a smile that disarmed his speech.

The outlaws guffawed.

"Git out, Jim, you're breakin' up the game," said Moze, who appeared loser.

"Wal, thet gurl would starve if it wasn't fer me," replied Wilson, genially, and he walked over toward her, beginning to address her, quite loudly, as he approached. "Wal, miss, I'm elected cook an' I'd shore like to heah what you fancy fer dinner."

The outlaws heard, for they guffawed again. "Haw! Haw! if Jim ain't funny!" exclaimed Anson.

The girl looked up amazed. Wilson was winking at her, and when he got near he began to speak rapidly and low.

"I jest met Dale down in the woods with his pet cougar. He's after you. I'm goin' to help him git you safe away. Now you do your part. I want you to pretend you've gone crazy. Savvy? Act out of your head! Shore I don't care what you do or say, only act crazy. An' don't be scared. We're goin' to scare the gang so I'll hev a chance to sneak you away. To-night or to-morrow - shore."

Before he began to speak she was pale, sad, dull of eye. Swiftly, with his words, she was transformed, and when he had ended she did not appear the same girl. She gave him one blazing flash of comprehension and nodded her head rapidly.

"Yes, I understand. I'll do it!" she whispered.

The outlaw turned slowly away with the most abstract air, confounded amid his shrewd acting, and he did not collect himself until half-way back to his comrades. Then, beginning to hum an old darky tune, he stirred up and replenished the fire, and set about preparation for the midday meal. But he did not miss anything going on around him. He saw the girl go into her shelter and come out with her hair all down over her face. Wilson, back to his comrades, grinned his glee, and he wagged his head as if he thought the situation was developing.

The gambling outlaws, however, did not at once see the girl preening herself and smoothing her long hair in a way calculated to startle.

"Busted!" ejaculated Anson, with a curse, as he slammed down his cards. "If I ain't hoodooed I'm a two-bit of a gambler!"

"Sartin you're hoodooed," said Shady Jones, in scorn. "Is thet jest dawnin' on you?"

"Boss, you play like a cow stuck in the mud," remarked Moze, laconically.

"Fellars, it ain't funny," declared Anson, with pathetic gravity. "I'm jest gittin' on to myself. Somethin's wrong. Since 'way last fall no luck - nothin' but the wust end of everythin'. I ain't blamin' anybody. I'm the boss. It's me thet's off."

"Snake, shore it was the gurl deal you made," rejoined Wilson, who had listened. "I told you. Our troubles hev only begun. An' I can see the wind-up. Look!"

Wilson pointed to where the girl stood, her hair flying wildly all over her face and shoulders. She was making most elaborate bows to an old stump, sweeping the ground with her tresses in her obeisance.

Anson started. He grew utterly astounded. His amaze was ludicrous. And the other two men looked to stare, to equal their leader's bewilderment.

"What 'n hell's come over her?" asked Anson, dubiously. "Must hev perked up. . . . But she ain't feelin' thet gay!"

Wilson tapped his forehead with a significant finger.

"Shore I was scared of her this mawnin'," he whispered.

"Naw!" exclaimed Anson, incredulously.

"If she hain't queer I never seen no queer wimmin," vouchsafed Shady Jones, and it would have been judged, by the way he wagged his head, that he had been all his days familiar with women.

Moze looked beyond words, and quite alarmed.

"I seen it comin'," declared Wilson, very much excited. "But I was scared to say so. You-all made fun of me aboot her. Now I shore wish I had spoken up."

Anson nodded solemnly. He did not believe the evidence of his sight, but the facts seemed stunning. As if the girl were a dangerous and incomprehensible thing, he approached her step by step. Wilson followed, and the others appeared drawn irresistibly.

"Hey thar - kid!" called Anson, hoarsely.

The girl drew her slight form up haughtily. Through her spreading tresses her eyes gleamed unnaturally upon the outlaw leader. But she deigned not to reply.

"Hey thar - you Rayner girl!" added Anson, lamely. "What's ailin' you?"

"My lord! did you address me?" she asked, loftily.

Shady Jones got over his consternation and evidently extracted some humor from the situation, as his dark face began to break its strain.

"Aww!" breathed Anson, heavily.

"Ophelia awaits your command, my lord. I've been gathering flowers," she said, sweetly, holding up her empty hands as if they contained a bouquet.

Shady Jones exploded in convulsed laughter. But his merriment was not shared. And suddenly it brought disaster upon him. The girl flew at him.

"Why do you croak, you toad? I will have you

whipped and put in irons, you scullion!" she cried, passionately.

Shady underwent a remarkable change, and stumbled in his backward retreat. Then she snapped her fingers in Moze's face.

"You black devil! Get hence! Avaunt!"

Anson plucked up courage enough to touch her.

"Aww! Now, Ophelyar -"

Probably he meant to try to humor her, but she screamed, and he jumped back as if she might burn him. She screamed shrilly, in wild, staccato notes.

"You! You!" she pointed her finger at the outlaw leader. "You brute to women! You ran off from your wife!"

Anson turned plum-color and then slowly white. The girl must have sent a random shot home.

"And now the devil's turned you into a snake. A long, scaly snake with green eyes! Uugh! You'll crawl on your belly soon - when my cowboy finds you. And he'll tramp you in the dust."

She floated away from them and began to whirl gracefully, arms spread and hair flying; and then, apparently oblivious of the staring men, she broke into a low, sweet song. Next she danced around a pine, then danced into her little green inclosure. From which presently she sent out the most doleful moans. "Aww! What a shame!" burst out Anson. "Thet fine, healthy, nervy kid! Clean gone! Daffy! Crazy 'n a bedbug!"

"Shore it's a shame," protested Wilson." But it's wuss for us. Lord! if we was hoodooed before, what will we be now? Didn't I tell you, Snake Anson? You was warned. Ask Shady an' Moze - they see what's up."

"No luck 'll ever come our way ag'in," predicted Shady, mournfully.

"It beats me, boss, it beats me," muttered Moze.

"A crazy woman on my hands! If thet ain't the last straw!" broke out Anson, tragically, as he turned away. Ignorant, superstitious, worked upon by things as they seemed, the outlaw imagined himself at last beset by malign forces. When he flung himself down upon one of the packs his big red-haired hands shook. Shady and Moze resembled two other men at the end of their ropes.

Wilson's tense face twitched, and he averted it, as apparently he fought off a paroxysm of some nature. Just then Anson swore a thundering oath.

"Crazy or not, I'll git gold out of thet kid!" he roared.

"But, man, talk sense. Are you gittin' daffy, too? I declare this outfit's been eatin' loco. You can't git gold fer her!" said Wilson, deliberately.

"Why can't I?"

"'Cause we're tracked. We can't make no dickers. Why, in another day or so we'll be dodgin' lead."

"Tracked! Whar 'd you git thet idee? As soon as this?" queried Anson, lifting his head like a striking snake. His men, likewise, betrayed sudden interest.

"Shore it's no idee. I 'ain't seen any one. But I feel it in my senses. I hear somebody comin' - a step on our trail - all the time - night in particular. Reckon there's a big posse after us."

"Wal, if I see or hear anythin' I'll knock the girl on the head an' we'll dig out of hyar," replied Anson, sullenly.

Wilson executed a swift forward motion, violent and passionate, so utterly unlike what might have been looked for from him, that the three outlaws gaped.

"Then you'll shore hev to knock Jim Wilson on the haid first," he said, in voice as strange as his action.

"Jim! You wouldn't go back on me!" implored Anson, with uplifted hands, in a dignity of pathos.

"I'm losin' my haid, too, an' you shore might as well knock it in, an' you'll hev to before I'll stand you murderin' thet pore little gurl you've drove crazy."

"Jim, I was only mad," replied Anson. "Fer thet matter, I'm growin' daffy myself. Aw! we all need a good stiff drink of whisky."

So he tried to throw off gloom and apprehension, but he failed. His comrades did not rally to his help. Wilson walked away, nodding his head.

"Boss, let Jim alone," whispered Shady. "It's orful the way you buck ag'in' him - when you seen he's stirred up. Jim's true blue. But you gotta be careful."

Moze corroborated this statement by gloomy nods.

When the card-playing was resumed, Anson did not join the game, and both Moze and Shady evinced little of that whole-hearted obsession which usually attended their gambling. Anson lay at length, his head in a saddle, scowling at the little shelter where the captive girl kept herself out of sight. At times a faint song or laugh, very unnatural, was wafted across the space. Wilson plodded at the cooking and apparently heard no sounds. Presently he called the men to eat, which office they surlily and silently performed, as if it was a favor bestowed upon the cook.

"Snake, hadn't I ought to take a bite of grub over to the gurl?" asked Wilson.

"Do you hev to ask me thet?" snapped Anson. "She's gotta be fed, if we hev to stuff it down her throat."

"Wal, I ain't stuck on the job," replied Wilson. "But I'll tackle it, seein' you-all got cold feet."

With plate and cup be reluctantly approached the little lean-to, and, kneeling, he put his head inside. The girl, quick-eyed and alert, had evidently seen him coming. At any rate, she greeted him with a cautious smile.

"Jim, was I pretty good?" she whispered.

"Miss, you was shore the finest aktress I ever seen," he responded, in a low voice. "But you dam near overdid it. I'm goin' to tell Anson you're sick now - poisoned or somethin' awful. Then we'll wait till night. Dale shore will help us out."

"Oh, I'm on fire to get away," she exclaimed. "Jim Wilson, I'll never forget you as long as I live!"

He seemed greatly embarrassed.

"Wal - miss - I - I'll do my best licks. But I ain't gamblin' none on results. Be patient. Keep your nerve. Don't get scared. I reckon between me an' Dale you'll git away from heah."

Withdrawing his head, he got up and returned to the camp-fire, where Anson was waiting curiously.

"I left the grub. But she didn't touch it. Seems sort of sick to me, like she was poisoned."

"Jim, didn't I hear you talkin'?" asked Anson.

"Shore. I was coaxin' her. Reckon she ain't so ranty as she was. But she shore is doubled-up, an' sickish."

"Wuss an' wuss all the time," said Anson, between his teeth. "An' where's Burt? Hyar it's noon an' he left early. He never was no woodsman. He's got lost."

"Either thet or he's run into somethin'," replied Wilson, thoughtfully.

Anson doubled a huge fist and cursed deep under his breath - the reaction of a man whose accomplices and partners and tools, whose luck, whose faith in himself had failed him. He flung himself down under a tree, and after a while, when his rigidity relaxed, he probably fell asleep. Moze and Shady kept at their game. Wilson paced to and fro, sat down, and then got up to bunch the horses again, walked around the dell and back to camp. The afternoon hours were long. And they were waiting hours. The act of waiting appeared on the surface of all these outlaws did.

At sunset the golden gloom of the glen changed to a vague, thick twilight. Anson rolled over, yawned, and sat up. As he glanced around, evidently seeking Burt, his face clouded.

"No sign of Burt?" he asked.

Wilson expressed a mild surprise. "Wal, Snake, you ain't expectin' Burt now?"

"I am, course I am. Why not?" demanded Anson. "Any other time we'd look fer him, wouldn't we?"

"Any other time ain't now. . . . Burt won't ever come back!" Wilson spoke it with a positive finality."

"A-huh! Some more of them queer feelin's of yourn - operatin' again, hey? Them onnatural kind thet you can't explain, hey?"

Anson's queries were bitter and rancorous.

"Yes. An', Snake, I tax you with this heah. Ain't any of them queer feelin's operatin' in you? "

"No!" rolled out the leader, savagely. But his passionate denial was a proof that he lied. From the moment of this outburst, which was a fierce clinging to the old, brave instincts of his character, unless a sudden change marked the nature of his fortunes, he would rapidly deteriorate to the breaking-point. And in such brutal, unrestrained natures as his this breaking-point meant a desperate stand, a desperate forcing of events, a desperate accumulation of passions that stalked out to deal and to meet disaster and blood and death.

Wilson put a little wood on the fire and he munched a biscuit. No one asked him to cook. No one made any effort to do so. One by one each man went to the pack to get some bread and meat.

Then they waited as men who knew not what they waited for, yet hated and dreaded it.

Twilight in that glen was naturally a strange, veiled condition of the atmosphere. It was a merging of shade and light, which two seemed to make gray, creeping shadows.

Suddenly a snorting and stamping of the horses startled the men.

"Somethin' scared the hosses," said Anson, rising. "Come on."

Moze accompanied him, and they disappeared in the gloom. More trampling of hoofs was heard, then a cracking of brush, and the deep voices of men. At length the two outlaws returned, leading three of the horses, which they haltered in the open glen.

The camp-fire light showed Anson's face dark and serious.

"Jim, them hosses are wilder 'n deer," he said. "I ketched mine, an' Moze got two. But the rest worked away whenever we come close. Some varmint has scared them bad. We all gotta rustle out thar quick."

Wilson rose, shaking his head doubtfully. And at that moment the quiet air split to a piercing, horrid neigh of a terrified horse. Prolonged to a screech, it broke and ended. Then followed snorts of fright, pound and crack and thud of hoofs, and crash of brush; then a gathering thumping, crashing roar, split by piercing sounds.

"Stampede!" yelled Anson, and he ran to hold his own horse, which he had haltered right in camp. It was big and wild-looking, and now reared and plunged to break away. Anson just got there in time, and then it took all his weight to pull the horse down. Not until the crashing, snorting, pounding melee had subsided and died away over the rim of the glen did Anson dare leave his frightened favorite.

"Gone! Our horses are gone! Did you hear 'em?" he exclaimed, blankly.

"Shore. They're a cut-up an' crippled bunch by now," replied Wilson.

"Boss, we'll never git 'em back, not 'n a hundred years," declared Moze.

"Thet settles us, Snake Anson," stridently added Shady Jones. "Them hosses are gone! You can kiss your hand to them. . . . They wasn't hobbled. They hed an orful scare. They split on thet stampede an' they'll never git together. . . . See what you've fetched us to!"

Under the force of this triple arraignment the outlaw leader dropped to his seat, staggered and silenced. In fact, silence fell upon all the men and likewise enfolded the glen.

Night set in jet-black, dismal, lonely, without a star. Faintly the wind moaned. Weirdly the brook babbled through its strange chords to end in the sound that was hollow. It was never the same - a rumble, as if faint, distant thunder - a deep gurgle, as of water drawn into a vortex - a rolling, as of a stone in swift current. The black cliff was invisible, yet seemed to have many weird faces; the giant pines loomed spectral; the shadows were thick, moving, changing. Flickering lights from the camp-fire circled the huge trunks and played fantastically over the brooding men. This camp-fire did not burn or blaze cheerily; it had no glow, no sputter, no white heart, no red, living embers. One by one the outlaws, as if with common consent, tried their hands at making the fire burn aright. What little wood had been collected was old; it would burn up with false flare, only to die quickly.

After a while not one of the outlaws spoke or stirred. Not one smoked. Their gloomy eyes were fixed on the fire. Each one was concerned with his own thoughts, his own lonely soul unconsciously full of a doubt of the future. That brooding hour severed him from comrade.

At night nothing seemed the same as it was by day. With success and plenty, with full-blooded action past and more in store, these outlaws were as different from their present state as this black night was different from the bright day they waited for. Wilson, though he played a deep game of deceit for the sake of the helpless girl - and thus did not have haunting and superstitious fears on her account - was probably more conscious of impending catastrophe than any of them.

The evil they had done spoke in the voice of nature, out of the darkness, and was interpreted by each according to his hopes and fears. Fear was their predominating sense. For years they had lived with some species of fear - of honest men or vengeance, of pursuit, of starvation, of lack of drink or gold, of blood and death, of stronger men, of luck, of chance, of fate, of mysterious nameless force. Wilson was the type of fearless spirit, but he endured the most gnawing and implacable fear of all - that of himself - that he must inevitably fall to deeds beneath his manhood.

So they hunched around the camp-fire, brooding because hope was at lowest ebb; listening because the weird, black silence, with its moan of wind and hollow laugh of brook, compelled them to hear; waiting for sleep, for the hours to pass, for whatever was to come.

And it was Anson who caught the first intimation of an impending doom.

CHAPTER XXIII

"Listen!"

Anson whispered tensely. His poise was motionless, his eyes roved everywhere. He held up a shaking, bludgy finger, to command silence.

A third and stranger sound accompanied the low, weird moan of the wind, and the hollow mockery of the brook - and it seemed a barely perceptible, exquisitely delicate wail or whine. It filled in the lulls between the other sounds.

"If thet's some varmint he's close," whispered Anson.

"But shore, it's far off," said Wilson.

Shady Jones and Moze divided their opinions in the same way.

All breathed freer when the wail ceased, relaxing to their former lounging positions around the fire. An impenetrable wall of blackness circled the pale space lighted by the camp-fire; and this circle contained the dark, somber group of men in the center, the dying camp-fire, and a few spectral trunks of pines and the tethered horses on the outer edge. The horses scarcely moved from their tracks, and their erect, alert heads attested to their sensitiveness to the peculiarities of the night.

Then, at an unusually quiet lull the strange sound gradually arose to a wailing whine.

"It's thet crazy wench cryin'," declared the outlaw leader.

Apparently his allies accepted that statement with as much relief as they had expressed for the termination of the sound.

"Shore, thet must be it," agreed Jim Wilson, gravely.

"We'll git a lot of sleep with thet gurl whinin' all night," growled Shady Jones.

"She gives me the creeps," said Moze.

Wilson got up to resume his pondering walk, head bent, hands behind his back, a grim, realistic figure of perturbation.

"Jim - set down. You make me nervous," said Anson, irritably.

Wilson actually laughed, but low, as if to keep his strange mirth well confined.

"Snake, I'll bet you my hoss an' my gun ag'in' a biscuit thet in aboot six seconds more or less I'll be stampedin like them hosses."

Anson's lean jaw dropped. The other two outlaws stared with round eyes. Wilson was not drunk, they evidently knew; but what he really was appeared a mystery.

"Jim Wilson, are you showin' yellow?" queried Anson, hoarsely.

"Mebbe. The Lord only knows. But listen heah. . . . Snake, you've seen an' heard people croak?"

"You mean cash in - die?"

"Shore."

"Wal, yes - a couple or so," replied Anson, grimly.

"But you never seen no one die of shock - of an orful scare?"

"No, I reckon I never did."

"I have. An' thet's what's ailin' Jim Wilson," and he resumed his dogged steps.

Anson and his two comrades exchanged bewildered glances with one another.

"A-huh! Say, what's thet got to do with us hyar? asked Anson, presently.

"Thet gurl is dyin'!" retorted Wilson, in a voice cracking like a whip.

The three outlaws stiffened in their seats, incredulous, yet irresistibly swayed by emotions that stirred to this dark, lonely, ill-omened hour.

Wilson trudged to the edge of the lighted circle,

muttering to himself, and came back again; then he trudged farther, this time almost out of sight, but only to return; the third time he vanished in the impenetrable wall of light. The three men scarcely moved a muscle as they watched the place where he had disappeared. In a few moments he came stumbling back.

"Shore she's almost gone," he said, dismally. "It took my nerve, but I felt of her face. . . . Thet orful wail is her breath chokin' in her throat. . . . Like a death-rattle, only long instead of short."

"Wal, if she's gotta croak it's good she gits it over quick," replied Anson. "I 'ain't hed sleep fer three nights. . . . An' what I need is whisky."

"Snake, thet's gospel you're spoutin'," remarked Shady Jones, morosely.

The direction of sound in the glen was difficult to be assured of, but any man not stirred to a high pitch of excitement could have told that the difference in volume of this strange wail must have been caused by different distances and positions. Also, when it was loudest, it was most like a whine. But these outlaws heard with their consciences.

At last it ceased abruptly.

Wilson again left the group to be swallowed up by the night. His absence was longer than usual, but he returned hurriedly.

"She's daid!" he exclaimed, solemnly. "Thet innocent kid - who never harmed no one - an' who'd make any man better fer seein' her - she's daid! . . . Anson, you've shore a heap to answer fer when your time comes."

"What's eatin' you?" demanded the leader, angrily. "Her blood ain't on my hands."

"It shore is," shouted Wilson, shaking his hand at Anson. "An' you'll hev to take your medicine. I felt thet comin' all along. An' I feel some more."

"Aw! She's jest gone to sleep," declared Anson, shaking his long frame as he rose. "Gimme a light."

"Boss, you're plumb off to go near a dead gurl thet's jest died crazy," protested Shady Jones.

"Off! Haw! Haw! Who ain't off in this outfit, I'd like to know?" Anson possessed himself of a stick blazing at one and, and with this he stalked off toward the lean-to where the girl was supposed to be dead. His gaunt figure, lighted by the torch, certainly fitted the weird, black surroundings. And it was seen that once near the girl's shelter he proceeded more slowly, until he halted. He bent to peer inside.

"SHE'S GONE!" he yelled, in harsh, shaken accents.

Than the torch burned out, leaving only a red glow. He whirled it about, but the blaze did not rekindle. His comrades, peering intently, lost sight of his tall form and the end of the red-ended stick. Darkness like pitch swallowed him. For a moment no sound intervened. Again the moan of wind, the strange little mocking hollow roar, dominated the place. Then there came a rush of something, perhaps of air, like the soft swishing of spruce branches swinging aside. Dull, thudding footsteps followed it. Anson came running back to the fire. His aspect was wild, his face pale, his eyes were fierce and starting from their sockets. He had drawn his gun.

"Did - ye - see er hear - anythin'?" he panted, peering back, then all around, and at last at his man.

"No. An' I shore was lookin' an' listenin'," replied Wilson.

"Boss, there wasn't nothin'," declared Moze.

"I ain't so sartin," said Shady Jones, with doubtful, staring eyes. "I believe I heerd a rustlin'."

"She wasn't there!" ejaculated Anson, in wondering awe. "She's gone! . . . My torch went out. I couldn't see. An' jest then I felt somethin' was passin'. Fast! I jerked 'round. All was black, an' yet if I didn't see a big gray streak I'm crazier 'n thet gurl. But I couldn't swear to anythin' but a rushin' of wind. I felt thet."

"Gone!" exclaimed Wilson, in great alarm. "Fellars, if thet's so, then mebbe she wasn't daid an' she wandered off. . . . But she was daid! Her heart hed quit beatin'. I'll swear to thet."

"I move to break camp," said Shady Jones, gruffly, and he stood up. Moze seconded that move by an expressive flash of his black visage.

"Jim, if she's dead - an' gone - what 'n hell's come off?" huskily asked Anson. "It, only seems thet way. We're all worked up. . . . Let's talk sense."

"Anson, shore there's a heap you an' me don't know," replied Wilson. "The world come to an end once. Wal, it can come to another end. . . . I tell you I ain't surprised -"

"Thar!" cried Anson, whirling, with his gun leaping out.

Something huge, shadowy, gray against the black rushed behind the men and trees; and following it came a perceptible acceleration of the air.

"Shore, Snake, there wasn't nothin'," said Wilson, presently."

"I heerd," whispered Shady Jones.

"It was only a breeze blowin' thet smoke," rejoined Moze.

"I'd bet my soul somethin' went back of me," declared Anson, glaring into the void.

"Listen an' let's make shore," suggested Wilson.

The guilty, agitated faces of the outlaws showed plain enough in the flickering light for each to see a convicting dread in his fellow. Like statues they stood, watching and listening.

Few sounds stirred in the strange silence. Now and then the horses heaved heavily, but stood still; a dismal, dreary note of the wind in the pines vied with a hollow laugh of the brook. And these low sounds only fastened attention upon the quality of the silence. A breathing, lonely spirit of solitude permeated the black dell. Like a pit of unplumbed depths the dark night yawned. An evil conscience, listening there, could have heard the most peaceful, beautiful, and mournful sounds of nature only as strains of a calling hell.

Suddenly the silent, oppressive, surcharged air split to a short, piercing scream.

Anson's big horse stood up straight, pawing the air, and came down with a crash. The other horses shook with terror.

"Wasn't - thet - a cougar?" whispered Anson, thickly.

"Thet was a woman's scream," replied Wilson, and he appeared to be shaking like a leaf in the wind.

"Then - I figgered right - the kid's alive - wonderin' around - an' she let out thet orful scream," said Anson.

"Wonderin' 'round, yes - but she's daid!"

"My Gawd! it ain't possible!"

"Wal, if she ain't wonderin' round daid she's almost daid," replied Wilson. And he began to whisper to himself.

"If I'd only knowed what thet deal meant I'd hev plugged Beasley instead of listenin'. . . . An' I ought to hev knocked thet kid on the head an' made sartin she'd croaked. If she goes screamin' 'round thet way -"

His voice failed as there rose a thin, splitting, high-pointed shriek, somewhat resembling the first scream, only less wild. It came apparently from the cliff.

From another point in the pitch-black glen rose the wailing, terrible cry of a woman in agony. Wild, haunting, mournful wail!

Anson's horse, loosing the halter, plunged back, almost falling over a slight depression in the rocky ground. The outlaw caught him and dragged him nearer the fire. The other horses stood shaking and straining. Moze ran between them and held them. Shady Jones threw green brush on the fire. With sputter and crackle a blaze started, showing Wilson standing tragically, his arms out, facing the black shadows.

The strange, live shriek was not repeated. But the cry, like that of a woman in her death-throes, pierced the silence again. It left a quivering ring that softly died away. Then the stillness clamped down once more and the darkness seemed to thicken. The men waited, and when they had begun to relax the cry burst out appallingly close, right behind the trees. It was human - the personification of pain and terror - the tremendous struggle of precious life against horrible death. So pure, so exquisite, so wonderful was the cry that the listeners writhed as if they saw an innocent, tender, beautiful girl torn frightfully before their eyes. It was full of suspense; it thrilled for death; its marvelous potency was the wild note - that beautiful and ghastly note of self-preservation.

In sheer desperation the outlaw leader fired his gun at the black wall whence the cry came. Then he had to fight his horse to keep him from plunging away. Following the shot was an interval of silence; the horses became tractable; the men gathered closer to the fire, with the halters still held firmly.

"If it was a cougar - thet 'd scare him off," said Anson.

"Shore, but it ain't a cougar," replied Wilson. "Wait an' see!"

They all waited, listening with ears turned to different points, eyes roving everywhere, afraid of their very shadows. Once more the moan of wind, the mockery of brook, deep gurgle, laugh and babble, dominated the silence of the glen.

"Boss, let's shake this spooky hole," whispered Moze.

The suggestion attracted Anson, and he pondered it while slowly shaking his head.

"We've only three hosses. An' mine 'll take ridin' - after them squalls," replied the leader. "We've got packs, too. An' hell 'ain't nothin' on this place fer bein' dark."

"No matter. Let's go. I'll walk an' lead the way," said Moze, eagerly. "I got sharp eyes. You fellars can ride an' carry a pack. We'll git out of here an' come back in daylight fer the rest of the outfit."

"Anson, I'm keen fer thet myself," declared Shady Jones.

"Jim, what d'ye say to thet?" queried Anson. "Rustlin' out of this black hole?"

"Shore it's a grand idee," agreed Wilson.

"Thet was a cougar," avowed Anson, gathering courage as the silence remained unbroken. "But jest the same it was as tough on me as if it hed been a woman screamin' over a blade twistin' in her gizzards."

"Snake, shore you seen a woman heah lately?" delibe-rately asked Wilson.

"Reckon I did. Thet kid," replied Anson, dubiously.

"Wal, you seen her go crazy, didn't you?"

"Yes."

"'An' she wasn't heah when you went huntin' fer her?"

"Correct."

"Wal, if thet's so, what do you want to blab about cougars for?"

Wilson's argument seemed incontestable. Shady and Moze nodded gloomily and shifted restlessly from foot to foot. Anson dropped his head.

"No matter - if we only don't hear -" he began, suddenly to grow mute.

Right upon them, from some place, just out the circle of light, rose a scream, by reason of its proximity the most piercing and agonizing yet heard, simply petrifying the group until the peal passed. Anson's huge horse reared, and with a snort of terror lunged in tremendous leap, straight out. He struck Anson with thudding impact, knocking him over the rocks into the depression back of the camp-fire, and plunging after him. Wilson had made a flying leap just in time to avoid being struck, and he turned to see Anson go down. There came a crash, a groan, and then the strike and pound of hoofs as the horse struggled up. Apparently he had rolled over his master.

"Help, fellars!" yelled Wilson, quick to leap down over the little bank, and in the dim light to grasp the halter. The three men dragged the horse out and securely tied him close to a tree. That done, they peered down into the depression. Anson's form could just barely be distinguished in the gloom. He lay stretched out. Another groan escaped him.

"Shore I'm scared he's hurt," said Wilson.

"Hoss rolled right on top of him. An' thet hoss's heavy," declared Moze.

They got down and knelt beside their leader. In the darkness his face looked dull gray. His breathing was not right.

"Snake, old man, you ain't - hurt?" asked Wilson, with a tremor in his voice. Receiving no reply, he said to his comrades, "Lay hold an' we'll heft him up where we can see."

The three men carefully lifted Anson up on the bank and laid him near the fire in the light. Anson was conscious. His face was ghastly. Blood showed on his lips.

Wilson knelt beside him. The other outlaws stood up, and with one dark gaze at one another damned Anson's chance of life. And on the instant rose that terrible distressing scream of acute agony - like that of a woman being dismembered. Shady Jones whispered something to Moze. Then they stood up, gazing down at their fallen leader.

"Tell me where you're hurt?" asked Wilson.

"He - smashed - my chest," said Anson, in a broken, strangled whisper.

Wilson's deft hands opened the outlaw's shirt and felt of his chest.

"No. Shore your breast-bone ain't smashed," replied Wilson, hopefully. And he began to run his hand around one side of Anson's body and then the other. Abruptly he stopped, averted his gaze, then slowly ran the hand all along that side. Anson's ribs had been broken and crushed in by the weight of the horse. He was bleeding at the mouth, and his slow, painful expulsions of breath brought a bloody froth, which showed that the broken bones had penetrated the lungs. An injury sooner or later fatal!

"Pard, you busted a rib or two," said Wilson.

"Aw, Jim - it must be - wuss 'n thet!" he whispered. "I'm - in orful - pain. An' I can't - git any - breath."

"Mebbe you'll be better," said Wilson, with a cheerfulness his face belied.

Moze bent close over Anson, took a short scrutiny of that ghastly face, at the blood-stained lips, and the lean hands plucking at nothing. Then he jerked erect.

"Shady, he's goin' to cash. Let's clear out of this."

"I'm yours pertickler previous," replied Jones.

Both turned away. They untied the two horses and led them up to where the saddles lay. Swiftly the blankets went on, swiftly he saddles swung up, swiftly the cinches snapped. Anson lay gazing up at Wilson, comprehending this move. And Wilson stood strangely grim and silent, somehow detached coldly from that self of the past few hours.

"Shady, you grab some bread an' I'll pack a bunk of meat," said Moze. Both men came near the fire, into the light, within ten feet of where the leader lay.

"Fellars - you ain't - slopin'?" he whispered, in husky amaze.

"Boss, we air thet same. We can't do you no good an' this hole ain't healthy," replied Moze.

Shady Jones swung himself astride his horse, all about him sharp, eager, strung.

"Moze, I'll tote the grub an' you lead out of hyar, till we git past the wust timber," he said.

"Aw, Moze -you wouldn't leave - Jim hyar - alone," implored Anson.

"Jim can stay till he rots," retorted Moze. "I've hed enough of this hole."

"But, Moze - it ain't square -" panted Anson. "Jim wouldn't - leave me. I'd stick - by you. . . . I'll make it - all up to you."

"Snake, you're goin' to cash," sardonically returned Moze.

A current leaped all through Anson's stretched frame. His ghastly face blazed. That was the great and the terrible moment which for long had been in abeyance. Wilson had known grimly that it would come, by one means or another. Anson had doggedly and faithfully struggled against the tide of fatal issues. Moze and Shady Jones, deep locked in their self-centered motives, had not realized the inevitable trend of their dark lives.

Anson, prostrate as he was, swiftly drew his gun and shot Moze. Without sound or movement of hand Moze fell. Then the plunge of Shady's horse caused Anson's second shot to miss. A quick third shot brought no apparent result but Shady's cursing resort to his own weapon. He tried to aim from his plunging horse. His bullets spattered dust and gravel over Anson. Then Wilson's long arm stretched and his heavy gun banged. Shady collapsed in the saddle, and the frightened horse, throwing him, plunged out of the circle of light. Thudding hoofs, crashings of brush, quickly ceased.

"Jim - did you - git him?" whispered Anson.

"Shore did, Snake," was the slow, halting response. Jim Wilson must have sustained a sick shudder as he replied. Sheathing his gun, he folded a blanket and put it under Anson's head.

"Jim - my feet - air orful cold," whispered Anson.

"Wal, it's gittin' chilly," replied Wilson, and, taking a second blanket, he laid that over Anson's limbs. "Snake, I'm feared Shady hit you once."

"A-huh! But not so I'd care - much - if I hed - no wuss hurt."

"You lay still now. Reckon Shady's hoss stopped out heah a ways. An' I'll see."

"Jim - I 'ain't heerd - thet scream fer - a little."

"Shore it's gone. . . . Reckon now thet was a cougar."

"I knowed it!"

Wilson stalked away into the darkness. That inky wall did not seem so impenetrable and black after he had gotten out of the circle of light. He proceeded carefully and did not make any missteps. He groped from tree to tree toward the cliff and presently brought up against a huge flat rock as high as his head. Here the darkness was blackest, yet he was able to see a light form on the rock.

"Miss, are you there - all right?" he called, softly.

"Yes, but I'm scared to death," she whispered in reply.

"Shore it wound up sudden. Come now. I reckon your trouble's over."

He helped her off the rock, and, finding her unsteady on her feet, he supported her with one arm and held the other out in front of him to feel for objects. Foot by foot they worked out from under the dense shadow of the cliff, following the course of the little brook. It babbled and gurgled, and almost drowned the low whistle Wilson sent out. The girl dragged heavily upon him now, evidently weakening. At length he reached the little open patch at the head of the ravine. Halting here, he whistled. An answer came from somewhere behind him and to the right. Wilson waited, with the girl hanging on his arm.

"Dale's heah," he said. "An' don't you keel over now - after all the nerve you hed."

A swishing of brush, a step, a soft, padded footfall; a looming, dark figure, and a long, low gray shape, stealthily moving - it was the last of these that made Wilson jump.

"Wilson!" came Dale's subdued voice.

"Heah. I've got her, Dale. Safe an sound," replied Wilson, stepping toward the tall form. And he put the drooping girl into Dale's arms.

"Bo! Bo! You're all right?" Dale's deep voice was tremulous.

She roused up to seize him and to utter little cries of joy

"Oh, Dale! . . . Oh, thank Heaven! I'm ready to drop now. . . . Hasn't it been a night - an adventure? . . . I'm well - safe - sound. . . . Dale, we owe it to this Jim Wilson."

"Bo, I - we'll all thank him - all our lives," replied Dale. "Wilson, you're a man! . . . If you'll shake that gang -"

"Dale, shore there ain't much of a gang left, onless you let Burt git away," replied Wilson.

"I didn't kill him - or hurt him. But I scared him so I'll bet he's runnin' yet. . . . Wilson, did all the shootin' mean a fight?"

"Tolerable."

"Oh, Dale, it was terrible! I saw it all. I -"

"Wal, Miss, you can tell him after I go. . . . I'm wishin' you good luck."

His voice was a cool, easy drawl, slightly tremulous.

The girl's face flashed white in the gloom. She pressed against the outlaw - wrung his hands.

"Heaven help you, Jim Wilson! You are from Texas! . . . I'll remember you - pray for you all my life!"

Wilson moved away, out toward the pale glow of light under the black pines.

CHAPTER XXIV

As Helen Rayner watched Dale ride away on a quest perilous to him, and which meant almost life or death for her, it was surpassing strange that she could think of nothing except the thrilling, tumultuous moment when she had put her arms round his neck.

It did not matter that Dale - splendid fellow that he was - had made the ensuing moment free of shame by taking her action as he had taken it - the fact that she had actually done it was enough. How utterly impossible for her to anticipate her impulses or to understand them, once they were acted upon! Confounding realization then was that when Dale returned with her sister, Helen knew she would do the same thing over again!"

"If I do - I won't be two-faced about it," she soliloquized, and a hot blush flamed her cheeks.

She watched Dale until he rode out of sight.

When he had gone, worry and dread replaced this other confusing emotion. She turned to the business of meeting events. Before supper she packed her valuables and books, papers, and clothes, together with Bo's, and had them in readiness so if she was forced to vacate the premises she would have her personal possessions.

The Mormon boys and several other of her trusted men slept in their tarpaulin beds on the porch of the ranch-house that night, so that Helen at least would not be surprised. But the day came, with its manifold duties undisturbed by any event. And it passed slowly with the leaden feet of listening, watching vigilance.

Carmichael did not come back, nor was there news of him to be had. The last known of him had been late the afternoon of the preceding day, when a sheep-herder had seen him far out on the north range, headed for the hills. The Beemans reported that Roy's condition had improved, and also that there was a subdued excitement of suspense down in the village.

This second lonely night was almost unendurable for Helen. When she slept it was to dream horrible dreams; when she lay awake it was to have her heart leap to her throat at a rustle of leaves near the window, and to be in torture of imagination as to poor Bo's plight. A thousand times Helen said to herself that Beasley could have had the ranch and welcome, if only Bo had been spared. Helen absolutely connected her enemy with her sister's disappearance. Riggs might have been a means to it.

Daylight was not attended by so many fears; there were things to do that demanded attention. And thus it was that the next morning, shortly before noon, she was recalled to her perplexities by a shouting out at the corrals and a galloping of horses somewhere near. From the window she saw a big smoke.

"Fire! That must be one of the barns - the old one, farthest out," she said, gazing out of the window.

"Some careless Mexican with his everlasting cigarette!"

Helen resisted an impulse to go out and see what had happened. She had decided to stay in the house. But when footsteps sounded on the porch and a rap on the door, she unhesitatingly opened it. Four Mexicans stood close. One of them, quick as thought, flashed a hand in to grasp her, and in a single motion pulled her across the threshold.

"No hurt, Señora," he said, and pointed - making motions she must go.

Helen did not need to be told what this visit meant. Many as her conjectures had been, however, she had not thought of Beasley subjecting her to this outrage. And her blood boiled.

"How dare you!" she said, trembling in her effort to control her temper. But class, authority, voice availed nothing with these swarthy Mexicans. They grinned. Another laid hold of Helen with dirty, brown hand. She shrank from the contact.

"Let go!" she burst out, furiously. And instinctively she began to struggle to free herself. Then they all took hold of her. Helen's dignity might never have been! A burning, choking rush of blood was her first acquaintance with the terrible passion of anger that was her inheritance from the Auchinclosses. She who had resolved never to lay herself open to indignity now fought like a tigress. The Mexicans, jabbering in their excitement, had all they could do, until they lifted her bodily from the porch. They handled her as if she had been a half-empty sack of corn. One holding each hand

and foot they packed her, with dress disarranged and half torn off, down the path to the lane and down the lane to the road. There they stood upright and pushed her off her property.

Through half-blind eyes Helen saw them guarding the gateway, ready to prevent her entrance. She staggered down the road to the village. It seemed she made her way through a red dimness - that there was a congestion in her brain - that the distance to Mrs. Cass's cottage was insurmountable. But she got there, to stagger up the path, to hear the old woman's cry. Dizzy, faint, sick, with a blackness enveloping all she looked at, Helen felt herself led into the sitting-room and placed in the big chair.

Presently sight and clearness of mind returned to her. She saw Roy, white as a sheet, questioning her with terrible eyes. The old woman hung murmuring over her, trying to comfort her as well as fasten the disordered dress.

"Four greasers - packed me down - the hill - threw me off my ranch - into the road!" panted Helen.

She seemed to tell this also to her own consciousness and to realize the mighty wave of danger that shook her whole body.

"If I'd known - I would have killed them!"

She exclaimed that, full-voiced and hard, with dry, hot eyes on her friends. Roy reached out to take her hand, speaking huskily. Helen did not distinguish what he said. The frightened old woman knelt, with unsteady fingers fumbling over the rents in Helen's dress. The moment came when Helen's quivering began to subside, when her blood quieted to let her reason sway, when she began to do battle with her rage, and slowly to take fearful stock of this consuming peril that had been a sleeping tigress in her veins.

"Oh, Miss Helen, you looked so turrible, I made sure you was hurted," the old woman was saying.

Helen gazed strangely at her bruised wrists, at the one stocking that hung down over her shoe-top, at the rent I which had bared her shoulder to the profane gaze of those grinning, beady-eyed Mexicans.

"My body's - not hurt," she whispered.

Roy had lost some of his whiteness, and where his eyes had been fierce they were now kind.

"Wal, Miss Nell, it's lucky no harm's done. . . . Now if you'll only see this whole deal clear! . . . Not let it spoil your sweet way of lookin' an' hopin'! If you can only see what's raw in this West - an' love it jest the same!"

Helen only half divined his meaning, but that was enough for a future reflection. The West was beautiful, but hard. In the faces of these friends she began to see the meaning of the keen, sloping lines, and shadows of pain, of a lean, naked truth, cut as from marble.

"For the land's sakes, tell us all about it," importuned Mrs. Cass.

Whereupon Helen shut her eyes and told the brief narrative of her expulsion from her home.

"Shore we-all expected thet," said Roy. "An' it's jest as well you're here with a whole skin. Beasley's in possession now an' I reckon we'd all sooner hev you away from thet ranch."

"But, Roy, I won't let Beasley stay there," cried Helen.

"Miss Nell, shore by the time this here Pine has growed big enough fer law you'll hev gray in thet pretty hair. You can't put Beasley off with your honest an' rightful claim. Al Auchincloss was a hard driver. He made enemies an' he made some he didn't kill. The evil men do lives after them. An' you've got to suffer fer Al's sins, though Al was as good as any man who ever prospered in these parts."

"Oh, what can I do? I won't give up. I've been robbed. Can't the people help me? Must I meekly sit with my hands crossed while that half-breed thief - Oh, it's unbelievable!"

"I reckon you'll jest hev to be patient fer a few days," said Roy, calmly. "It'll all come right in the end."

"Roy! You've had this deal, as you call it, all worked out in mind for a long time!" exclaimed Helen.

"Shore, an' I 'ain't missed a reckonin' yet."

"Then what will happen - in a few days?"

"Nell Rayner, are you goin' to hev some spunk an' not lose your nerve again or go wild out of your head?"

"I'll try to be brave, but - but I must be prepared," she replied, tremulously.

"Wal, there's Dale an' Las Vegas an' me fer Beasley to reckon with. An', Miss Nell, his chances fer long life are as pore as his chances fer heaven!"

"But, Roy, I don't believe in deliberate taking of life," replied Helen, shuddering. "That's against my religion. I won't allow it. . . . And - then - think, Dale, all of you - in danger!"

"Girl, how 're you ever goin' to help yourself ? Shore you might hold Dale back, if you love him, an' swear you won't give yourself to him. . . . An' I reckon I'd respect your religion, if you was goin' to suffer through me. . . . But not Dale nor you - nor Bo - nor love or heaven or hell can ever stop thet cowboy Las Vegas!"

"Oh, if Dale brings Bo back to me - what will I care for my ranch?" murmured Helen.

"Reckon you'll only begin to care when thet happens. Your big hunter has got to be put to work," replied Roy, with his keen smile.

Before noon that day the baggage Helen had packed at home was left on the porch of Widow Cass's cottage, and Helen's anxious need of the hour was satisfied. She was made comfortable in the old woman's one spare room, and she set herself the task of fortitude and endurance.

To her surprise, many of Mrs. Cass's neighbors came unobtrusively to the back door of the little cottage and made sympathetic inquiries. They appeared a subdued and apprehensive group, and whispered to one another as they left. Helen gathered from their visits a conviction that the wives of the men dominated by

Beasley believed no good could come of this high-handed taking over of the ranch. Indeed, Helen found at the end of the day that a strength had been borne of her misfortune.

The next day Roy informed her that his brother John had come down the preceding night with the news of Beasley's descent upon the ranch. Not a shot had been fired, and the only damage done was that of the burning of a hay-filled barn. This had been set on fire to attract Helen's men to one spot, where Beasley had ridden down upon them with three times their number. He had boldly ordered them off the land, unless they wanted to acknowledge him boss and remain there in his service. The three Beemans had stayed, having planned that just in this event they might be valuable to Helen's interests. Beasley had ridden down into Pine the same as upon any other day. Roy reported also news which had come in that morning, how Beasley's crowd had celebrated late the night before.

The second and third and fourth days endlessly wore away, and Helen believed they had made her old. At night she lay awake most of the time, thinking and praying, but during the afternoon she got some sleep. She could think of nothing and talk of nothing except her sister, and Dale's chances of saving her.

"Well, shore you pay Dale a pore compliment," finally protested the patient Roy. "I tell you - Milt Dale can do anythin' he wants to do in the woods. You can believe thet. . . . But I reckon he'll run chances after he comes back."

This significant speech thrilled Helen with its assurance of hope, and made her blood curdle at the implied peril awaiting the hunter.

On the afternoon of the fifth day Helen was abruptly awakened from her nap. The sun had almost set. She heard voices - the shrill, cackling notes of old Mrs. Cass, high in excitement, a deep voice that made Helen tingle all over, a girl's laugh, broken but happy. There were footsteps and stamping of hoofs. Dale had brought Bo back! Helen knew it. She grew very weak, and had to force herself to stand erect. Her heart began to pound in her very ears. A sweet and perfect joy suddenly flooded her soul. She thanked God her prayers had been answered. Then suddenly alive with sheer mad physical gladness, she rushed out.

She was just in time to see Roy Beeman stalk out as if he had never been shot, and with a yell greet a big, gray-clad, gray-faced man - Dale.

"Howdy, Roy! Glad to see you up," said Dale. How the quiet voice steadied Helen! She beheld Bo. Bo, looking the same, except a little pale and disheveled! Then Bo saw her and leaped at her, into her arms.

"Nell! I'm here! Safe - all right! Never was so happy in my life. . . . Oh-h! talk about your adventures! Nell, you dear old mother to me - I've had e-enough forever!"

Bo was wild with joy, and by turns she laughed and cried. But Helen could not voice her feelings. Her eyes were so dim that she could scarcely see Dale when he loomed over her as she held Bo. But he found the hand she put shakily out.

"Nell! . . . Reckon it's been harder - on you." His voice

was earnest and halting. She felt his searching gaze upon her face. "Mrs. Cass said you were here. An' I know why."

Roy led them all indoors.

"Milt, one of the neighbor boys will take care of thet hoss," he said, as Dale turned toward the dusty and weary Ranger. "Where'd you leave the cougar?"

"I sent him home," replied Date.

"Laws now, Milt, if this ain't grand!" cackled Mrs. Cass. "We've worried some here. An' Miss Helen near starved a-hopin' fer you."

"Mother, I reckon the girl an' I are nearer starved than anybody you know," replied Dale, with a grim laugh.

"Fer the land's sake! I'll be fixin' supper this minit."

"Nell, why are you here?" asked Bo, suspiciously.

For answer Helen led her sister into the spare room and closed the door. Bo saw the baggage. Her expression changed. The old blaze leaped to the telltale eyes.

"He's done it!" she cried, hotly.

"Dearest - thank God. I've got you - back again!" murmured Helen, finding her voice. "Nothing else matters! . . . I've prayed only for that!"

"Good old Nell!" whispered Bo, and she kissed and embraced Helen. "You really mean that, I know. But nix for yours truly! I'm back alive and kicking, you bet.

. . . Where's my - where's Tom?".

"Bo, not a word has been heard of him for five days. He's searching for you, of course."

"And you've been - been put off the ranch?"

"Well, rather," replied Helen, and in a few trembling words she told the story of her eviction.

Bo uttered a wild word that had more force than elegance, but it became her passionate resentment of this outrage done her sister.

"Oh! . . . Does Tom Carmichael know this?" she added, breathlessly.

"How could he?"

"When he finds out, then - Oh, won't there be hell? I'm glad I got here first. . . . Nell, my boots haven't been off the whole blessed time. Help me. And oh, for some soap and hot water and some clean clothes! Nell, old girl, I wasn't raised right for these Western deals. Too luxurious!"

And then Helen had her ears filled with a rapid-fire account of running horses and Riggs and outlaws and Beasley called boldly to his teeth, and a long ride and an outlaw who was a hero - a fight with Riggs - blood and death - another long ride – a wild camp in black woods - night - lonely, ghostly sounds - and day again - plot - a great actress lost to the world - Ophelia - Snakes and Ansons - hoodooed outlaws - mournful moans and terrible cries - cougar - stampede - fight and shots, more blood and death - Wilson hero - another

Tom Carmichael - fallen in love with outlaw gun-fighter if – black night and Dale and horse and rides and starved and, "Oh, Nell, he was from Texas!"

Helen gathered that wonderful and dreadful events had hung over the bright head of this beloved little sister, but the bewilderment occasioned by Bo's fluent and remarkable utterance left only that last sentence clear.

Presently Helen got a word in to inform Bo that Mrs. Cass had knocked twice for supper, and that welcome news checked Bo's flow of speech when nothing else seemed adequate.

It was obvious to Helen that Roy and Dale had exchanged stories. Roy celebrated this reunion by sitting at table the first time since he had been shot; and despite Helen's misfortune and the suspended waiting balance in the air the occasion was joyous. Old Mrs. Cass was in the height of her glory. She sensed a romance here, and, true to her sex, she radiated to it.

Daylight was still lingering when Roy got up and went out on the porch. His keen ears had heard something. Helen fancied she herself had heard rapid hoof-beats.

"Dale, come out!" called Roy, sharply.

The hunter moved with his swift, noiseless agility. Helen and Bo followed, halting in the door.

"Thet's Las Vegas," whispered Dale.

To Helen it seemed that the cowboy's name changed the very atmosphere.

Voices were heard at the gate; one that, harsh and quick, sounded like Carmichael's. And a spirited horse was pounding and scattering gravel. Then a lithe figure appeared, striding up the path. It was Carmichael - yet not the Carmichael Helen knew. She heard Bo's strange little cry, a corroboration of her own impression.

Roy might never have been shot, judging from the way he stepped out, and Dale was almost as quick. Carmichael reached them - grasped them with swift, hard hands.

"Boys - I jest rode in. An' they said you'd found her!"

"Shore, Las Vegas. Dale fetched her home safe an' sound. . . . There she is."

The cowboy thrust aside the two men, and with a long stride he faced the porch, his piercing eyes on the door. All that Helen could think of his look was that it seemed terrible. Bo stepped outside in front of Helen. Probably she would have run straight into Carmichael's arms if some strange instinct had not withheld her. Helen judged it to be fear; she found her heart lifting painfully.

"Bo!" he yelled, like a savage, yet he did not in the least resemble one.

"Oh - Tom!" cried Bo, falteringly. She half held out her arms.

"You, girl?" That seemed to be his piercing query, like the quivering blade in his eyes. Two more long strides carried him close up to her, and his look chased the red out of Bo's cheek. Then it was beautiful to see his face marvelously change until it was that of the well remembered Las Vegas magnified in all his old spirit.

"Aw!" The exclamation was a tremendous sigh. "I shore am glad!"

That beautiful flash left his face as he wheeled to the men. He wrung Dale's hand long and hard, and his gaze confused the older man.

"Riggs!" he said, and in the jerk of his frame as he whipped out the word disappeared the strange, fleeting signs of his kindlier emotion.

"Wilson killed him," replied Dale.

"Jim Wilson - that old Texas Ranger! . . . Reckon he lent you a hand?"

"My friend, he saved Bo," replied Dale, with emotion. "My old cougar an' me - we just hung 'round."

"You made Wilson help you?" cut in the hard voice.

"Yes. But he killed Riggs before I come up an' I reckon he'd done well by Bo if I'd never got there."

"How about the gang?"

"All snuffed out, I reckon, except Wilson."

"Somebody told me Beasley hed ran Miss Helen off the ranch. Thet so?"

"Yes. Four of his greasers packed her down the hill -

most tore her clothes off, so Roy tells me."

"Four greasers! . . . Shore it was Beasley's deal clean through?"

"Yes. Riggs was led. He had an itch for a bad name, you know. But Beasley made the plan. It was Nell they wanted instead of Bo."

Abruptly Carmichael stalked off down the darkening path, his silver heel-plates ringing, his spurs jingling.

"Hold on, Carmichael," called Dale, taking a step.

"Oh, Tom!" cried Bo.

"Shore folks callin' won't be no use, if anythin would be," said Roy. "Las Vegas has hed a look at red liquor."

"He's been drinking! Oh, that accounts! . . . he never - never even touched me!"

For once Helen was not ready to comfort Bo. A mighty tug at her heart had sent her with flying, uneven steps toward Dale. He took another stride down the path, and another.

"Dale - oh - please stop!" she called, very low.

He halted as if he had run sharply into a bar across the path. When he turned Helen had come close. Twilight was deep there in the shade of the peach-trees, but she could see his face, the hungry, flaring eyes.

"I - I haven't thanked you - yet - for bringing Bo

home," she whispered.

"Nell, never mind that," he said, in surprise. "If you must - why, wait. I've got to catch up with that cowboy."

"No. Let me thank you now," she whispered, and, stepping closer, she put her arms up, meaning to put them round his neck. That action must be her self-punishment for the other time she had done it. Yet it might also serve to thank him. But, strangely, her hands got no farther than his breast, and fluttered there to catch hold of the fringe of his buckskin jacket. She felt a heave of his deep chest.

"I - I do thank you - with all my heart," she said, softly. "I owe you now - for myself and her - more than I can ever repay."

"Nell, I'm your friend," he replied, hurriedly. "Don't talk of repayin' me. Let me go now - after Las Vegas."

"What for?" she queried, suddenly.

"I mean to line up beside him - at the bar - or wherever he goes," returned Dale.

"Don't tell me that. I know. You're going straight to meet Beasley."

"Nell, if you hold me up any longer I reckon I'll have to run - or never get to Beasley before that cowboy."

Helen locked her fingers in the fringe of his jacket - leaned closer to him, all her being responsive to a bursting gust of blood over her.

"I'll not let you go," she said.

He laughed, and put his great hands over hers. "What 're you sayin', girl? You can't stop me."

"Yes, I can. Dale, I don't want you to risk your life."

He stared at her, and made as if to tear her hands from their hold.

"Listen - please - oh - please!" she implored. "If you go deliberately to kill Beasley - and do it - that will be murder. . . .It's against my religion. . . . I would be unhappy all my life."

"But, child, you'll be ruined all your life if Beasley is not dealt with - as men of his breed are always dealt with in the West," he remonstrated, and in one quick move he had freed himself from her clutching fingers.

Helen, with a move as swift, put her arms round his neck and clasped her hands tight.

"Milt, I'm finding myself," she said. "The other day, when I did - this - you made an excuse for me. . . . I'm not two-faced now."

She meant to keep him from killing Beasley if she sacrificed every last shred of her pride. And she stamped the look of his face on her heart of hearts to treasure always. The thrill, the beat of her pulses, almost obstructed her thought of purpose.

"Nell, just now - when you're overcome - rash with feelin's - don't say to me - a word - a -"

He broke down huskily.

"My first friend - my - Oh Dale, I know you love me! she whispered. And she hid her face on his breast, there to feel a tremendous tumult.

"Oh, don't you?" she cried, in low, smothered voice, as his silence drove her farther on this mad, yet glorious purpose.

"If you need to be told - yes - I reckon I do love you, Nell Rayner," he replied.

It seemed to Helen that he spoke from far off. She lifted her face, her heart on her lips.

"If you kill Beasley I'll never marry you," she said.

"Who's expectin' you to?" he asked, with low, hoarse laugh. "Do you think you have to marry me to square accounts? This's the only time you ever hurt me, Nell Rayner. . . . I'm 'shamed you could think I'd expect you - out of gratitude -"

"Oh - you - you are as dense as the forest where you live," she cried. And then she shut her eyes again, the better to remember that transfiguration of his face, the better to betray herself.

"Man - I love you!" Full and deep, yet tremulous, the words burst from her heart that had been burdened with them for many a day.

Then it seemed, in the throbbing riot of her senses, that she was lifted and swung into his arms, and handled with a great and terrible tenderness, and hugged and kissed with the hunger and awkwardness of a bear, and held with her feet off the ground, and rendered blind, dizzy, rapturous, and frightened, and utterly torn asunder from her old calm, thinking self.

He put her down - released her.

"Nothin' could have made me so happy as what you said." He finished with a strong sigh of unutterable, wondering joy.

"Then you will not go to - to meet -"

Helen's happy query froze on her lips.

"I've got to go!" he rejoined, with his old, quiet voice. "Hurry in to Bo. . . . An' don't worry. Try to think of things as I taught you up in the woods."

Helen heard his soft, padded footfalls swiftly pass away. She was left there, alone in the darkening twilight, suddenly cold and stricken, as if turned to stone.

Thus she stood an age-long moment until the upflashing truth galvanized her into action. Then she flew in pursuit of Dale. The truth was that, in spite of Dale's' early training in the East and the long years of solitude which had made him wonderful in thought and feeling, he had also become a part of this raw, bold, and violent West.

It was quite dark now and she had run quite some distance before she saw Dale's tall, dark form against the yellow light of Turner's saloon.

Somehow, in that poignant moment, when her flying feet kept pace with her heart, Helen felt in herself a force opposing itself against this raw, primitive justice of the West. She was one of the first influences emanating from civilized life, from law and order. In that flash of truth she saw the West as it would be some future time, when through women and children these wild frontier days would be gone forever. Also, just as clearly she saw the present need of men like Roy Beeman and Dale and the fire-blooded Carmichael. Beasley and his kind must be killed. But Helen did not want her lover, her future husband, and the probable father of her children to commit what she held to be murder.

At the door of the saloon she caught up with Dale.

"Milt - oh - wait!' - wait!" she panted.

She heard him curse under his breath as he turned. They were alone in the yellow flare of light. Horses were champing bits and drooping before the rails.

"You go back!" ordered Dale, sternly. His face was pale, his eyes were gleaming.

"No! Not till - you take me - or carry me!" she replied, resolutely, with all a woman's positive and inevitable assurance.

Then he laid hold of her with ungentle hands. His violence, especially the look on his face, terrified Helen, rendered her weak. But nothing could have shaken her resolve. She felt victory. Her sex, her love, and her presence would be too much for Dale.

As he swung Helen around, the low hum of voices inside the saloon suddenly rose to sharp, hoarse roars, accompanied by a scuffling of feet and crashing of violently sliding chairs or tables. Dale let go of Helen and leaped toward the door. But a silence inside, quicker and stranger than the roar, halted him. Helen's heart contracted, then seemed to cease beating. There was absolutely not a perceptible sound. Even the horses appeared, like Dale, to have turned to statues.

Two thundering shots annihilated this silence. Then quickly came a lighter shot - the smash of glass. Dale ran into the saloon. The horses began to snort, to rear, to pound. A low, muffled murmur terrified Helen even as it drew her. Dashing at the door, she swung it in and entered.

The place was dim, blue-hazed, smelling of smoke. Dale stood just inside the door. On the floor lay two men. Chairs and tables were overturned. A motley, dark, shirt-sleeved, booted, and belted crowd of men appeared hunched against the opposite wall, with pale, set faces, turned to the bar. Turner, the proprietor, stood at one end, his face livid, his hands aloft and shaking. Carmichael leaned against the middle of the bar. He held a gun low down. It was smoking.

With a gasp Helen flashed her eyes back to Dale. He had seen her - was reaching an arm toward her. Then she saw the man lying almost at her feet. Jeff Mulvey - her uncle's old foreman! His face was awful to behold. A smoking gun lay near his inert hand. The other man had fallen on his face. His garb proclaimed him a Mexican. He was not yet dead. Then Helen, as she felt Dale's arm encircle her, looked farther, because she could not prevent it - looked on at that strange figure against the bar - this boy who had been such a friend in her hour of need - this naïve and frank sweetheart of her sister's.

She saw a man now - wild, white, intense as fire, with some terrible cool kind of deadliness in his mien. His left elbow rested upon the bar, and his hand held a glass of red liquor. The big gun, low down in his other hand, seemed as steady as if it were a fixture.

"Heah's to thet - half-breed Beasley an' his outfit!"

Carmichael drank, while his flaming eyes held the crowd; then with savage action of terrible passion he flung the glass at the quivering form of the still living Mexican on the floor.

Helen felt herself slipping. All seemed to darken around her. She could not see Dale, though she knew he held her. Then she fainted.

CHAPTER XXV

Las Vegas Carmichael was a product of his day.

The Pan Handle of Texas, the old Chisholm Trail along which were driven the great cattle herds northward, Fort Dodge, where the cowboys conflicted with the card-sharps - these hard places had left their marks on Carmichael. To come from Texas was to come from fighting stock. And a cowboy's life was strenuous, wild, violent, and generally brief. The exceptions were the fortunate and the swiftest men with guns; and they drifted from south to north and west, taking with them the reckless, chivalrous, vitriolic spirit peculiar to their breed.

The pioneers and ranchers of the frontier would never have made the West habitable had it not been for these wild cowboys, these hard-drinking, hard-riding, hard-living rangers of the barrens, these easy, cool, laconic, simple young men whose blood was tinged with fire and who possessed a magnificent and terrible effrontery toward danger and death.

Las Vegas ran his horse from Widow Cass's cottage to Turner's saloon, and the hoofs of the goaded steed crashed in the door. Las Vegas's entrance was a leap. Then he stood still with the door ajar and the horse pounding and snorting back. All the men in that saloon who saw the entrance of Las Vegas knew what it portended. No thunderbolt could have more quickly checked the drinking, gambling, talking crowd. They recognized with kindred senses the nature of the man and his arrival. For a second the blue-hazed room was perfectly quiet, then men breathed, moved, rose, and suddenly caused a quick, sliding crash of chairs and tables.

The cowboy's glittering eyes flashed to and fro, and then fixed on Mulvey and his Mexican companion. That glance singled out these two, and the sudden rush of nervous men proved it. Mulvey and the sheep-herder were left alone in the center of the floor.

"Howdy, Jeff ! Where's your boss?" asked Las Vegas. His voice was cool, friendly; his manner was easy, natural; but the look of him was what made Mulvey pale and the Mexican livid.

"Reckon he's home," replied Mulvey.

"Home? What's he call home now?"

"He's hangin' out hyar at Auchincloss's," replied Mulvey. His voice was not strong, but his eyes were steady, watchful.

Las Vegas quivered all over as if stung. A flame that seemed white and red gave his face a singular hue.

"Jeff, you worked for old Al a long time, an' I've heard of your differences," said Las Vegas. "Thet ain't no mix of mine. . . . But you double-crossed Miss Helen!"

Mulvey made no attempt to deny this. He gulped slowly. His hands appeared less steady, and he grew paler. Again Las Vegas's words signified less than his look. And that look now included the Mexican.

"Pedro, you're one of Beasley's old hands," said Las Vegas, accusingly. "An' - you was one of them four greasers thet -"

Here the cowboy choked and bit over his words as if they were a material poison. The Mexican showed his guilt and cowardice. He began to jabber.

"Shet up!" hissed Las Vegas, with a savage and significant jerk of his arm, as if about to strike. But that action was read for its true meaning. Pell-mell the crowd split to rush each way and leave an open space behind the three.

Las Vegas waited. But Mulvey seemed obstructed. The Mexican looked dangerous through his fear. His fingers twitched as if the tendons running up into his arms were being pulled.

An instant of suspense - more than long enough for Mulvey to be tried and found wanting - and Las Vegas, with laugh and sneer, turned his back upon the pair and stepped to the bar. His call for a bottle made Turner jump and hold it out with shaking hands. Las Vegas poured out a drink, while his gaze was intent on the scarred old mirror hanging behind the bar.

This turning his back upon men he had just dared to draw showed what kind of a school Las Vegas had been trained in. If those men had been worthy antagonists of his class he would never have scorned them. As it was, when Mulvey and the Mexican jerked at their guns, Las Vegas swiftly wheeled and shot twice. Mulvey's gun went off as he fell, and the Mexican doubled up in a heap on the floor. Then Las Vegas reached around with his left hand for the drink he had poured out.

At this juncture Dale burst into the saloon, suddenly to check his impetus, to swerve aside toward the bar and halt. The door had not ceased swinging when again it was propelled inward, this time to admit Helen Rayner, white and wide-eyed.

In another moment then Las Vegas had spoken his deadly toast to Beasley's gang and had fiercely flung the glass at the writhing Mexican on the floor. Also Dale had gravitated toward the reeling Helen to catch her when she fainted.

Las Vegas began to curse, and, striding to Dale, he pushed him out of the saloon.

"-! What 're you doin' heah?" he yelled, stridently. "Hevn't you got thet girl to think of? Then do it, you big Indian! Lettin' her run after you heah - riskin' herself thet way! You take care of her an' Bo an' leave this deal to me!"

The cowboy, furious as he was at Dale, yet had keen, swift eyes for the horses near at hand, and the men out in the dim light. Dale lifted the girl into his arms, and, turning without a word, stalked away to disappear in the darkness. Las Vegas, holding his gun low, returned to the bar-room. If there had been any change in the crowd it was slight. The tension had relaxed. Turner no longer stood with hands up.

"You-all go on with your fun," called the cowboy, with

a sweep of his gun. "But it'd be risky fer any one to start leavin'."

With that he backed against the bar, near where the black bottle stood. Turner walked out to begin righting tables and chairs, and presently the crowd, with some caution and suspense, resumed their games and drinking. It was significant that a wide berth lay between them and the door. From time to time Turner served liquor to men who called for it.

Las Vegas leaned with back against the bar. After a while he sheathed his gun and reached around for the bottle. He drank with his piercing eyes upon the door. No one entered and no one went out. The games of chance there and the drinking were not enjoyed. It was a hard scene - that smoky, long, ill-smelling room, with its dim, yellow lights, and dark, evil faces, with the stealthy-stepping Turner passing to and fro, and the dead Mulvey staring in horrible fixidity at the ceiling, and the Mexican quivering more and more until he shook violently, then lay still, and with the drinking, somber, waiting cowboy, more fiery and more flaming with every drink, listening for a step that did not come.

Time passed, and what little change it wrought was in the cowboy. Drink affected him, but he did not become drunk. It seemed that the liquor he drank was consumed by a mounting fire. It was fuel to a driving passion. He grew more sullen, somber, brooding, redder of eye and face, more crouching and restless. At last, when the hour was so late that there was no probability of Beasley appearing, Las Vegas flung himself out of the saloon.

All lights of the village had now been extinguished.

The tired horses drooped in the darkness. Las Vegas found his horse and led him away down the road and out a lane to a field where a barn stood dim and dark in the starlight. Morning was not far off. He unsaddled the horse and, turning him loose, went into the barn. Here he seemed familiar with his surroundings, for he found a ladder and climbed to a loft, where be threw himself on the hay.

He rested, but did not sleep. At daylight he went down and brought his horse into the barn. Sunrise found Las Vegas pacing to and fro the short length of the interior, and peering out through wide cracks between the boards. Then during the succeeding couple of hours he watched the occasional horse-man and wagon and herder that passed on into the village.

About the breakfast hour Las Vegas saddled his horse and rode back the way he had come the night before. At Turner's he called for something to eat as well as for whisky. After that he became a listening, watching machine. He drank freely for an hour; then he stopped. He seemed to be drunk, but with a different kind of drunkenness from that usual in drinking men. Savage, fierce, sullen, he was one to avoid. Turner waited on him in evident fear.

At length Las Vegas's condition became such that action was involuntary. He could not stand still nor sit down. Stalking out, he passed the store, where men slouched back to avoid him, and he went down the road, wary and alert, as if he expected a rifle-shot from some hidden enemy. Upon his return down that main thoroughfare of the village not a person was to be seen. He went in to Turner's. The proprietor was there at his post, nervous and pale. Las Vegas did not order any more liquor.

"Turner, I reckon I'll bore you next time I run in heah," he said, and stalked out.

He had the stores, the road, the village, to himself; and he patrolled a beat like a sentry watching for an Indian attack.

Toward noon a single man ventured out into the road to accost the cowboy.

"Las Vegas, I'm tellin' you - all the greasers air leavin' the range," he said.

"Howdy, Abe!" replied Las Vegas. "What 'n hell you talkin' about?"

The man repeated his information. And Las Vegas spat out frightful curses.

"Abe - you heah what Beasley's doin'?"

"Yes. He's with his men - up at the ranch. Reckon he can't put off ridin' down much longer."

That was where the West spoke. Beasley would be forced to meet the enemy who had come out single-handed against him. Long before this hour a braver man would have come to face Las Vegas. Beasley could not hire any gang to bear the brunt of this situation. This was the test by which even his own men must judge him. All of which was to say that as the wildness of the West had made possible his crimes, so it now held him responsible for them.

"Abe, if thet - greaser don't rustle down heah I'm goin' after him."

"Sure. But don't be in no hurry," replied Abe.

"I'm waltzin' to slow music. . . . Gimme a smoke."

With fingers that slightly trembled Abe rolled a cigarette, lit it from his own, and handed it to the cowboy.

"Las Vegas, I reckon I hear hosses," he said, suddenly.

"Me, too," replied Las Vegas, with his head high like that of a listening deer. Apparently he forgot the cigarette and also his friend. Abe hurried back to the store, where he disappeared.

Las Vegas began his stalking up and down, and his action now was an exaggeration of all his former movements. A rational, ordinary mortal from some Eastern community, happening to meet this red-faced cowboy, would have considered him drunk or crazy. Probably Las Vegas looked both. But all the same he was a marvelously keen and strung and efficient instrument to meet the portending issue. How many thousands of times, on the trails, and in the wide-streeted little towns all over the West, had this stalk of the cowboy's been perpetrated! Violent, bloody, tragic as it was, it had an importance in that pioneer day equal to the use of a horse or the need of a plow.

At length Pine was apparently a deserted village, except for Las Vegas, who patrolled his long beat in many ways - he lounged while he watched; he stalked like a mountaineer; he stole along Indian fashion, stealthily, from tree to tree, from corner to corner; he disappeared in the saloon to reappear at the back; he slipped round behind the barns to come out again in the main road; and time after time he approached his horse as if deciding to mount.

The last visit he made into Turner's saloon he found no one there. Savagely he pounded on the bar with his gun. He got no response. Then the long-pent-up rage burst. With wild whoops he pulled another gun and shot at the mirror, the lamps. He shot the neck off a bottle and drank till be choked, his neck corded, bulging, and purple. His only slow and deliberate action was the reloading of his gun. Then he crashed through the doors, and with a wild yell leaped sheer into the saddle, hauling his horse up high and goading him to plunge away.

Men running to the door and windows of the store saw a streak of dust flying down the road. And then they trooped out to see it disappear. The hour of suspense ended for them. Las Vegas had lived up to the code of the West, had dared his man out, had waited far longer than needful to prove that man a coward. Whatever the issue now, Beasley was branded forever. That moment saw the decline of whatever power he had wielded. He and his men might kill the cowboy who had ridden out alone to face him, but that would not change the brand.

The preceding night Beasley bad been finishing a late supper at his newly acquired ranch, when Buck Weaver, one of his men, burst in upon him with news of the death of Mulvey and Pedro.

"Who's in the outfit? How many?" he had questioned, quickly.

"It's a one-man outfit, boss," replied Weaver.

Beasley appeared astounded. He and his men had prepared to meet the friends of the girl whose property he had taken over, and because of the superiority of his own force he had anticipated no bloody or extended feud. This amazing circumstance put the case in very much more difficult form.

"One man!" he ejaculated.

"Yep. Thet cowboy Las Vegas. An,' boss, he turns out to be a gun-slinger from Texas. I was in Turner's. Hed jest happened to step in the other room when Las Vegas come bustin' in on his boss an' jumped off. . . . Fust thing he called Jeff an' Pedro. They both showed yaller. An' then, damn if thet cowboy didn't turn his back on them an' went to the bar fer a drink. But he was lookin' in the mirror an' when Jeff an' Pedro went fer their guns why he whirled quick as lightnin' an' bored them both. . . . I sneaked out an -"

"Why didn't you bore him?" roared Beasley.

Buck Weaver steadily eyed his boss before he replied. "I ain't takin' shots at any fellar from behind doors. An' as fer meetin' Las Vegas - excoose me, boss! I've still a hankerin' fer sunshine an' red liquor. Besides, I 'ain't got nothin' ag'in' Las Vegas. If he's rustled over here at the head of a crowd to put us off I'd fight, jest as we'd all fight. But you see we figgered wrong. It's between you an' Las Vegas! . . . You oughter seen him throw thet hunter Dale out of Turner's."

"Dale! Did he come?" queried Beasley.

"He got there just after the cowboy plugged Jeff. An' thet big-eyed girl, she came runnin' in, too. An' she keeled over in Dale's arms. Las Vegas shoved him out - cussed him so hard we all heerd. . . . So, Beasley, there ain't no fight comin, off as we figgered on."

Beasley thus heard the West speak out of the mouth of his own man. And grim, sardonic, almost scornful, indeed, were the words of Buck Weaver. This rider had once worked for Al Auchincloss and had deserted to Beasley under Mulvey's leadership. Mulvey was dead and the situation was vastly changed.

Beasley gave Weaver a dark, lowering glance, and waved him away. From the door Weaver sent back a doubtful, scrutinizing gaze, then slouched out. That gaze Beasley had not encountered before.

It meant, as Weaver's cronies meant, as Beasley's long-faithful riders, and the people of the range, and as the spirit of the West meant, that Beasley was expected to march down into the village to face his single foe.

But Beasley did not go. Instead he paced to and fro the length of Helen Rayner's long sitting-room with the nervous energy of a man who could not rest. Many times he hesitated, and at others he made sudden movements toward the door, only to halt. Long after midnight he went to bed, but not to sleep. He tossed and rolled all night, and at dawn arose, gloomy and irritable.

He cursed the Mexican serving-women who showed their displeasure at his authority. And to his amaze and rage not one of his men came to the house. He waited and waited. Then he stalked off to the corrals and stables carrying a rifle with him. The men were there, in a group that dispersed somewhat at his advent. Not a Mexican was in sight.

Beasley ordered the horses to be saddled and all hands to go down into the village with him. That order was disobeyed. Beasley stormed and raged. His riders sat or lounged, with lowered faces. An unspoken hostility seemed present. Those who had been longest with him were least distant and strange, but still they did not obey. At length Beasley roared for his Mexicans.

"Boss, we gotta tell you thet every greaser on the ranch hes sloped - gone these two hours - on the way to Magdalena," said Buck Weaver.

Of all these sudden-uprising perplexities this latest was the most astounding. Beasley cursed with his questioning wonder.

"Boss, they was sure scared of thet gun-slingin' cowboy from Texas," replied Weaver, imperturbably.

Beasley's dark, swarthy face changed its hue. What of the subtle reflection in Weaver's slow speech! One of the men came out of a corral leading Beasley's saddled and bridled horse. This fellow dropped the bridle and sat down among his comrades without a word. No one spoke. The presence of the horse was significant. With a snarling, muttered curse, Beasley took up his rifle and strode back to the ranch-house.

In his rage and passion he did not realize what his men had known for hours - that if he had stood any chance at all for their respect as well as for his life the hour was long past.

Beasley avoided the open paths to the house, and when he got there he nervously poured out a drink. Evidently something in the fiery liquor frightened him, for he threw the bottle aside. It was as if that bottle contained a courage which was false.

Again he paced the long sitting-room, growing more and more wrought-up as evidently he grew familiar with the singular state of affairs. Twice the pale serving-woman called him to dinner.

The dining-room was light and pleasant, and the meal, fragrant and steaming, was ready for him. But the women had disappeared. Beasley seated himself - spread out his big hands on the table.

Then a slight rustle - a clink of spur - startled him. He twisted his head.

"Howdy, Beasley!" said Las Vegas, who had appeared as if by magic.

Beasley's frame seemed to swell as if a flood had been loosed in his veins. Sweat-drops stood out on his pallid face.

"What - you - want?" he asked, huskily.

"Wal now, my boss, Miss Helen, says, seein' I am foreman heah, thet it'd be nice an' proper fer me to drop in an' eat with you - the last time!" replied the cowboy. His drawl was slow and cool, his tone was friendly and pleasant. But his look was that of a falcon ready to drive deep its beak.

Beasley's reply was loud, incoherent, hoarse.

Las Vegas seated himself across from Beasley.

"Eat or not, it's shore all the same to me," said Las Vegas, and he began to load his plate with his left hand. His right hand rested very lightly, with just the tips of his vibrating fingers on the edge of the table; and he never for the slightest fraction of a second took his piercing eyes off Beasley.

"Wal, my half-breed greaser guest, it shore roils up my blood to see you sittin' there - thinkin' you've put my boss, Miss Helen, off this ranch," began Las Vegas, softly. And then he helped himself leisurely to food and drink. "In my day I've shore stacked up against a lot of outlaws, thieves, rustlers, an' sich like, but fer an out an' out dirty low-down skunk, you shore take the dough! . . . I'm goin, to kill you in a minit or so, jest as soon as you move one of them dirty paws of yourn. But I hope you'll be polite an' let me say a few words. I'll never be happy again if you don't. . . . Of all the - yaller greaser dogs I ever seen, you're the worst! . . . I was thinkin' last night mebbe you'd come down an' meet me like a man, so 's I could wash my hands ever afterward without gettin' sick to my stummick. But you didn't come. . . . Beasley, I'm so ashamed of myself thet I gotta call you - when I ought to bore you, thet - I ain't even second cousin to my old self when I rode fer Chisholm. It don't mean nuthin' to you to call you liar! robber! blackleg! a sneakin' coyote! an' a cheat thet hires others to do his dirty work! . . . By Gawd! -"

"Carmichael, gimme a word in," hoarsely broke out Beasley. "You're right, it won't do no good to call me . . . . But let's talk. . . . I'll buy you off. Ten thousand dollars -"

"Haw! Haw! Haw!" roared Las Vegas. He was as tense as a strung cord and his face possessed a singular pale radiance. His right hand began to quiver more and more.

"I'll - double - it!" panted Beasley. "I'll - make over - half the ranch - all the stock -"

"Swaller thet!" yelled Las Vegas, with terrible strident ferocity.

"Listen - man! . . . I take - it back! . . . I'll give up - Auchincloss's ranch!" Beasley was now a shaking, whispering, frenzied man, ghastly white, with rolling eyes.

Las Vegas's left fist pounded hard on the table.

"Greaser, come on!" he thundered.

Then Beasley, with desperate, frantic action, jerked for his gun.

CHAPTER XXVI

For Helen Rayner that brief, dark period of expulsion from her home had become a thing of the past, almost forgotten.

Two months had flown by on the wings of love and work and the joy of finding her place there in the West. All her old men had been only too glad of the opportunity to come back to her, and under Dale and Roy Beeman a different and prosperous order marked the life of the ranch.

Helen had made changes in the house by altering the arrangement of rooms and adding a new section. Only once had she ventured into the old dining-room where Las Vegas Carmichael had sat down to that fatal dinner for Beasley. She made a store-room of it, and a place she would never again enter.

Helen was happy, almost too happy, she thought, and therefore made more than needful of the several bitter drops in her sweet cup of life. Carmichael had ridden out of Pine, ostensibly on the trail of the Mexicans who had executed Beasley's commands. The last seen of him had been reported from Show Down, where he had appeared red-eyed and dangerous, like a hound on a scent. Then two months had flown by without a word.

Dale had shaken his head doubtfully when interrogated about the cowboy's absence. It would be just like Las Vegas never to be heard of again. Also it would be more like him to remain away until all trace of his drunken, savage spell had departed from him and had been forgotten by his friends. Bo took his disappearance apparently less to heart than Helen. But Bo grew more restless, wilder, and more wilful than ever. Helen thought she guessed Bo's secret; and once she ventured a hint concerning Carmichael's return.

"If Tom doesn't come back pretty soon I'll marry Milt Dale," retorted Bo, tauntingly.

This fired Helen's cheeks with red.

"But, child," she protested, half angry, half grave. "Milt and I are engaged."

"Sure. Only you're so slow. There's many a slip - you know."

"Bo, I tell you Tom will come back," replied Helen, earnestly. "I feel it. There was something fine in that cowboy. He understood me better than you or Milt, either. . . . And he was perfectly wild in love with you."

"Oh! Was he?"

"Very much more than you deserved, Bo Rayner."

Then occurred one of Bo's sweet, bewildering, unexpected transformations. Her defiance, resentment, rebelliousness, vanished from a softly agitated face.

"Oh, Nell, I know that. . . . You just watch me if I ever get another chance at him! . . . Then - maybe he'd never drink again!"

"Bo, be happy - and be good. Don't ride off any more - don't tease the boys. It'll all come right in the end."

Bo recovered her equanimity quickly enough.

"Humph! You can afford to be cheerful. You've got a man who can't live when you're out of his sight. He's like a fish on dry land. . . . And you - why, once you were an old pessimist!"

Bo was not to be consoled or changed. Helen could only sigh and pray that her convictions would be verified.

The first day of July brought an early thunder-storm, just at sunrise. It roared and flared and rolled away, leaving a gorgeous golden cloud pageant in the sky and a fresh, sweetly smelling, glistening green range that delighted Helen's eye.

Birds were twittering in the arbors and bees were humming in the flowers. From the fields down along the brook came a blended song of swamp-blackbird and meadow-lark. A clarion-voiced burro split the air with his coarse and homely bray. The sheep were bleating, and a soft baa of little lambs came sweetly to Helen's ears. She went her usual rounds with more than usual zest and thrill. Everywhere was color, activity, life. The wind swept warm and pine-scented down from the mountain heights, now black and bold, and the great green slopes seemed to call to her.

At that very moment she came suddenly upon Dale, in his shirt-sleeves, dusty and hot, standing motionless, gazing at the distant mountains. Helen's greeting startled him.

"I - I was just looking away yonder," he said, smiling. She thrilled at the clear, wonderful light of his eyes.

"So was I - a moment ago," she replied, wistfully. "Do you miss the forest - very much?"

"Nell, I miss nothing. But I'd like to ride with you under the pines once more."

"We'll go," she cried.

"When?" he asked, eagerly.

"Oh - soon!" And then with flushed face and downcast eyes she passed on. For long Helen had cherished a fond hope that she might be married in Paradise Park, where she had fallen in love with Dale and had realized herself. But she had kept that hope secret. Dale's eager tone, his flashing eyes, had made her feel that her secret was there in her telltale face.

As she entered the lane leading to the house she encountered one of the new stable-boys driving a pack-mule.

"Jim, whose pack is that?" she asked.

"Ma'am, I dunno, but I heard him tell Roy he reckoned his name was mud," replied the boy, smiling.

Helen's heart gave a quick throb. That sounded like

Las Vegas. She hurried on, and upon entering the courtyard she espied Roy Beeman holding the halter of a beautiful, wild-looking mustang. There was another horse with another man, who was in the act of dismounting on the far side. When he stepped into better view Helen recognized Las Vegas. And he saw her at the same instant.

Helen did not look up again until she was near the porch. She had dreaded this meeting, yet she was so glad that she could have cried aloud.

"Miss Helen, I shore am glad to see you," he said, standing bareheaded before her, the same young, frank-faced cowboy she had seen first from the train.

"Tom!" she exclaimed, and offered her hands.

He wrung them hard while he looked at her. The swift woman's glance Helen gave in return seemed to drive something dark and doubtful out of her heart. This was the same boy she had known - whom she had liked so well - who had won her sister's love. Helen imagined facing him thus was like awakening from a vague nightmare of doubt. Carmichael's face was clean, fresh, young, with its healthy tan; it wore the old glad smile, cool, easy, and natural; his eyes were like Dale's - penetrating, clear as crystal, without a shadow. What had evil, drink, blood, to do with the real inherent nobility of this splendid specimen of Western hardihood? Wherever he had been, whatever he had done during that long absence, he had returned long separated from that wild and savage character she could now forget. Perhaps there would never again be call for it.

"How's my girl?" he asked, just as naturally as if he had been gone a few days on some errand of his employer's.

"Bo? Oh, she's well - fine. I - I rather think she'll be glad to see you," replied Helen, warmly.

"An' how's thet big Indian, Dale?" he drawled.

"Well, too - I'm sure."

"Reckon I got back heah in time to see you-all married?"

"I - I assure you I - no one around here has been married yet," replied Helen, with a blush.

"Thet shore is fine. Was some worried," he said, lazily. "I've been chasin' wild hosses over in New Mexico, an' I got after this heah blue roan. He kept me chasin' him fer a spell. I've fetched him back for Bo."

Helen looked at the mustang Roy was holding, to be instantly delighted. He was a roan almost blue in color, neither large nor heavy, but powerfully built, clean-limbed, and racy, with a long mane and tail, black as coal, and a beautiful head that made Helen love him at once.

"Well, I'm jealous," declared Helen, archly. "I never did see such a pony."

"I reckoned you'd never ride any hoss but Ranger," said Las Vegas.

"No, I never will. But I can be jealous, anyhow, can't I?"

"Shore. An I reckon if you say you're goin' to have him - wal, Bo 'd be funny," he drawled.

"I reckon she would be funny," retorted Helen. She was so happy that she imitated his speech. She wanted to hug him. It was too good to be true - the return of this cowboy. He understood her. He had come back with nothing that could alienate her. He had apparently forgotten the terrible rôle he had accepted and the doom he had meted out to her enemies. That moment was wonderful for Helen in its revelation of the strange significance of the West as embodied in this cowboy. He was great. But he did not know that.

Then the door of the living-room opened, and a sweet, high voice pealed out:

"Roy! Oh, what a mustang! Whose is he?"

"Wal, Bo, if all I hear is so he belongs to you," replied Roy with a huge grin.

Bo appeared in the door. She stepped out upon the porch. She saw the cowboy. The excited flash of her pretty face vanished as she paled.

"Bo, I shore am glad to see you," drawled Las Vegas, as he stepped forward, sombrero in hand. Helen could not see any sign of confusion in him. But, indeed, she saw gladness. Then she expected to behold Bo run right into the cowboys's arms. It appeared, however, that she was doomed to disappointment.

"Tom, I'm glad to see you," she replied.

They shook hands as old friends.

"You're lookin' right fine," he said.

"Oh, I'm well. . . . And how have you been these six months?" she queried.

"Reckon I though it was longer," he drawled. "Wal, I'm pretty tip-top now, but I was laid up with heart trouble for a spell."

"Heart trouble?" she echoed, dubiously.

"Shore. . . . I ate too much over heah in New Mexico."

"It's no news to me - where your heart's located," laughed Bo. Then she ran off the porch to see the blue mustang. She walked round and round him, clasping her hands in sheer delight.

"Bo, he's a plumb dandy," said Roy. "Never seen a prettier hoss. He'll run like a streak. An' he's got good eyes. He'll be a pet some day. But I reckon he'll always be spunky."

"Bo ventured to step closer, and at last got a hand on the mustang, and then another. She smoothed his quivering neck and called softly to him, until he submitted to her hold.

"What's his name?" she asked.

"Blue somethin' or other," replied Roy.

"Tom, has my new mustang a name?" asked Bo, turning to the cowboy.

"Shore."

"What then?"

"Wal, I named him Blue-Bo," answered Las Vegas, with a smile.

"Blue-Boy?"

"Nope. He's named after you. An' I chased him, roped him, broke him all myself."

"Very well. Blue-Bo he is, then. . . . And he's a wonderful darling horse. Oh, Nell, just look at him. . . . Tom, I can't thank you enough."

"Reckon I don't want any thanks," drawled the cowboy. "But see heah, Bo, you shore got to live up to conditions beforc you ride him."

"What!" exclaimed Bo, who was startled by his slow, cool, meaning tone, of voice.

Helen delighted in looking at Las Vegas then. He had never appeared to better advantage. So cool, careless, and assured! He seemed master of a situation in which his terms must be accepted. Yet he might have been actuated by a cowboy motive beyond the power of Helen to divine.

"Bo Rayner," drawled Las Vegas, "thet blue mustang will be yours, an' you can ride him - when you're Mrs. Tom Carmichael!"

Never had he spoken a softer, more drawling speech, nor gazed at Bo more mildly. Roy seemed thunderstruck. Helen endeavored heroically to restrain her delicious, bursting glee. Bo's wide eyes stared at her lover - darkened - dilated. Suddenly she left the mustang to confront the cowboy where he lounged on the porch steps.

"Do you mean that?" she cried.

"Shore do."

"Bah! It's only a magnificent bluff," she retorted. "You're only in fun. It's your - your darned nerve!"

"Why, Bo," began Las Vegas, reproachfully. "You shore know I'm not the four-flusher kind. Never got away with a bluff in my life! An' I'm jest in daid earnest aboot this heah."

All the same, signs were not wanting in his mobile face that he was almost unable to restrain his mirth.

Helen realized then that Bo saw through the cowboy - that the ultimatum was only one of his tricks.

"It is a bluff and I call you!" declared Bo, ringingly.

Las Vegas suddenly awoke to consequences. He essayed to speak, but she was so wonderful then, so white and blazing-eyed, that he was stricken mute.

"I'll ride Blue-Bo this afternoon," deliberately stated the girl.

Las Vegas had wit enough to grasp her meaning, and

he seemed about to collapse.

"Very well, you can make me Mrs. Tom Carmichael to-day - this morning - just before dinner. . . . Go get a preacher to marry us - and make yourself look a more presentable bridegroom - unless it was only a bluff!"

Her imperiousness changed as the tremendous portent of her words seemed to make Las Vegas a blank, stone image of a man. With a wild-rose color suffusing her face, she swiftly bent over him, kissed him, and flashed away into the house. Her laugh pealed back, and it thrilled Helen, so deep and strange was it for the wilful sister, so wild and merry and full of joy.

It was then that Roy Beeman recovered from his paralysis, to let out such a roar of mirth as to frighten the horses. Helen was laughing, and crying, too, but laughing mostly. Las Vegas Carmichael was a sight for the gods to behold. Bo's kiss had unclamped what had bound him. The sudden truth, undeniable, insupportable, glorious, made him a madman.

"Bluff - she called me - ride Blue-Bo saf'ternoon!" he raved, reaching wildly for Helen. "Mrs. - Tom - Carmichael - before dinner - preacher - presentable bridegroom! . . . Aw! I'm drunk again! I - who swore off forever!"

"No, Tom, you're just happy," said Helen.

Between her and Roy the cowboy was at length persuaded to accept the situation and to see his wonderful opportunity.

"Now - now, Miss Helen - what'd Bo mean by

pre - presentable bridegroom? . . . Presents? Lord, I'm clean busted flat!"

"She meant you must dress up in your best, of course," replied Helen.

"Where 'n earth will I get a preacher? . . . Show Down's forty miles. . . . Can't ride there in time. . . . Roy, I've gotta have a preacher. . . . Life or death deal fer me."

"Wal, old man, if you'll brace up I'll marry you to Bo," said Roy, with his glad grin.

"Aw!" gasped Las Vegas, as if at the coming of a sudden beautiful hope.

"Tom, I'm a preacher," replied Roy, now earnestly. "You didn't know thet, but I am. An' I can marry you an' Bo as good as any one, an' tighter 'n most."

Las Vegas reached for his friend as a drowning man might have reached for solid rock.

"Roy, can you really marry them - with my Bible - and the service of my church?" asked Helen, a happy hope flushing her face.

"Wal, indeed I can. I've married more 'n one couple whose religion wasn't mine."

"B-b-before - d-d-din-ner!" burst out Las Vegas, like a stuttering idiot.

"I reckon. Come on, now, an' make yourself pre-senttible," said Roy. "Miss Helen, you tell Bo thet it's all settled."

He picked up the halter on the blue mustang and turned away toward the corrals. Las Vegas put the bridle of his horse over his arm, and seemed to be following in a trance, with his dazed, rapt face held high.

"Bring Dale," called Helen, softly after them.

So it came about as naturally as it was wonderful that Bo rode the blue mustang before the afternoon ended.

Las Vegas disobeyed his first orders from Mrs. Tom Carmichael and rode out after her toward the green-rising range. Helen seemed impelled to follow. She did not need to ask Dale the second time. They rode swiftly, but never caught up with Bo and Las Vegas, whose riding resembled their happiness.

Dale read Helen's mind, or else his own thoughts were in harmony with hers, for he always seemed to speak what she was thinking. And as they rode homeward he asked her in his quiet way if they could not spare a few days to visit his old camp.

"And take Bo - and Tom? Oh, of all things I'd like to'" she replied.

"Yes - an' Roy, too," added Dale, significantly.

"Of course," said Helen, lightly, as if she had not caught his meaning. But she turned her eyes away, while her heart thumped disgracefully and all her body was aglow. "Will Tom and Bo go?"

"It was Tom who got me to ask you," replied Dale.

"John an' Hal can look after the men while we're gone."

"Oh - so Tom put it in your head? I guess - maybe - I won't go."

"It is always in my mind, Nell," he said, with his slow seriousness. "I'm goin' to work all my life for you. But I'll want to an' need to go back to the woods often. . . . An' if you ever stoop to marry me - an' make me the richest of men - you'll have to marry me up there where I fell in love with you."

"Ah! Did Las Vegas Tom Carmichael say that, too?" inquired Helen, softly.

"Nell, do you want to know what Las Vegas said?"

"By all means."

"He said this - an' not an hour ago. 'Milt, old hoss, let me give you a hunch. I'm a man of family now - an' I've been a devil with the wimmen in my day. I can see through 'em. Don't marry Nell Rayner in or near the house where I killed Beasley. She'd remember. An' don't let her remember thet day. Go off into the woods. Paradise Park! Bo an' me will go with you."

Helen gave him her hand, while they walked the horses homeward in the long sunset shadows. In the fullness of that happy hour she had time for a grateful wonder at the keen penetration of the cowboy Carmichael. Dale had saved her life, but it was Las Vegas who had saved her happiness.

Not many days later, when again the afternoon

shadows were slanting low, Helen rode out upon the promontory where the dim trail zigzagged far above Paradise Park.

Roy was singing as he drove the pack-burros down the slope; Bo and Las Vegas were trying to ride the trail two abreast, so they could hold hands; Dale had dismounted to stand beside Helen's horse, as she gazed down the shaggy black slopes to the beautiful wild park with its gray meadows and shining ribbons of brooks.

It was July, and there were no golden-red glorious flames and blazes of color such as lingered in Helen's memory. Black spruce slopes and green pines and white streaks of aspens and lacy waterfall of foam and dark outcroppings of rock-these colors and forms greeted her gaze with all the old enchantment. Wildness, beauty, and loneliness were there, the same as ever, immutable, like the spirit of those heights.

Helen would fain have lingered longer, but the others called, and Ranger impatiently snorted his sense of the grass and water far below. And she knew that when she climbed there again to the wide outlook she would be another woman.

"Nell, come on," said Dale, as he led on. "It's better to look up."

The sun had just sunk behind the ragged fringe of mountain-rim when those three strong and efficient men of the open had pitched camp and had prepared a bountiful supper. Then Roy Beeman took out the little worn Bible which Helen had given him to use when he married Bo, and as he opened it a light changed his dark face.

"Come, Helen an' Dale," he said.

They arose to stand before him. And he married them there under the great, stately pines, with the fragrant blue smoke curling upward, and the wind singing through the branches, while the waterfall murmured its low, soft, dreamy music, and from the dark slope came the wild, lonely cry of a wolf, full of the hunger for life and a mate.

"Let us pray," said Roy, as he closed the Bible, and knelt with them.

"There is only one God, an' Him I beseech in my humble office for the woman an' man I have just wedded in holy bonds. Bless them an' watch them an' keep them through all the comin' years. Bless the sons of this strong man of the woods an' make them like him, with love an' understandin' of the source from which life comes. Bless the daughters of this woman an' send with them more of her love an' soul, which must be the softenin' an' the salvation of the hard West. O Lord, blaze the dim, dark trail for them through the unknown forest of life! O Lord, lead the way across the naked range of the future no mortal knows! We ask in Thy name! Amen."

When the preacher stood up again and raised the couple from their kneeling posture, it seemed that a grave and solemn personage had left him. This young man was again the dark-faced, clear-eyed Roy, droll and dry, with the enigmatic smile on his lips.

"Mrs. Dale," he said, taking her hands, "I wish you joy

. . . . An' now, after this here, my crownin' service in your behalf – I reckon I'll claim a reward."

Then he kissed her. Bo came next with her warm and loving felicitations, and the cowboy, with characteristic action, also made at Helen.

"Nell, shore it's the only chance I'll ever have to kiss you," he drawled. "Because when this heah big Indian once finds out what kissin' is - !"

Las Vegas then proved how swift and hearty he could be upon occasions. All this left Helen red and confused and unutterably happy. She appreciated Dale's state. His eyes reflected the precious treasure which manifestly he saw, but realization of ownership had not yet become demonstrable.

Then with gay speech and happy laugh and silent look these five partook of the supper. When it was finished Roy made known his intention to leave. They all protested and coaxed, but to no avail. He only laughed and went on saddling his horse.

"Roy, please stay," implored Helen. "The day's almost ended. You're tired."

"Nope. I'll never be no third party when there's only two."

"But there are four of us."

"Didn't I just make you an' Dale one? . . . An', Mrs. Dale, you forget I've been married more 'n once."

Helen found herself confronted by an unanswerable

side of the argument. Las Vegas rolled on the grass in his mirth. Dale looked strange.

"Roy, then that's why you're so nice," said Bo, with a little devil in her eyes. "Do you know I had my mind made up if Tom hadn't come around I was going to make up to you, Roy. . . . I sure was. What number wife would I have been?"

It always took Bo to turn the tables on anybody. Roy looked mightily embarrassed. And the laugh was on him. He did not face them again until he had mounted.

"Las Vegas, I've done my best for you - hitched you to thet blue-eyed girl the best I know how," he declared. "But I shore ain't guaranteein' nothin'. You'd better build a corral for her."

"Why, Roy, you shore don't savvy the way to break these wild ones," drawled Las Vegas. "Bo will be eatin' out of my hand in about a week."

Bo's blue eyes expressed an eloquent doubt as to this extraordinary claim.

"Good-by, friends," said Roy, and rode away to disappear in the spruces.

Thereupon Bo and Las Vegas forgot Roy, and Dale and Helen, the camp chores to be done, and everything else except themselves. Helen's first wifely duty was to insist that she should and could and would help her husband with the work of cleaning up after the sumptuous supper. Before they had finished a sound startled them. It came from Roy, evidently high on the darkening slope, and was a long, mellow pealing halloo, that rang on the cool air, burst the dreamy silence, and rapped across from slope to slope and cliff to cliff, to lose its power and die away hauntingly in the distant recesses.

Dale shook his head as if he did not care to attempt a reply to that beautiful call. Silence once again enfolded the park, and twilight seemed to be born of the air, drifting downward.

"Nell, do you miss anythin'?" asked Dale.

"No. Nothing in all the world," she murmured. "I am happier than I ever dared pray to be."

"I don't mean people or things. I mean my pets."

"Ah! I had forgotten. . . . Milt, where are they?"

"Gone back to the wild," he said. "They had to live in my absence. An' I've been away long."

Just then the brooding silence, with its soft murmur of falling water and faint sigh of wind in the pines, was broken by a piercing scream, high, quivering, like that of a woman in exquisite agony.

"That's Tom!" exclaimed Dale.

"Oh - I was so - so frightened!" whispered Helen.

Bo came running, with Las Vegas at her heels.

"Milt, that was your tame cougar," cried Bo, excitedly.

"Oh, I'll never forget him! I'll hear those cries in my dreams!"

"Yes, it was Tom," said Dale, thoughtfully. "But I never heard him cry just like that."

"Oh, call him in!"

Dale whistled and called, but Tom did not come. Then the hunter stalked off in the gloom to call from different points under the slope. After a while be returned without the cougar. And at that moment, from far up the dark ravine, drifted down the same wild cry, only changed by distance, strange and tragic in its meaning.

"He scented us. He remembers. But he'll never come back," said Dale.

Helen felt stirred anew with the convictions of Dale's deep knowledge of life and nature. And her imagination seemed to have wings. How full and perfect her trust, her happiness in the realization that her love and her future, her children, and perhaps grandchildren, would come under the guidance of such a man! Only a little had she begun to comprehend the secrets of good and ill in their relation to the laws of nature. Ages before men had lived on the earth there had been the creatures of the wilderness, and the holes of the rocks, and the nests of the trees, and rain, frost, heat, dew, sunlight and night, storm and calm, the honey of the wildflower and the instinct of the bee - all the beautiful and multiple forms of life with their inscrutable design. To know something of them and to love them was to be close to the kingdom of earth - perhaps to the greater kingdom of heaven. For whatever breathed and moved was a part of that creation. The coo of the dove, the lichen on the mossy rock, the mourn of a hunting wolf, and the murmur of the waterfall, the ever-green and growing tips of the spruces, and the thunderbolts along the battlements of the heights - these one and all must be actuated by the great spirit - that incalculable thing in the universe which had produced man and soul.

And there in the starlight, under the wide-gnarled pines, sighing low with the wind, Helen sat with Dale on the old stone that an avalanche of a million years past had flung from the rampart above to serve as camp-table and bench for lovers in the wilderness; the sweet scent of spruce mingled with the fragrance of wood-smoke blown in their faces. How white the stars, and calm and true! How they blazed their single task! A coyote yelped off on the south slope, dark now as midnight. A bit of weathered rock rolled and tapped from shelf to shelf. And the wind moaned. Helen felt all the sadness and mystery and nobility of this lonely fastness, and full on her heart rested the supreme consciousness that all would some day be well with the troubled world beyond.

"Nell, I'll homestead this park," said Dale. "Then it'll always be ours."

"Homestead! What's that?" murmured Helen, dreamily. The word sounded sweet.

"The government will give land to men who locate an' build," replied Dale. "We'll run up a log cabin."

"And come here often. . . . Paradise Park!" whispered Helen.

Dale's first kisses were on her lips then, hard and cool and clean, like the life of the man, singularly exalting to her, completing her woman's strange and unutterable joy of the hour, and rendering her mute.

Bo's melodious laugh, and her voice with its old mockery of torment, drifted softly on the night breeze. And the cowboy's "Aw, Bo," drawling his reproach and longing, was all that the tranquil, waiting silence needed.

Paradise Park was living again one of its romances. Love was no stranger to that lonely fastness. Helen heard in the whisper of the wind through the pine the old-earth story, beautiful, ever new, and yet eternal. She thrilled to her depths. The spar-pointed spruces stood up black and clear against the noble stars. All that vast solitude breathed and waited, charged full with its secret, ready to reveal itself to her tremulous soul.